Introduction to Psychology for Law Enforcement

SECOND EDITION

Shahé S. Kazarian, PhD, and Michael J. Boisvert, PhD

2010
Emond Montgomery Publications
Toronto, Canada

Emond Montgomery Publications Limited
60 Shaftesbury Avenue
Toronto ON M4T 1A3
http://www.emp.ca/college

Printed in Canada.
Reprinted July 2016

We acknowledge the financial support of the Government of Canada through the Canada Book Fund for our publishing activities.

Acquisitions and development editor: Bernard Sandler
Marketing manager: Christine Davidson
Director, sales and marketing, higher education: Kevin Smulan
Supervising editor: Jim Lyons
Copy editor: Francine Geraci
Production editor: Debbie Gervais
Assistant production editor: David Handelsman
Proofreader: Deanna Dority
Indexer: Paula Pike
Cover designer: Tara Wells
Cover image: Susan Darrach, Darrach Design

Library and Archives Canada Cataloguing in Publication

Kazarian, Shahe S., 1945-
     Introduction to psychology for law enforcement / Shahé S. Kazarian and Michael J. Boisvert. — 2nd ed.

Includes index.
ISBN 978-1-55239-386-4

     1. Police psychology—Textbooks.   2. Law enforcement—Psychological aspects—Textbooks.   I. Boisvert, Michael J. (Michael James), 1973-   II. Title.

HV7936.P75K39 2010   363.201'9   C2010-901678-5

*Dedicated to all the psychologists whose work is relevant to law enforcement,
and to all aspiring law enforcement officers who apply psychology
for their own benefit and the benefit of society*

Contents

Preface to the Second Edition

Guided by positive feedback from instructors who used the first edition of *Introduction to Psychology for Law Enforcement*, the second edition retains the overall organization, pedagogy, and workbook format of the first edition. But the new edition differs from the original in a number of significant respects. Dr. Michael J. Boisvert, of the School of Language and Liberal Studies, Fanshawe College, and the Department of Psychology, University of Western Ontario, has brought new perspective and experience to the text. A new chapter on memory, intelligence, and problem solving (Chapter 6) has been added. All chapters have been updated or revised to reflect psychology's relevance to the increasing diversity within law enforcement and society. And all chapters also now include application boxes that highlight issues, controversies, or practices in law enforcement. The second edition is also accompanied by an updated instructor's guide, PowerPoint presentations, and a test bank.

Instructors and students using the second edition of this text are encouraged to consider that they are together on a voyage of discovery and that their journey can be best enjoyed when critical thinking and emotion in the learning process are openly embraced.

Work on the second edition has been laborious but also fun. My co-author and I sincerely thank Bernard Sandler of Emond Montgomery for his superb administrative skills and relentless support, encouragement, and guidance. We also thank the editorial and production team for their invaluable efforts in the preparation of the book for publication: Francine Geraci, Deanna Dority, Debbie Gervais, David Handelsman, Tara Wells, Jim Lyons, and Paula Pike.

Finally, I would like to thank the Department of the Social and Behavioral Sciences at the American University of Beirut, the former dean of the Faculty of Arts and Sciences, Professor Khalil Bitar, the Advisory Committee of the Faculty of Arts and Sciences, and the University for supporting my request for a sabbatical to work on this project. I would also like to express my special thanks to my children Nancy and Steve and the special people in their lives, Mark and Karri, respectively, for their hospitality, patience, and support while I finished this work. Thank you to my grandchildren, Zachary (two-and-three-quarters years old) and Kara (6 months old) for contributing to the fun in writing the chapters, and allowing the occasional breaks. Finally, I thank Levonty, my spouse, for her ongoing insights and unconditional support and love.

Shahé S. Kazarian
Port Perry and London, Ontario
March 2010

Preface to the First Edition

Law enforcement officers are variously described as crime fighters, social agents, law enforcers, and watchpeople. Regardless of their law enforcement style, officers perform specialist functions that include maintaining law and order, protecting life and property, making arrests, issuing summonses, providing information to the public and their respective police services, and working with the community to plan, organize, problem-solve, and serve as information links.

To perform these complex duties, law enforcement officers need a healthy body, mind, and character. They must be in excellent health and have physical strength, endurance, and agility; they must have good sight and normal colour vision, proper weight, and no conditions that restrict their ability to safely perform their duties. Law enforcement officers must also have communication, coping, motivation, role adaptability, and problem-solving abilities. In terms of character, officers must be honest, dependable, and personally and financially responsible; they must respect the law and the rights of others; they must have good driving records; and they must have mature judgment, including the use of drugs and intoxicants.

Psychology is the scientific study of the human body, mind, and character. As such, its methods and findings are highly relevant to the criminal justice system in general and to law enforcement in particular. *Introduction to Psychology for Law Enforcement* explains psychology's relevance to law enforcement. This introductory book consists of 11 chapters and covers such topics as the biological basis of behaviour, sensation and perception, states of consciousness, learning, motivation, psychological disorders, and social behaviour. The various topics are presented to inform law enforcement officers, present and future, of the relevance of psychology to their work and their personal lives.

Each chapter includes Chapter Objectives, Preview Scenarios, Points To Remember, Key Terms, References, and Exercises and Review. The Exercises and Review comprise a Self-Test and a Thinking About Psychology and Law Enforcement section. The Self-Test is designed to evaluate your comprehension of the material covered in the chapter, while Thinking About Psychology and Law Enforcement complements the text by applying principles of psychology to law enforcement practices.

In preparing *Introduction to Psychology for Law Enforcement*, every effort was made to use a writing style that is clear, understandable, engaging, and pertinent to law enforcement officers. It is my sincere hope that this book fulfills its promise and makes a positive difference not only to law enforcement work but also to the quality of life of officers, present and future.

Although this book holds the name of a single author, it is multi-authored in that the text is based on the contribution of numerous distinguished psychologists to the fields of psychology and law enforcement. I assume full responsibility for what I have written but I thank them for their invaluable and scholarly work. Thank you to the D.B. Weldon Library and the John and Dotsa Bitove Family Law Library of the University of Western Ontario for their invaluable resources and cheerful staff. Special thank you to Dr. David R. Evans for his contribution to shaping the content of the book and his assistance in writing parts of the first chapter, and for sharing all resource materials in his possession. I am also indebted to the wonderful people at Emond Montgomery for their contributions to the conception, birthing, and delivery of *Introduction to Psychology for Law Enforcement*: Paul Emond, Nora Rock, Marie Maidman, and David Stokaluk. At WordsWorth Communications, thank you to Claudia Kutchukian for her competent copy editing, supportive attitude, and unfailing guidance; to Nancy Ennis for formatting the text; and to Shani Sohn for drawing the diagrams. Finally, thank you to my wife Levonty, my son Seve Kazarian, my daughter Nancy Kazarian, and all my friends for tolerating my bouts of terminal seclusion from their lives.

Shahé S. Kazarian, PhD
London, Ontario
April 2001

CHAPTER 1

Psychology and the Scientific Method

CHAPTER OBJECTIVES

After completing this chapter, you should be able to:

- Define the field of psychology and its branches.

- Describe the research methods used in psychology.

- Discuss the ethics of research.

PREVIEW SCENARIO

Michelinne Pisarski was a 40-year-old woman with no previous criminal record but a history of psychiatric issues. In August 1999, she set her London, Ontario apartment building ablaze by starting two fires, one in her bed and the other in her living room. She fled the building after setting the fires and landed in a nearby pub. The blaze sent 100 people into the street and caused an estimated $35,000 in damage. Pisarski volunteered a videotaped statement to the police to the effect that she had set the fires and would be willing to pay for all the damage. She was convicted of arson and sentenced to 4 months in custody and 18 months' probation. The probation order stipulated that she seek counselling and refrain from returning to the apartment building. The assistant Crown attorney told the court that Pisarski's history of mental illness partly accounted for the arson. (Schuck, 1999)

THE PSYCHOLOGY ENTERPRISE

Psychology is a field that is highly relevant to the careers of law enforcement officers. Just as law enforcement officers serve citizens for the purpose of securing their safety and welfare, protecting them from harm, or improving their quality of life, human psychology is a science and a profession whose purpose is human welfare.

Psychology strives to understand human behaviour by studying all aspects of the human experience. It demystifies the world of the brain by probing into brain structure and function and by delving into the complex world of human development from conception to death. In addition to understanding the internal workings of the human experience, psychology tries to explain individual behaviour in cul-

psychology
science and profession that strives to understand human behaviour by studying all aspects of the human experience; the scientific study of behaviour and mental processes

tural and social contexts. It studies identity formation, adaptation to a new culture, conformity, compliance and obedience, persuasion, prejudice, racism and discrimination, attraction and love, the altruistic actions of groups and nations, the dynamics of genocide, war, and terrorism, and conflict resolution and peacemaking. In fact, it is difficult to imagine any aspect of individual, social, and cultural life that lies outside the science and practice of psychology. While psychology has its roots in Western Europe and North America, the discipline is striving for international application of its science and practice (see, for example, Kazarian, 2007).

This chapter defines the psychology enterprise and identifies four of its goals. It also discusses the branches of psychology and the specific scientific methods used to advance understanding of the human mind and human behaviour.

Psychology Defined

behaviour
observable actions; what people actually do

mental processes
internal activities (physiological activities, thoughts, and feelings) that cannot be observed directly but can be measured with recording instruments or inferred from self-report measures and performance

Psychology is the scientific study of behaviour and mental processes. **Behaviour** refers to observable actions—what people actually do. **Mental processes** are internal activities that cannot be observed directly but can be measured with recording instruments (for example, with magnetic resonance imaging) or inferred from self-report measures (what people tell you they are doing) and performance (for example, observing a person solving a puzzle). Mental processes include physiological activities (such as heart rate), cognitions (such as thoughts), and affect (such as expressions of feelings). Needless to say, behaviour and mental processes are interconnected—understanding a particular behaviour (such as sexual intimacy) requires understanding the mental processes (such as fantasies) associated with the behaviour.

Psychology is not just common sense or the study of common sense. Common-sense psychology may be adequate for many of the tasks performed by law enforcement officers, but it can also lead officers to false conclusions and less than effective actions. The ineffectiveness of some officers may be largely due to faulty assumptions they hold about human nature, personal biases and prejudices they may carry in their heads or on their shoulders, or passive acceptance of "truths" imparted by the media or self-professed experts.

Psychology thrives on facts. It attempts to foster an approach that questions personal assumptions, encourages accurate observation, weighs evidence objectively, and draws valid and reliable conclusions.

The Four Missions of the Psychology Enterprise: DEPC

The scientific method in psychology has four goals:

- *Description* of behaviour and mental processes. Description is the "what" of behaviour and mental processes. Psychology offers explicit, accurate, and complete descriptions for the purpose of scientific scrutiny and understanding of the human experience.

- *Explanation* of behaviour and mental processes. Explanation is the "why" of behaviour and mental processes. For example, Gendreau, Goggin, and

Cullen (1999) studied the effect of prison on criminal behaviour among low-risk and high-risk offenders. They found that long prison sentences (in comparison to short sentences) *increased* recidivism—the tendency to return to criminal behaviour—slightly. Gendreau et al. explained this paradox by suggesting that prison may serve as a school for crime for some offenders. It is important to underscore that this theory must be tested empirically and confirmed, and other causes of the increase in recidivism must be ruled out before this explanation is accepted.

- *Prediction* of behaviour and mental processes. Prediction refers to the "when" of behaviour and mental processes—the conditions under which they are likely to occur. When one of Albert Einstein's headmasters proclaimed that Einstein would amount to nothing, the headmaster was making a prediction on the basis of his assessment and knowledge of his student. Needless to say, this prediction failed miserably.

  Prediction has heuristic, or problem-solving, value. For example, being able to predict an offender's risk of committing new crimes is important for the police, courts, correctional workers, and general public (Andrews & Bonta, 1998). The knowledge that sex offenders are more likely to reoffend when they show sexual preoccupation, negative peer influence, and poor self-management (Hanson & Harris, 1998) allows the development and implementation of meaningful approaches to assessing offender risk potential, disposition (when the offender can be safely released), supervision, rehabilitation, and intervention.

- *Control* of behaviour and mental processes. Control refers to the "how" of behaviour and mental processes—the application of psychological principles or conditions to bring about positive outcomes or prevent negative outcomes. In dealing with criminal behaviour and its impact on victims of crime, restorative justice programs may be developed and implemented for the benefit of crime victims, individual offenders, and the community at large (Bonta, Wallace-Capretta, & Rooney, 1998; Forget, 2002; Gilman, n.d.). The positive outcomes expected from such programs include alternatives to prison, increased victim participation in the criminal justice process, significant restitution payments, and offender contribution to society through community service. Preventing negative outcomes may mean programs to reduce offender recidivism.

Branches of Psychology: Diversity in Unity and Unity in Diversity

The field of psychology consists of several branches and subspecialties within the branches. For example, within clinical psychology are the subspecialties of clinical child psychology, geropsychology, clinical neuropsychology, and clinical health psychology. Here are brief descriptions of ten select branches of psychology:

- Clinical neuropsychology: Applying knowledge of brain–behaviour relationships to assess, diagnose, and treat people with known or suspected central nervous system dysfunction.

- Clinical psychology: Applying knowledge of human behaviour to assess, diagnose, and treat disorders of behaviour, emotions, and thought.

- Counselling psychology: Applying knowledge of human behaviour to foster and improve normal human functioning. Generally, counselling psychologists work with reasonably well-adjusted people to help them solve problems, make decisions, and cope with everyday life stresses.

- Cultural psychology: Applying cultural processes and outcomes in human behaviour.

- Developmental psychology: Applying knowledge of changes in human behaviour that occur as a result of developmental processes (for example, growth).

- Forensic psychology: Applying knowledge of human behaviour to processes in the criminal justice system, such as causes of criminal behaviour; assessment, treatment, rehabilitation, recidivism, and community reintegration of offenders; the workings of a jury; and witness behaviour.

- Health psychology: Applying knowledge of holistic processes in physical disorders (causes, assessment, treatment, rehabilitation, community reintegration, quality of life).

- Industrial/organizational psychology: Applying knowledge of human behaviour to the workplace, such as processes in productivity, quality of work life, employee–management relations, personnel selection and training, and advertising and marketing.

- School psychology: Applying knowledge of human behaviour to help educators and others promote the intellectual, social, and emotional development of children, adolescents, and adults, and to create environments that facilitate learning and mental health.

- Social psychology: Applying processes pertaining to how people think about, influence, and relate to one another (see Chapter 12).

Despite their different orientations and specialties, psychologists are committed to a perspective that encompasses diversity in research and practice, particularly in multicultural contexts (Kazarian & Evans, 1998, 2001). They are also committed to placing the welfare of society and individual members of that society above their own welfare or that of the psychology discipline (CPA, 2000; APA, 2002; International Union of Psychological Science, 2008).

SCIENCE OF THE PSYCHOLOGY ENTERPRISE

Psychology is committed to scientific research. Good scientific research depends on critical thinking (Sternberg, Roediger, & Halpern, 2006). While critical thinking may mean different things to different people, it certainly does not mean negative thinking, assigning blame, or criticizing or bullying those who hold views different from one's own. **Critical thinking** means the ability and willingness to ask questions, to wonder, to assess claims, to evaluate assumptions, biases, and evidence to make

critical thinking
ability and willingness to ask questions, to wonder, to assess claims, to evaluate assumptions, biases, and evidence to make objective judgments on the basis of well-supported reasons, to look for flaws in arguments and resist claims that have no supporting evidence, and to tolerate uncertainty

objective judgments on the basis of well-supported reasons, to look for flaws in arguments and resist claims that have no supporting evidence, and to tolerate uncertainty. Critical thinkers strive for clarity, precision, accuracy, relevance, depth, breadth, and logic.

As a group, psychologists tend to embrace critical thinking. They espouse and nurture a "show me," "prove it to me" attitude and critical-thinking approach. This approach is of value to individuals and society in several ways: it minimizes the risk of being taken in by false claims or quackery; it helps separate the wheat from the chaff—sense from nonsense; and it allows the use of appropriate evaluative standards to determine the true worth, merit, or value of ideas and claims (Paul & Elder, 1999). In the absence of critical thinking, it is more likely for people to gravitate toward prejudice, overgeneralization, common fallacies, self-deception, rigidity, and narrowness, and to commit human errors, blunders, and distortions of thought (Paul, Elder, & Bartell, 1997; Wade & Tavris, 2000).

The Knowledge Pursuit: Pure and Applied

Psychology relies on the scientific approach to understand human behaviour. Psychology research can be pure or applied. **Pure** (or basic) **research** aims to develop new knowledge without immediate concern for the practical uses of this knowledge. Studies that examine the brain structure of hard-core criminals are examples of pure psychological research. The researchers are seeking basic knowledge to describe, explain, and possibly predict criminal behaviour rather than to offer the world immediate solutions on how to deal with hard-core criminals. Solutions to real-world problems may come in the long term and with sufficient knowledge of criminality.

pure research
basic research that aims to develop new knowledge without immediate concern for the practical uses of this knowledge

Applied research, on the other hand, aims to advance new knowledge that has immediate real-world uses. Research to develop assessment tools and rehabilitation approaches to identify offenders at high risk for recidivism and to reduce their chances of reoffending is one example of applied research. The positive findings of such research have direct application to the control of criminal behaviour. For another example, see Box 1.1.

applied research
research that aims to advance new knowledge that has immediate real-world uses

The Scientific Method

The **scientific method** involves four basic steps:

scientific method
method of doing research that involves (1) forming a research question, (2) framing the research question as a hypothesis, (3) developing the methodology for testing the hypothesis, and (4) drawing conclusions about the hypothesis

- Step 1: Forming a research question. For example, "Does class attendance have anything to do with a student's marks?"

- Step 2: Framing the research question as a hypothesis. For example, "Academic achievement is influenced by class attendance. Students who attend classes regularly obtain higher marks than those who attend irregularly."

- Step 3: Developing the methodology for testing the hypothesis. For example, "The introductory psychology class will be divided into two groups—those who attend classes regularly (Regulars) and those who attend classes irregularly (Irregulars)—and their final marks will be compared at the end of the course."

BOX 1.1   Traditional Interviews Versus Cognitive Interviews of Witnesses of Crimes

Police spend much of their time solving crimes by interviewing witnesses and getting them to remember details about events or a series of events. The traditional police interview of witnesses of crimes entails experienced detectives asking many closed-ended questions to extract as much factual information as possible from cooperative witnesses. Nevertheless, the traditional police interview has been shown to be limited in that it tends to extract rather than elicit information, and that it allows considerable inaccuracies in witnesses' memories.

The cognitive interview (CI) is an innovative technique for questioning witnesses of crime, and an alternative to evidence from forensic hypnosis, which may not be admissible in court. It is considered an improvement over the traditional interview approach in that it asks fewer questions and elicits more detailed and more accurate information. CI was developed in the United States by R. Edward Geiselman, Ronald P. Fisher, and their colleagues in the early 1980s on the basis of research on memory. In CI, police investigators are trained to give four instructions to witnesses during the interview process.

First, investigators ask witnesses to try to mentally reconstruct the physical (external) and personal (internal) circumstances that surrounded the crime event. The interviewer is allowed to help witnesses recreate the environment in which the crime occurred by asking them to form an image or impression of the environmental aspects of the original scene (for example, the location of objects in a room), to comment on their emotional reactions and feelings (surprise, anger, etc.) at the time, and to describe any sounds, smells, and physical conditions (hot, humid, smoky, etc.) that were present.

Second, investigators ask witnesses to report everything they can remember, even those things that they consider unimportant or irrelevant, and not to leave anything out. In addition to facilitating recall, this technique is likely to yield information that may be valuable in piecing together details from different witnesses to the same crime.

Third, investigators instruct witnesses to report the events from a variety of perspectives in order to encourage them to place themselves in the shoes of the victim (if the witness is not a victim) or of another witness and to report what they saw or would have seen.

Finally, investigators ask witnesses to report the events from different starting points—from the end, from the middle, or from the beginning, to encourage more focused and more extensive retrieval of events. This technique, like the change-of-perspective instruction, is assumed to change the retrieved account, resulting in the recall of additional details.

Studies comparing CI with traditional interviews in the United States, United Kingdom, Spain, Germany, and Australia tend to favour CI because this approach produces between 35 and 60 percent more information than the traditional interview does.

Sources: Geiselman and Fisher (1988) NTSB Academy (n.d.).

■ Step 4: Drawing conclusions about the hypothesis. For example, "The hypothesis that class attendance does make a difference in academic achievement seems supported in that Regulars show a higher average mark than do Irregulars."

The first step entails posing a research question based on theory, astute observation, an inquisitive mind, or a combination of these. A **theory** in science is a statement of a general principle or a set of principles whose purpose is to explain how a number of separate facts are interrelated. "Depression is caused by child abuse" is an example of a theory. Theories in psychology serve the functions of organizing known facts and generating hypotheses for scientific scrutiny. A **hypothesis** is a statement of prediction that can be verified through observation or experiment. "Child abuse influences negative mood" is an example of a hypothesis. Needless to say, psychological theories abound, and the hypotheses or questions they breed can be intriguing.

theory
statement of a general principle or set of principles for the purpose of explaining how a number of separate facts are interrelated

hypothesis
statement of prediction that can be tested empirically

Scientific Methods: The Magnificent Seven

In psychology, there are many roads to discovery. The seven scientific roads that are most travelled are described in Table 1.1. Note that variations of many of these research methods are used by the average person every day.

NATURALISTIC OBSERVATION

Naturalistic observation is a descriptive approach to the study of behaviour. It involves observing and recording behaviour as the behaviour occurs in a natural setting with minimal researcher influence or control. Observation may be done with or without the knowledge of whomever is being observed. An investigator who hires research assistants to observe the eating patterns of customers in a fast-food restaurant is employing this method. The "participants" in such a study are unaware that the amount of food they are eating or how much time they are taking to eat the food is being monitored and recorded. On the other hand, prisoners who consent to being observed unobtrusively in group discussions through a one-way mirror are participating in a naturalistic observation study with full awareness.

naturalistic observation
research approach that involves observing and recording behaviour as it occurs in a natural setting, with minimal researcher influence or control

The strength in this method is its approach to studying real (natural, spontaneous) rather than artificial (created in a laboratory environment) behaviour (see below). A psychologist from York University, Dr. Debra Pepler, studied school violence by observing children in elementary schoolyards for a total of 52 hours. In addition to documenting some 400 episodes of bullying, Dr. Pepler reported incidents of knives being drawn and attacks on children by a group of self-appointed playground vigilantes for the purpose of teaching other children "a lesson" (Goff, 1997). Examples of other natural and spontaneous behaviours of considerable importance to psychology include street or prison riots, and people's reactions in the face of natural disasters such as floods and earthquakes and serious accidents such as airplane crashes.

Observer bias is the major weakness of naturalistic observation. Observer bias refers to the potential distortion introduced by the researcher—seeing what one wants to see and not seeing what one does not want to see, for instance. Of course, the ones who are observed can also distort reality by doing what they think the

TABLE 1.1   Psychology Research Methods

Method	Description	Advantages	Disadvantages
Naturalistic observation	Systematically observing and recording behaviours or events in a natural environment with or without participant knowledge	Behaviours or events studied in a natural setting; may generate hypotheses for testing; provides clues to the causes of behaviours	Possible observer bias; behaviours or events may be influenced by presence of observer; ethical problem of observing people without their knowledge
Laboratory observation	Systematically observing and recording behaviour in a laboratory setting	More control than in natural setting	Observer bias; behaviour may be different from that in natural setting
Epidemiological method	Assessing incidence or prevalence of behaviours or events and possible determinants and causes, based on medical, social, and personal indicators	Identification of extent of behaviours or events; monitoring of behaviours or events over time for trends; rational approach to resource allocation; clues for interventions	Determinants or causes of behaviours or events may be difficult to establish
Survey method	Using questionnaires, interviews, and opinion polls to assess attitudes, opinions, beliefs, and feelings of survey participants	Identification and monitoring of attitudes over time for trends; use of information for education and policy development and implementation	Costly; possible socially desirable responding; falsification of information
Case study	Gathering and analyzing a life history to understand and explain the behaviour of an individual	Excellent source for observing the co-occurrence of two or more events (for example, experiencing sexual abuse and developing an eating disorder)	Susceptible to researcher bias; difficulty in generalizing findings to other cases
Correlational method	Using many case studies to assess the degree to which two or more events or behaviours are related (correlated)	Identifies the co-occurrence of events that are real (not due to chance); permits prediction; some events can be studied only using the correlational method (for example, child abuse)	Difficulty in establishing cause-and-effect relationship
Experimental method	Randomly assigning participants to two or more experimental groups to compare them on one or more indicators	Permits cause-and-effect inferences	Difficulty in generalizing findings to the real world

observers want them to do, refusing the "guinea pig" role, or presenting a favourable image. An obvious result of observer bias and observee distortions is incorrect description or inference about the observed behaviour. Another weakness of the naturalistic observation approach is the ethical problem of observing people without their knowledge or consent.

Naturalistic observation is a common and inherent part of law enforcement work. Officers are trained to constantly scan their environment, develop hypotheses in split seconds (for example, "This is a high-risk situation"), and execute their action plans immediately. Similarly, corrections officers observe the behaviour of prisoners, develop personality profiles based on their observations, and suggest prisoner management plans.

LABORATORY OBSERVATION

Laboratory observation is a descriptive approach to the study of behaviour in a laboratory setting for the purpose of observing and recording behaviour. The laboratory environment, such as a sleep laboratory, allows more control for observation and recording of behaviour than does the naturalistic setting. The willing participants in the laboratory observation also have knowledge of the fact that their behaviours are being observed and recorded.

Mary Ainsworth studied the attachment of babies to their mothers in a controlled laboratory observation setting. On the basis of her laboratory observations of children's interactions with their mothers and strangers, Ainsworth was able to distinguish between securely attached children and two types of insecurely attached children, the anxious/avoidant attached type and the anxious/resistant attached type. Securely attached children behaved comfortably in their parent's presence, played well with other children, responded positively to strangers, became upset when the parent left, and were easily calmed when the parent returned. Anxious/ avoidant children, on the other hand, either cried or did not cry when the parent left the room, were comforted as effectively by a stranger as the parent when upset, and turned or looked away when the parent returned. Finally, the anxious/resistant children tended to stay close to their parent, were anxious even when the parent was near, and became very upset when the parent left yet resisted comfort when it was offered.

The laboratory experiments conducted by Ainsworth and others on attachment between babies and mothers have important implications for child development. They suggest that securely attached children are likely to have good relationships with their mothers, making them feel confident and able to explore novel environments and to value the mother as a secure base from which to venture into the outside world.

While the laboratory observation method has the advantage of allowing the researcher more control than the naturalistic observation method, an important disadvantage is that behaviour in the laboratory setting may differ from that in the natural setting.

EPIDEMIOLOGICAL METHOD

The **epidemiological method** is a descriptive and potentially explanatory research approach that is based on medical and health issues in a population. This method

laboratory observation research approach that involves observing and recording behaviour as it occurs in a laboratory rather than in a natural setting, with minimal researcher influence or control

epidemiological method research approach that uses data on incidence or prevalence of behaviours or events to determine their extent, possible causes, and trends over time allows psychologists to discover the extent of physical, psychological, or criminal behaviours or issues in the population, their trends over time, and their causes.

Morbidity and *mortality* are two common indicators used in the epidemiological method. Morbidity refers to the number of people with a particular condition or disease at a given time. It may be represented as an *incidence* (the number of new cases) or a *prevalence* (the total number of cases, old and new). Mortality refers to the number of people who die from a particular condition, disease, or cause. For example, inmate suicide is the leading cause of death in Canadian prisons (Goff, 1997). Also, the number of law enforcement officers killed in the line of duty is higher in certain situations than in others (CBC News, 2007). For example, a US study showed that a total of 1,744 officers were killed in the line of duty between 1976 and 1997 (US Department of Justice, 1998). The conditions that contributed to police deaths were disturbance calls (16 percent of the deaths), investigations of suspicious individuals or circumstances (14 percent), robbery arrests (14 percent), traffic pursuits/stops (13 percent), ambush situations (10 percent), drug-related arrests (7 percent), burglary arrests (5 percent), other arrests (14 percent), and other situations (6 percent).

Morbidity and mortality indicators are important to intervention and prevention. For example, knowing that the suicide rate of inmates in Canada's federal prisons is significantly higher than the suicide rate in the non-prison population has led to the creation of a suicide prevention program by Correctional Service of Canada. Similarly, knowledge of high-risk police situations is useful for preventing the deaths of officers.

Archival data (information that is routinely collected by organizations) and the survey method (discussed below) are two approaches to obtaining epidemiological statistics.

SURVEY METHOD

survey method
research approach that uses questionnaires, interviews, and opinion polls to learn about people's attitudes, beliefs, values, opinions, feelings, actions, and experiences

The **survey method** is another descriptive research approach. It involves using questionnaires, interviews, and opinion polls to learn about people's attitudes—their beliefs, values, opinions, feelings, actions, and experiences. An example of the survey method is the US Bureau of Justice Statistics' 1999 study in which the attitudes of residents of 12 cities toward their neighbourhood, their city, and the local police service were examined. Residents were asked to rate, on a scale from "very satisfied" to "very dissatisfied," their satisfaction with police. The survey showed that resident satisfaction with police ranged from 97 percent in Madison, Wisconsin to 78 percent in Washington, DC. Only about 3 percent of respondents indicated a very high level of dissatisfaction with police (US Department of Justice, 1999).

A second example of the survey method is a study on Canadian citizen attitudes toward the police. In this study, O'Conner (2008) reported findings consistent with much of similar research conducted in the United States. Young people, visible minorities, males, those who had experienced criminal victimization, those dissatisfied with their safety, and those who perceived their neighbourhoods as being high in crime held negative views toward the police.

Researchers do not have to survey all members of the population of interest for their study. Thus, surveying all 34 million Canadians or 308 million Americans to find out how they feel about law enforcement officers would not only be an incredible amount of work, but also costly and foolish. To reach meaningful conclusions, all the researchers need to do is select a *representative sample* of the population: a sample that includes subgroups in the same proportion as they are found in the larger population of interest. For example, if 54 percent of the people within the larger population are male, then males should constitute 54 percent of the representative sample.

The survey method is a useful approach for describing people's attitudes and changes in attitudes over time.

The survey method has the major disadvantage of relying primarily on self-reports—that is, what people *say* rather than what they *do*. For example, those surveyed may try to present themselves in a positive light by giving socially desirable answers to survey questions. People who are surveyed want to look good in the eyes of the surveyor. Participants may also falsify information either to please surveyors—tell the surveyors what they think the surveyors want to hear—or to deliberately mislead them.

CASE STUDY

The **case study** is another descriptive research method. It involves exploring a single individual in depth to create a detailed portrayal of a particular behaviour or phenomenon, or to identify the co-occurrences of two or more events or variables—for example, alcoholism and domestic violence. Case studies are popular in psychology and medicine. They are used to support a theory or to help generate hypotheses and theories.

case study
research approach that involves exploring a single individual in depth to obtain a detailed portrayal of a particular behaviour or phenomenon, or to identify the co-occurrences of two or more events or variables

Similarly, people analyze the behaviour of their peers to make sense of their conduct. When John, a law enforcement officer, attempts suicide, Jane, another officer, tries to figure out why John took this drastic self-destructive action. When she discovers that John has recently been under tremendous pressure, including financial and marital problems, and that he has attempted suicide in the past under similar circumstances, Jane puts the two events together (stress and suicide seem to co-occur) and offers the connection as an explanation for her friend's behaviour.

Linking two or more events is a strength of the case study approach. However, the two weaknesses of this approach are possible observer bias and generalizability. Again, observer bias—seeing only what one wants to see—can creep into the analysis of case studies. For example, Jane may selectively focus on stress factors in John's life and ignore information such as a family history of suicide.

Generalizability refers to the ability of a researcher to apply findings from one case to all other cases in the population. For example, if John attempted suicide because he was depressed about his marital problems, the researcher cannot universalize this connection by saying that everyone with marital problems is at risk of committing suicide. The researcher may, however, be able to show a link between significant stress in people's lives and the rate of suicide.

CORRELATIONAL METHOD

The **correlational method** is the "cloning" of the case study—that is, gathering multiple case studies to identify co-occurrences of events that are generalizable to more than one individual. A study that examines the length of time spent in prison (in number of days) and the criminal behaviour of offenders after they leave prison

correlational method
research approach that involves gathering multiple case studies to identify co-occurrences of events that are generalizable to more than one individual

(in number of offences committed in the one-year period after leaving prison) for, say, 40 individuals (40 case studies) represents the correlational method. The strength and direction of the relationship can be presented statistically in the form of a *correlation coefficient*. Correlation coefficients range from +1.0 to −1.0. The larger the coefficient (regardless of whether it is positive or negative), the greater the strength of the relationship. In the example on prison duration and frequency of criminal behaviour, a positive correlation would indicate that the more time offenders spend in prison, the more criminal behaviour they are likely to show after being released into the community. On the other hand, a negative correlation would mean that the longer offenders are imprisoned, the less criminal behaviour they are likely to show after their release from prison. Also, a correlation coefficient of 0.90 would indicate a strong relationship between the two variables, regardless of whether the relationship is positive or negative. Conversely, a correlation coefficient of 0.20 would indicate a weak relationship between length of time spent in prison and recidivism.

The correlational method has been used to study humour styles and psychological well-being among Belgians, Canadians, Chinese, Lebanese, and Armenian-Lebanese (Martin, 2007). Contrary to the commonsensical belief that all humour is good for well-being, the studies on humour styles suggest that aggressive and self-defeating humour styles tend to be associated with poorer reports of psychological well-being, whereas affiliative and self-enhancing humour styles tend to be associated with better reports of psychological well-being.

One advantage of the correlational method is that the statistically significant finding of a relationship can be construed as real rather than due to chance. A second advantage is that it allows prediction: the stronger the statistical relationship, the better the prediction. The disadvantage of this method, however, is its inability to allow conclusive cause–effect inferences. In any correlational study, three plausible explanations may account for the relationship found between two variables (see Figure 1.1). The first possibility is that variable *x* causes variable *y*. The second possibility is that *y* causes *x*. The last possibility is that a third variable, *z*, is common to both *x* and *y*, and accounts for their relationship.

Examples of false relationships and the cause–effect limitation of the correlational method abound. You are probably familiar with some of the more popular ones: "Watching television makes you stupid" and "Playing violent video games makes you violent" are only two examples.

EXPERIMENTAL METHOD

The **experimental method** is an explanatory research method. It involves randomly assigning experimental participants to two or more groups or conditions to compare them on one or more measures. As the gold standard of the scientific methods, the experimental approach allows psychologists to make cause-and-effect inferences.

The experimental method has three major elements: an independent variable, a dependent variable, and random assignment. A **variable** is any factor or condition that can be manipulated, controlled, or measured. The **independent variable** is the condition that is manipulated to examine its effect on the dependent variable. The **dependent variable** is a measurable indicator that is presumed to change (increase or decrease) at the conclusion of the experiment. The change in the dependent variable is attributed to the independent variable.

experimental method
research approach that randomly assigns experimental participants to two or more groups or conditions to compare them on one or more measures

variable
any factor or condition that can be manipulated, controlled, or measured

independent variable
condition that is manipulated to examine its effect on the dependent variable

dependent variable
measurable indicator that is presumed to change (increase or decrease) at the conclusion of an experiment; the change in this variable is attributed to the independent variable

FIGURE 1.1   Three Explanations for a Correlational Finding

Hypothesis: The more people view TV that is aggressive in content (*x*),
    the more aggressive they become (*y*).

Explanation 1

$x \longrightarrow y$

Watching TV shows that have violent content causes aggression.

Explanation 2

$y \longrightarrow x$

Aggressive people tend to watch TV shows that have violent content.

Explanation 3

People with a brain defect (*z*) view TV that is violent *and* are more aggressive.

Random assignment fills the function of an equalizer. The random assignment process ensures that changes in the dependent variable are attributable to the independent variable. In random assignment, each research participant has an equal chance of being in the various groups or conditions comprising the independent variable. This equal opportunity ensures that participants representing the independent variable are equal in all respects at the beginning of the experiment.

In an experiment investigating the deterrent effect of long prison sentences on offenders, the independent variable is length of prison sentence. In this case, length of sentence is manipulated to represent two levels: short and long (a third level, medium, could also be added). To ensure that the two groups are equal at the beginning of the experiment, participants are randomly assigned to the groups so that the effect of the independent variable on the dependent variable (recidivism, in this case) can be attributed solely to the independent variable. A group of Canadian researchers that randomly assigns a representative sample of offenders into the long- and short-sentence groups and finds that recidivism is significantly lower for offenders who receive short prison sentences may conclude that long prison sentences have no advantage over short prison sentences. Nevertheless, this conclusion would be limited to the offender population of interest and the recidivism indicator. The findings would be silent with respect to other offender populations (for example, in the United States) and outcome measures other than recidivism (for example, homelessness).

Lack of generalization is a potential limitation of the experimental method. Results from an experimental study in the laboratory or involving a particular sample of participants (for example, college students) may not apply in the real world or with a different group of participants. The ability to replicate the experiment's findings outside the laboratory or with different participants is necessary for generalization.

RESEARCH ETHICS

code of ethics
set of rules by which a group of people, often members of a profession, agree to abide

To protect research participants from potential rights violations, strict **codes of ethics** for conducting scientific investigations have been developed in Canada and other countries. The CPA (2000) and the APA (2002) advocate protecting research participants from physical and psychological harm, and upholding the rights of participants to informed consent and privacy. *Informed consent* entails properly and fully disclosing to research participants all relevant information about the proposed study: the purpose of the study, procedures involved, risks and benefits associated with the study, and freedom to withdraw from the study for any reason without negative consequences. Research participants must understand the information they are given and be competent to give consent—that is, they must have the mental capacity to make a competent decision. Finally, research participants must give their consent freely without being coerced, unduly influenced, misled, lied to, threatened, or pressured.

POINTS TO REMEMBER

Psychology is the scientific study of behaviour and mental processes. Its four goals are description, explanation, prediction, and control. Psychology has several branches and subspecialties that have evolved over time.

There are four steps to the scientific method, and several research methods: naturalistic observation, laboratory observation, epidemiological method, survey method, case study, correlational method, and experimental method. No matter which approach is used, good psychology entails critical thinking, an orientation toward diversity, ethical practice, research methodology, research ethics, and internationalization.

KEY TERMS

applied research	independent variable
behaviour	laboratory observation
case study	mental processes
code of ethics	naturalistic observation
correlational method	psychology
critical thinking	pure research
dependent variable	scientific method
epidemiological method	survey method
experimental method	theory
hypothesis	variable

REFERENCES

American Psychological Association (APA). (2002). *Ethical principles of psychologists and code of conduct.* Washington, DC: Author. http://www.apa.org/ethics/code.html.

Andrews, D.A., & J. Bonta. (1998). *The psychology of criminal conduct* (2nd ed.). Cincinnati: Anderson.

Bonta, J., S. Wallace, & J. Rooney. (1999, May). *Electronic monitoring in Canada.* Ottawa: Solicitor General Canada. http://www.sgc.gc.ca/epub/corr/eem/eem.htm.

Bonta, J., S. Wallace-Capretta, & J. Rooney. (1998, October). *Restorative justice: An evaluation of the Restorative Resolutions Project.* User Report 1998-05. Ottawa: Solicitor General Canada.

CBC News. (2007, November 6). *In the line of duty: Deaths of RCMP officers.* http://www.cbc.ca/news/background/ rcmp/inthelineofduty.html.

Canadian Psychological Association (CPA). (2000). *Canadian code of ethics for psychologists* (3rd ed.). Ottawa: Author. http://www.cpa.ca/ethics.html.

Forget, M. (2002). *The restorative approach.* http://www.sfu.ca/cfrj/fulltext/forget2.pdf.

Geiselman, R.E., & R.P. Fisher. (1988). The cognitive interview: An innovative technique for questioning witnesses of crime. *Journal of Police and Criminal Psychology, 4* (2), 2–5.

Gendreau, P., C. Goggin, & F.T. Cullen. (1999). *The effects of prison sentences on recidivism.* Ottawa: Solicitor General Canada.

Gilman, E. (n.d.). *What is restorative justice?* http://www.sfu.ca/cfrj/fulltext/gilman.pdf.

Goff, C. (1997). *Criminal justice in Canada.* Toronto: Nelson.

Hanson, R.K., & A. Harris. (1998). *Dynamic predictors of sexual recidivism.* Ottawa: Solicitor General of Canada.

International Union of Psychological Science. (2008). *Universal declaration of ethical principles for psychologists.* http://www.am.org/iupsys/resources/ethics/univdecl2008.html.

Kazarian, S.S. (2007). Psychological interventions and assessments. In D. Bhugra and K. Bhui (Eds.), *Textbook of cultural psychiatry* (pp. 424–31). London, UK: Cambridge University Press.

Kazarian, S.S., & Evans, D.R. (Eds.). (1998). *Cultural clinical psychology: Theory, research and practice.* New York: Oxford University Press.

Kazarian, S.S., & Evans, D.R. (2001). *Handbook of cultural health psychology.* San Diego: Academic Press.

Martin, R.A. (2007). *The psychology of humor: An integrative approach.* New York: Academic Press.

NTSB Academy. (n.d.). *Q & A with Ron Fisher: The cognitive interview.* Ashburn, VA: Author. http://www.ntsb.gov/tc/courseinfo/qanda_fisher.pdf.

O'Conner, C.D. (2008). Citizen attitudes toward the police in Canada. *Policing: An International Journal of Police Strategies & Management, 31,* 578–95. http://demo1.emeraldinsight.com/Insight/viewContentItem.do?contentType =Article&hdAction=lnkhtml&contentId=1753881&history=false.

Paul, R., and L. Elder. (1999). *Critical thinking handbook: Basic theory and instructional structures.* http://www.criticalthinking.org.

Paul, R., L. Elder, and T. Bartell. (1997). *California teacher preparation for instruction in critical thinking: Research findings and policy recommendations.* Sacramento: California Commission on Teacher Credentialing. http://www.criticalthinking.org.

Schuck, P. (1999, December 20). East London arsonist freed on probation. *The London Free Press,* p. A5.

Sternberg, R.J., H.L. Roediger, & D.F. Halpern. (2006). *Critical thinking in psychology.* London, UK: Cambridge University Press.

United States Department of Justice. Bureau of Justice Statistics. (1998, December 11). *Homicide trends in the US: Law enforcement officers killed.* http://www.ojp.usdoj.gov/bjs/homicide/leok.htm.

United States Department of Justice. Bureau of Justice Statistics. (1999, June 3). *Surveys in 12 cities show widespread community support for police.* Press release. http://www.ojp.usdoj.gov/bjs/pub/press/cvpcs98.pr.

Wade, C., & C. Tavris. (2000). *Psychology* (6th ed.). Upper Saddle River, NJ: Prentice Hall.

Wilson, J.Q. (1968). *Varieties of criminal behavior.* Cambridge, MA: Harvard University Press.

EXERCISES AND REVIEW

Self-Test

Circle the correct answer.

1. The statement "Smiling influences the impressions that people have about law enforcement officers" is an example of

    a. a hypothesis

    b. a theory

    c. a case study

    d. all of the above

2. Which of the following represents an ethical issue for a researcher?

    a. a new drug being tested for its effectiveness is showing harmful effects in research participants

    b. in observational study the researcher has to invade the participant's privacy to get meaningful results

    c. a study on aggression causes research participants to become aggressive

    d. all of the above

3. Informed consent requires that research participants

    a. know the purpose of the study, the procedures involved, and the risks and benefits associated with the study

    b. be able to withdraw from the study for any reason without negative consequences

    c. must understand the information provided

    d. all of the above

4. A researcher selects at random one out of every five names from a list of offenders in the country. The researcher is attempting to obtain

    a. a representative sample of the offender population

    b. an unrepresentative sample of the offender population

    c. an experimental and a control group

    d. a homogeneous subsample of offenders

5. A researcher is studying the effects of prison crowding on inmate aggressive behaviour. In this study, crowding is the

    a. dependent variable

    b. independent variable

    c. random assignment

    d. mysterious third variable

6. In the above study, the dependent variable is

  a. aggressive behaviour

  b. crowding

  c. the inmate

  d. the prison

7. Which of the following research methods allows cause–effect inferences?

  a. case study

  b. epidemiological method

  c. experimental method

  d. correlational method

8. A psychologist involved in basic research seeks to accomplish the goal of

  a. description

  b. explanation

  c. prediction

  d. all of the above

9. A cultural psychologist is likely to be interested in

  a. international studies

  b. immigrant and refugee adjustment issues

  c. diversity issues

  d. all of the above

10. A forensic psychologist is most likely to be involved in

  a. telling a jury what to do

  b. assessment and treatment of offenders

  c. counselling high school students

  d. none of the above

Thinking About Psychology and Law Enforcement

1. Electronic monitoring programs (EMPs) were first developed in the United States in the 1980s for the purpose of enforcing the house arrest of offenders. The advantages of EMPs are that offenders can be sentenced to remain in their homes and their whereabouts can be monitored by having them wear electronic equipment that emits signals, such as an electronic ankle bracelet. An added advantage is that EMPs offer potentially inexpensive alternatives to housing offenders in jail. However, the jury is still out on the effectiveness of such programs (Bonta et al., 1999).

   Design a study to evaluate the impact of EMPs on recidivism and their value as true alternatives to prisons.

2. Wilson (1968) classified law enforcement into three main styles: legalistic (law enforcement to the limits of authority), watchman (order maintenance with discretion not to arrest), and social service (meeting the service needs of the community). Formulate a research question on styles of law enforcement and design a research method to answer the hypothesis you develop.

3. Which of the seven research methods would you use to address the following questions? Why?

   a. Should there be mandatory sentences for everyone convicted of a crime?

   b. Do tall, heavy, and blond recruits make better law enforcement officers than those who are short, light, and dark-haired?

   c. Should countries ban probation and parole?

   d. Is the answer to decreasing crime rates hiring more law enforcement officers?

CHAPTER 2

Biological Basis of Behaviour

,

CHAPTER OBJECTIVES

After completing this chapter, you should be able to:

- Understand the biological basis of human behaviour.
- Describe the structure of the nervous system, its basic elements, and the channels of communication.
- Understand the role of the endocrine system.

PREVIEW SCENARIO

Marilyn Sheppard was assaulted and murdered in July 1954. Dr. Sam Sheppard, her husband, was charged and convicted of murdering his wife. Mrs. Sheppard's body was found in a position suggesting she had been raped. The fact that she had been sexually assaulted was not revealed by the prosecution at the doctor's trial. Also, prosecutors argued that the blood found at the murder scene came from a knife that Dr. Sheppard used to kill his wife. However, the knife was not presented as evidence. In fact, no knife was ever found, and no other suspect was ever investigated.

After Dr. Sheppard served ten years in prison, the US Supreme Court ordered a retrial on the basis that the original trial had been "tainted by excessive press attention and a carnival-like atmosphere in the courtroom." The retrial resulted in Dr. Sheppard's acquittal. He had always claimed that the real murderer was a bushy-haired stranger with whom he had struggled on the night of the murder. Dr. Sheppard died in 1970. His ordeal inspired the television program The Fugitive *and a movie of the same name.*

Four decades later, DNA testing of blood and tissue samples taken from Dr. Sheppard's exhumed body provided evidence that he had been wrongfully convicted of murdering his wife. The DNA evidence pointed to Richard Eberling, a former window washer at the Sheppards' lakeside house. Eberling first came under suspicion in 1959, when a ring of Mrs. Sheppard's was found in his home. His DNA type was found in semen taken from Mrs. Sheppard. Eberling is now in prison for the 1984 murder of an elderly widow. Dr. Sheppard's son, Sam Reese Sheppard, is seeking a declaration of innocence for his father from a court before he can collect damages, which could run as high as $2 million. (Butterfield, 1998)

Dr. Sheppard's case is not isolated. In Canada, Guy Paul Morin was wrongly convicted of murder and finally acquitted on the basis of DNA evidence.

INTRODUCTION

Human behaviour and mental processes are influenced by biological structures and functions. This chapter explores the biology–psychology connection with a particular focus on the structures and functions of the human nervous system. While biology is not destiny, all human behaviour has some biological basis.

THE NERVOUS SYSTEM

An officer observes a car failing to stop at a stop sign and decides to pursue it. She sets her own car in motion and starts the chase. In this common scenario, a lot of information is transmitted and processed by the officer's nervous system. For example, the nervous system takes in information from the environment (the failure of a vehicle to stop at a stop sign), interprets the perceived information (a traffic violation), and regulates the officer's response (setting her own vehicle in motion) to the environmental event (vehicle failure to stop at a stop sign).

The **nervous system** is a communication network of the body. Electrical signals that control physical reactions are transmitted through neurons, or nerve cells (explained in detail later in the chapter). The various functions performed by the nervous system are complex. A useful way of understanding them is to look at the structural divisions within the nervous system. The two main divisions are the peripheral nervous system and the central nervous system (Figure 2.1).

Peripheral Nervous System (PNS)

The **peripheral nervous system** (PNS) is a system of inputs and outputs. On the input side, *afferent nerves* (bundles of neurons) carry information from the sensory receptors—for example, the eyes and ears—to the central nervous system (CNS). On the output side, *efferent nerves* carry signals from the CNS to the voluntary muscles (**somatic nervous system**) and the involuntary muscles and glands (**autonomic nervous system**). In the introductory example, the visual sensory information about the law-breaking motorist is carried by the officer's afferent nerves to her CNS. The brain interprets the sensory information, makes a decision on the officer's response to the situation, and sends signals through the efferent nerves to appropriate muscles to initiate the officer's response of setting her vehicle in motion.

The autonomic system has two general divisions. The **sympathetic system** takes control when there is an internal or external threat. It makes a person more alert and readies the body for combat and use of energy. For example, the sympathetic system dilates the pupils, inhibits the salivary glands (causing dry mouth), speeds up the heart, and inhibits digestion when an officer confronts a dangerous suspect or is involved in a raid. This pattern of arousal is often called the *fight or flight* response.

The **parasympathetic system** is the opposite of the sympathetic system. It turns off a person's alert state, calms the person down, and promotes recuperation from "battle." For example, the parasympathetic system constricts the pupils, stimulates the salivary glands, and slows down the heart after an officer has successfully handled a dangerous suspect or raid.

nervous system
communication network of the body that controls thoughts, feelings, and actions

peripheral nervous system
major division of the nervous system that relays information from sensory receptors to central nervous system

somatic nervous system
division of the peripheral nervous system that controls the voluntary muscles

autonomic nervous system
division of the peripheral nervous system that controls the involuntary muscles and glands

sympathetic system
division of the autonomic nervous system that makes a person alert and ready to use energy when there is an internal or external threat

parasympathetic system
division of the autonomic nervous system that restores the body to a normal state after a threat has passed

FIGURE 2.1   Divisions of the Nervous System

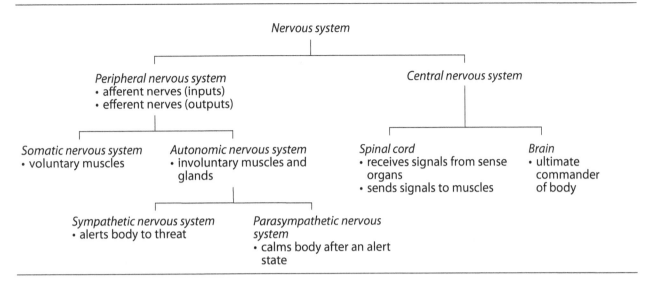

Central Nervous System (CNS)

The **central nervous system** (CNS) is the body's major control centre. It interprets sensory information taken in by the eyes, ears, mouth, nose, and skin and sends orders to the body to respond to this information. The CNS consists of the spinal cord and the brain.

central nervous system
major division of the nervous system that interprets sensory information and sends orders to the body to respond

THE SPINAL CORD

The *spinal cord*, which is made up of neural tissue and brain cells, runs from the base of the brain down the centre of the spinal column. It is protected from injury by vertebrae (bones) and is surrounded by spinal fluid, which acts as a shock absorber. The spinal cord is an extension of the brain, receiving signals from the sense organs and sending them to the muscles. It can operate both independently from and in cooperation with the brain. For example, a reflex such as a knee jerk can be automatic, without the brain's involvement. More complex behaviours, however, require the spinal cord to work with the ultimate commander of the body, the brain.

THE BRAIN

The *brain* is protected by the skull. Various areas of the brain have different functions. The brain is made up of three parts: the hindbrain, the midbrain, and the forebrain.

Hindbrain

The *hindbrain* is at the top of the spinal cord. It is made up of three important areas: the medulla, the pons, and the cerebellum (Figure 2.2). The **medulla** is located between the spinal cord and the pons. Its main function is to coordinate the basic life-support systems of the body (Levinthal, 1996): blood pressure, heart activity, breathing, swallowing, coughing, digestion, and vomiting. Abnormal functioning of the medulla can lead to death.

medulla
part of hindbrain that coordinates the basic life-support systems of the body

FIGURE 2.2   Parts of the Brain

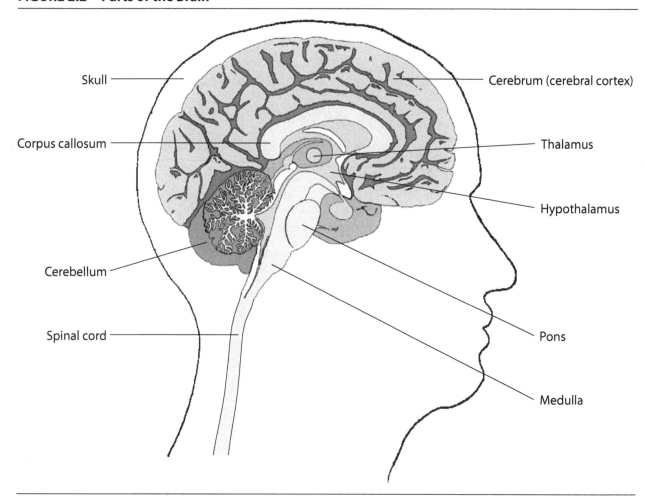

Skull — Cerebrum (cerebral cortex)

Corpus callosum — Thalamus

Hypothalamus

Cerebellum

Spinal cord — Pons

Medulla

pons
part of hindbrain involved in maintaining a state of alertness

Pons means bridge in Latin. The pons is located above the medulla and contains a network of fibres called the reticular formation, which has a number of important functions, including regulating attention and sleep, and modulating pain. It is also involved in energizing the rest of the brain and maintaining its state of alertness for incoming information (Levinthal, 1996). The reticular formation of Officer Sanjay, who is startled by a sudden noise, increases his bodily arousal and prepares his body for appropriate action. Similarly, the reticular formation of Officer Monica screens out background noise to help her sleep soundly after a long shift.

cerebellum
part of hindbrain involved in maintaining balance, coordinating movement, and regulating muscle tone

Cerebellum means little brain. The cerebellum is located behind the medulla and the pons. It is involved in maintaining balance, coordinating movement, and regulating muscle tone. Damage to the cerebellum makes it difficult to perform smooth, skilled activities and everyday functions such as walking in a straight line and feeding oneself. Intoxicated drivers may have difficulty walking a straight line due to impairment of the cerebellum by alcohol.

Midbrain

substantia nigra
part of the midbrain involved in controlling body movements

The *midbrain* is above the hindbrain and serves as a centre of control of motor and sensory reflexes. A specific region of the midbrain, the **substantia nigra**, controls body movements. Degeneration of the substantia nigra may result in Parkinson's disease, a disorder in which weakness, poor balance, rigidity of the limbs, tremors, and other motor difficulties such as with initiating movements are seen. Former boxing champion Muhammad Ali and actor Michael J. Fox suffer from Parkinson's disease.

Forebrain

The *forebrain* sits on top of the midbrain and is the most complex section of the brain. It has two main areas: the hypothalamus and the limbic system, and the cerebrum or cerebral cortex. The **hypothalamus** is small but is one of the most influential structures in the brain. It regulates a wide range of bodily functions and emotional behaviours: hunger, thirst, sexual behaviour, body temperature, and bodily changes associated with strong emotions. Electrical stimulation of the hypothalamus can trigger aggression or pleasant sensations. Similarly, damage to the hypothalamus can result in major behavioural abnormalities such as overindulging in enormous amounts of food or starving to death. The **suprachiasmatic nucleus**, located in the hypothalamus, has been identified as the primary structure that controls circadian (daily) rhythms, such as the sleep–wakefulness cycle.

Limbus is Latin for border. The **limbic system** surrounds the hypothalamus and plays a vital role in emotional behaviour during periods of stress. This system is made up of the amygdala (Latin for almond) and the hippocampus (Greek for sea horse). The **amygdala** is involved in reactions to unpleasant sensations and the learning of fear. Damage to the amygdala can result in an inability to recognize facial expressions of emotion, such as anger. The **hippocampus** plays an important role in memory. Damage to this part of the brain can result in an inability to store or recall new information, or to remember events that were stored before damage occurred.

The **cerebral cortex** is the second area of the forebrain (Figure 2.3). *Cortex* is Latin for bark, and the cerebral cortex can be thought of as the "bark" that covers the rest of the brain. It looks like a giant walnut and is divided into three areas: sensory, motor, and association. The sensory area is involved in registering sensory information such as sound, pressure, temperature, touch sensations, and visual images. The motor area is involved in controlling voluntary movement. The association area is involved in language, memory storage, perception, and thought.

The cerebral cortex has a left and a right hemisphere. Each cerebral hemisphere has four important areas: the occipital lobe, the temporal lobe, the parietal lobe, and the frontal lobe. The two hemispheres are connected by the *corpus callosum*, which supports the transmission of information between the two brain hemispheres.

The **occipital lobes** are at the back of the cerebral cortex and are involved in registering visual information. The occipital lobes consist of the primary visual cortex and the visual association areas. The primary visual cortex enables us to see. Damage to this area may result in visual agnosia, the inability to combine individual parts of an object into the complete object. For example, a person may not recognize a bicycle even though he may see parts of the bicycle, such as the crossbar, one front wheel, and one back wheel. Damage to the visual association areas results in losing the visual ability to recognize familiar objects. A person may be unable to identify objects visually but have no difficulty identifying them with her other senses, such as touch.

Temporal means near the temples. The **temporal lobes** are on the side of the cerebral cortex and are involved in registering auditory information (sounds). The temporal lobes consist of the primary auditory cortex, Wernicke's area, and the

hypothalamus
part of forebrain that regulates a wide range of bodily functions and emotional behaviours, including hunger, thirst, and sexual behaviour

suprachiasmatic nucleus
part of the hypothalamus that controls circadian (daily) rhythmic cycles, such as the sleep–wake cycle

limbic system
part of forebrain that plays a vital role in emotional behaviour during periods of stress

amygdala
part of limbic system involved in unpleasant sensations and learning of fear

hippocampus
part of limbic system involved in memory

cerebral cortex
part of forebrain involved in language, memory, and thinking

occipital lobe
part of cerebral cortex involved in vision

temporal lobe
part of cerebral cortex involved in audition

FIGURE 2.3   Areas of the Cerebral Cortex

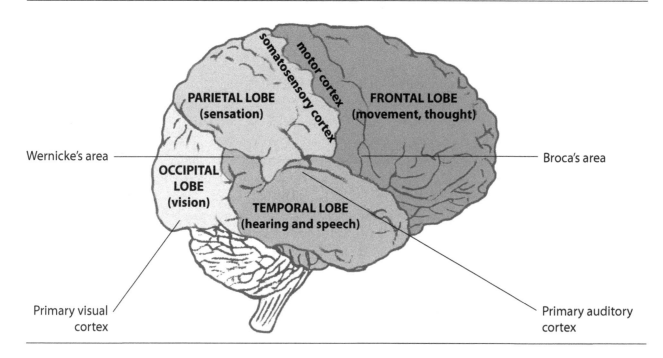

temporal association areas. The primary auditory cortex enables us to hear. Damage to this part of the brain may result in hearing loss or total deafness. Wernicke's area is involved in understanding speech and in choosing words for speaking or writing. Damage to this area may result in Wernicke's aphasia, a disorder in which a person can speak fluently but the content of his or her speech is either vague or incomprehensible. The temporal association areas are involved in storing memories and interpreting sounds. Damage to these areas results in major changes to these aspects of human behaviour.

The **parietal lobes** sit on top of the cerebral cortex and are involved in registering somatosensory information (physical and touch sensations). The parietal lobes contain the somatosensory cortex and the parietal association areas. The somatosensory cortex is involved in processing such information as touch, pressure, temperature, and pain. Damage to this area of the brain may result in loss of sensitivity to touch, inability to tell textures apart on the basis of touch, and numbness in a body part. The parietal association areas are involved in spatial orientation (awareness of position and location of the body), sense of direction, and memory storage. Damage to these areas results in the inability to identify objects by touch alone, even though the sense of touch still exists.

Finally, the **frontal lobes** are on top and in front of the cerebral cortex and contain the motor cortex, Broca's area, and the frontal association areas. The motor cortex is involved in controlling voluntary body movement. The right motor cortex controls voluntary movement on the left side of the body, while the left motor cortex controls voluntary movement on the right side of the body. Damage to the motor cortex may result in paralysis, loss of coordination, or grand mal epilepsy (epilepsy that involves major seizures). **Broca's area** is involved in the muscle movements that produce speech or verbal sounds. Damage to this area leads to Broca's aphasia, a loss

parietal lobe
part of cerebral cortex involved in touch, pressure, temperature, pain, body awareness, and spatial orientation

frontal lobe
part of cerebral cortex involved in voluntary body movement, thinking, motivation, and planning

Broca's area
part of frontal lobe involved in muscle movements that produce speech or verbal sounds

or impairment in the ability to use or understand language. People with Broca's aphasia know what they want to say but are unable to say it. When they do speak, their speech is very slow, laborious, and unclear. The frontal association areas are involved in emotional responses, impulse control, motivation, and planning. The region closest to the front of the brain is the **prefrontal cortex**, which is involved in intellectual abilities and personality traits. Damage to the frontal and prefrontal association areas results in major changes to these higher-order behaviours.

prefrontal cortex
part of frontal lobe involved in intellectual abilities and personality traits

Left Brain, Right Brain

As mentioned earlier, there are two sides to the brain, a left side and a right side. The **left** and **right hemispheres** of the brain are mirror images of each other and are connected by the corpus callosum. Each hemisphere controls the opposite side of the body: the left hemisphere controls the right side of the body, and the right hemisphere controls the left side of the body. This means that damage to the left side of the brain is likely to result in impairment in the right side of the body, and vice versa.

left hemisphere
side of brain involved in verbal ability

right hemisphere
side of brain involved in visual–spatial abilities

Even though the two cerebral hemispheres have similar structures, they have some functional differences. **Lateralization** is a term used to describe the functional differences between the two halves. Verbal ability (speech, language), logic, and mathematical abilities generally and calculation particularly seem to fall within the realm of the left brain. In contrast, non-verbal, visual–spatial abilities, recognition and expression of emotion, and musical abilities are all within the realm of the right brain.

lateralization
functional differences between the two brain hemispheres

Normally, the two hemispheres of the brain collaborate in sensing, interpreting, and responding to the world. Still, each hemisphere also has a mind of its own—that is, its own efficiencies in sensing, interpreting, and responding to the environment (Sperry, 1984). A *split-brain operation* involves surgically separating the hemispheres by cutting the corpus callosum. Split-brain operations are performed on patients with severe grand mal epilepsy to eliminate seizures. People who undergo these operations seem to show no major changes in intelligence or personality.

Split-brain operations allow researchers to investigate the independent functioning of the two cerebral hemispheres. An image shown to the right visual field of a split-brain patient will be sent to the left hemisphere while an image shown to the left visual field will be sent to the right hemisphere. Split-brain patients are unable to verbally name an object registered in the right hemisphere, but are able to correctly grasp the object with their left (but not right) hand!

Methods of Studying the Brain

Doctors and scientists use several technological methods to examine the brain and its activity, and to gain an understanding of how the brain works.

The *electroencephalogram* (EEG) records the electrical activity of the brain through electrodes placed on the scalp beside each lobe. Computer programs convert the electrical signals into a "picture" of brain activity (lines of brainwaves). The EEG is used extensively in diagnosing epilepsy and sleep disorders.

Dr. John Connolly, a Dalhousie University researcher, uses a modified EEG approach to assess patients who cannot move, speak, or communicate in any other way because of stroke, cerebral palsy, or accident, and those who are in a coma or persistent vegetative state. Connolly's technique involves presenting nonsensical sentences (for example, "The pizza was too hot to sing") and monitoring the brain's electrical response to these sentences (McIlroy, 2001). People with properly working brains respond to the nonsensical sentences (the singing pizza, in this case) and send out a distinct electrical signal called *event-related potential* (ERP). ERP in a person who has an active mind trapped inside a paralyzed body indicates that the person is capable of comprehending speech. Those with non-functional brains do not react to the nonsensical sentences—they do not show ERP. The measurement of particular event-related potentials is a major aspect of some technologies designed to detect deception (see Box 2.1).

The *magnetic resonance imaging* (MRI) scanner uses a powerful magnetic field to produce a computer-generated image of the brain. It can also be used to study individual bundles of nerves in other areas of the body. An MRI scan can show any tumours, tissue degeneration, and blood clots or leaks that may signal a stroke.

The *superconducting quantum interference device* (SQUID) scanner is sensitive to changes in magnetic fields that occur when neurons fire (see the section on neurons that follows). This method identifies the location of neural activity.

The *positron emission tomography* (PET) scanner shows biochemical activity in the brain after radioactive substances are introduced through the bloodstream. Brain cells that are active take up more of the radioactive material and emit more subatomic particles called positrons. However, because of the need for radioactive substances, PET scans cannot be used to capture rapidly changing brain activity.

The *functional MRI* (fMRI) scanner operates on the principle that active neurons require more oxygen and thus more blood flow is directed toward those sites. The fMRI scanner has been connected to three-dimensional virtual reality displays that allow observation of the brain while it is working on cognitive tasks, including activity that occurs in less than a second.

The *magnetoencephalograph* (MEG) is used to measure weak magnetic fields generated by the activity of neurons in the brain. Unlike PET and fMRI scans, MEG measures this activity as it occurs. One disadvantage is that while the MEG accurately measures brain activity close to the surface of the brain, it is less accurate when activity in deep structures (such as the thalamus) is being measured. When the MEG output is projected onto MRI scans, both the location and the function of brain activity can be identified.

NEURONS AND NEUROTRANSMITTERS

Neurons

neuron
specialized cell that transmits electrical signals throughout the nervous system through an electrochemical process

As the basic units of the nervous system, **neurons** are specialized cells that transmit electrical signals throughout the system through an electrochemical process. The many neurons in the body have various shapes and sizes, depending on their function. The brain alone contains about 100 billion neurons.

A typical neuron is made up of four parts: dendrites, cell body, axon, and terminal buttons (Figure 2.4). The *dendrites* are a cluster of fibres that branch out from the cell body, providing increased surface area for receiving signals from other neurons. Dendrites carry these chemical signals to the *cell body*, or soma, which contains the cell nucleus. The nucleus is the control centre of the cell and houses the *chromosomes*, long strands of deoxyribonucleic acid (DNA) molecules that carry genetic information, or genes. All human DNA is contained within 23 pairs of chromo-

BOX 2.1   Brain Fingerprinting

Technology has long been used to assist police officers in detecting deception. In 1921, a police department in California began using a device that measured respiration, pulse, and blood pressure. Modern polygraphs typically record heart rate, blood pressure, respiration, and electrical conductance of the skin as subjects are asked a series of questions. The basic logic behind tests like the polygraph is that there are involuntary behavioural or physiological patterns of activity that can be used to indicate deception. Although polygraph tests are commonly conducted by police during investigations, the consensus among psychologists is that the polygraph is not a valid means of detecting deception and thus polygraph results should not be admissible in court proceedings.

Some efforts to assist police officers in detecting deception have explored new ways of relating involuntary physical responses to knowledge of meaningful information. One recent approach, **brain fingerprinting**, uses brain activity as a physical marker to infer deception. An electroencephalogram (EEG) measures the electrical activity of the brain through electrodes placed on the scalp. The EEG produces a number of distinctive brainwave patterns. One of these patterns, called the P300 event-related potential (ERP), may result when a person is shown meaningful information (that is, information the person already knows). If the perpetrator of a crime is shown a picture of a crime scene and denies recognizing it, but the P300 ERP occurs, the indication is that the person is lying.

Brain fingerprinting may seem an innovative way to assess deception, but it is not without problems. Some evidence suggests that brain fingerprinting is, like the polygraph, susceptible to countermeasures. The difference in brainwave patterns between meaningful and non-meaningful items might be minimized by, for example, imagining a particular stimulus whenever a non-meaningful item is shown. Brain fingerprinting has been admitted as evidence in one case (*Harrington v. Iowa*, 2003) in which an individual convicted of murder two decades earlier appealed for a reversal, partly on the basis of a brain fingerprinting test that appeared to show he did not recognize some details of the crime. Ultimately, the Iowa Supreme Court ordered a new trial. However, the test results were not a primary factor in this decision.

Sources: Iacono and Lykken (1997); Rosenfeld (2005); Rosenfeld et al. (2004).

brain fingerprinting
the use of brain activity as a physical marker indicating deception

somes. *Genes* are the recipe, or instructions, for making a human being. Through complex interactions with the internal and external environment, they determine everything about a person, including looks, eye colour, and foot size. In 2003, scientists around the world completed mapping and describing the human genetic code as part of the Human Genome Project. This project involved identifying all of the approximately 30,000 genes in human DNA, plus the 3 billion chemicals involved, and then putting all this information into a database.

FIGURE 2.4   Structure of a Neuron and Communication Between Neurons

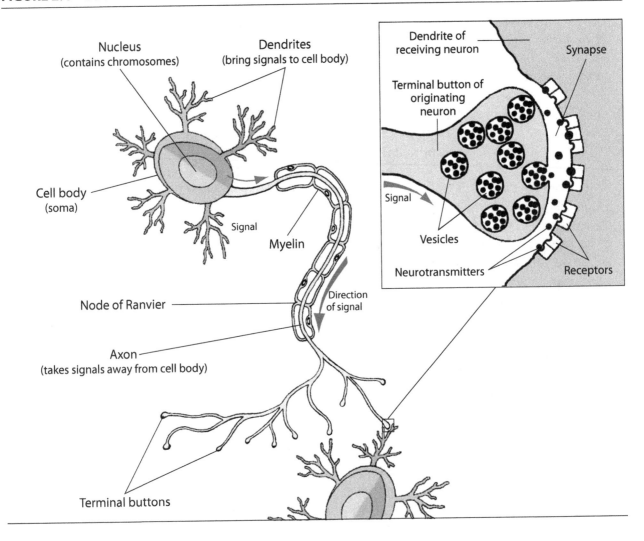

The cell body integrates the signals from the dendrites. If an integrated signal reaches a certain threshold, then an action potential is generated and transmitted down the axon (see the section below). The *axon* is a tube-like structure that carries action potentials from the cell body to the axon terminals. *Terminal buttons* are small branches at the end of axons that relay messages from neuron to neuron.

Axons are either myelinated or unmyelinated. *Myelinated axons* are wrapped in a myelin sheath, which is a white fatty substance. There are small gaps, called nodes of Ranvier, in the myelin wrapping along the axon. The myelin sheath has two functions: it protects the longer axons from electrical interference from other neurons, and the sheath and the gaps in it allow signals to be transmitted more rapidly along the axon. Multiple sclerosis is a disease of progressive degeneration of the myelin sheaths along the axons, which results in a variety of symptoms including pain sensations, cognitive disruptions, and jerky, uncoordinated movements, among others.

Action Potentials

As mentioned earlier, neurons send messages through an electrochemical process. Basically, chemicals in the body (such as calcium, sodium, and potassium) are electrically charged. The electrically charged molecules in the chemicals are called ions, and the charge can be positive or negative. **Action potentials** explain how and when information is transmitted from one neuron to another. When a neuron is at rest (not sending a signal), it works to maintain a resting potential by pumping out positive ions and retaining negative ions. As a result, there is a negative charge of –70 millivolts (mV, or one-thousandth of a volt) inside the neuron compared with outside the neuron. When a neuron is stimulated by either an external stimulus (light, noise, or pressure) or other neurons, a graded potential occurs. As their name implies, *graded potentials* vary in intensity depending on the strength of the stimulus or the chemical signal from other neurons. Usually, graded potentials travel down the dendrites of the neuron to the cell body.

> **action potential**
> the firing of a neuron

If the electrical activity of graded potentials travelling down the dendrites has a magnitude above the threshold of that neuron, causing it to move toward 0 mV, at about –55 mV an action potential is initiated in the axon. (If this threshold is not reached, no action potential occurs.) The action potential is an explosion of electrical activity that moves down the axon in a chain reaction that is similar to a row of dominoes falling. As the action potential travels down the axon, positive ions enter the neuron through pores called ion channels. As the positive ions enter a section of the axon, the resting potential is disturbed and the interior of the cell becomes positively charged (up to +40 mV) at that point. After about 1 millisecond, the neuron pumps positive ions out of that section of the axon and negative ions re-enter the neuron. Once the resting potential is re-established along the axon, the neuron is ready to fire again.

Action potentials travel more quickly down myelinated and larger-diameter axons. A law enforcement officer who is hit by a bullet feels the bullet before feeling the pain associated with the bullet hitting her or him. This is because the axons of the sensory neurons for pressure are large and myelinated, whereas the axons in the pain neurons are thin and unmyelinated. Action potentials follow an all-or-none law: they occur at full strength down the length of the axon or not at all, depending on whether or not the threshold of –55 mV is reached. This action is similar to firing a gun: once the trigger has passed a certain point (threshold), the gun will fire regardless of the pressure and speed applied to the trigger.

Neurotransmitters

Knowing the structure of a neuron and how it functions or "fires" is important when considering how messages pass from one neuron to another. When a neuron fires, the action potential travels to the terminal button. In each terminal button are sacs called vesicles that contain **neurotransmitters**, chemicals manufactured by the body. Different neurotransmitters affect different brain activities, from emotions to learning to muscle actions. The arrival of the action potential stimulates the vesicles to move to the surface of the terminal button of the sending neuron, and to discharge the neurotransmitters into the narrow space between the surface of the terminal

> **neurotransmitter**
> chemical that transmits messages between neurons

button and the dendrite or cell body of the next or receiving neuron. This space into which the neurotransmitters are released is called a *synapse*, the Greek word for junction.

Three things happen to the neurotransmitters once they have had their impact on the receiving neuron. Some neurotransmitters are deactivated by enzymes that break them down into their chemical components, and are removed. Other neurotransmitters diffuse away from the synapse. However, most neurotransmitters are reused in a process called *synaptic reuptake*. They are pulled back into the axon terminal button by molecular pumps and formed into new vesicles. The neurotransmitters must be removed from the synapse; if not, they would continue to affect the receiving neuron.

Neurotransmitters can either excite or inhibit the receiving neuron. If the neurotransmitter is *excitatory*, then it causes positive ions to enter the receiving neuron. Thus, an excitatory message provides chemical information that makes the firing of the receiving neuron and the travel of the action potential down its axon more likely. An *inhibitory* neurotransmitter allows negative ions to enter the receiving neuron. An inhibitory message provides chemical information to either prevent or make it less likely for the receiving neuron to fire. The brain controls the entire communication system, with each neuron receiving thousands of signals at once and responding based on the pattern of excitatory and inhibitory signals. If the system breaks down, illnesses such as epilepsy and memory disorders can result.

Table 2.1 provides an overview of the universally recognized neurotransmitters and their location and function in the nervous system. (For explanations of the disorders mentioned in the table, see Chapter 10.)

THE ENDOCRINE SYSTEM

endocrine system
chemical communication network of the body that stimulates and regulates human behaviour through hormones produced by the glands

gland
organ that secretes hormones into the bloodstream

hormone
chemical substance produced and released into the bloodstream for the purpose of affecting the growth and functioning of other parts of the body

The **endocrine system** is another chemical communication network that stimulates and regulates human behaviour. The endocrine system consists of **glands**, organs that secrete chemicals called hormones into the bloodstream. A **hormone** is a substance that is produced and released into the bloodstream for the purpose of affecting the growth and functioning of other parts of the body. Different hormones perform different functions. For example, the hormone oxytocin stimulates cuddling and production of breast milk in mothers of newborn babies.

The glands that constitute the endocrine system from the head down are the pituitary gland, pineal gland, thyroid gland, parathyroid glands, thymus, adrenal glands, pancreas, and sex glands, or gonads (ovaries in females and testes in males) (Figure 2.5).

Pituitary Gland

The *pituitary gland* is located in the brain just below the hypothalamus. It is involved in producing growth hormones. A person who does not produce enough growth hormone is likely to become a dwarf. Conversely, a person who produces too much growth hormone is likely to become a giant.

The pituitary gland is also considered the master gland, even though it is only the size of a pea and is regulated by the hypothalamus. It is the master gland because it releases hormones that activate the remaining endocrine glands.

TABLE 2.1   Universally Recognized Neurotransmitters

Neurotransmitter	Location	Function
Acetylcholine	Central nervous system, autonomic nervous system, neuromuscular junctions	Involved in attention, learning, and memory, and produces muscle contraction; implicated in Alzheimer's disease
Glutamate	Most prevalent excitatory neurotransmitter in the brain and the retina of the eye	Important in long-term memory and perception of pain
Gamma-amino butyric acid (GABA)	Most prevalent inhibitory neurotransmitter in the central nervous system	Involved in eating, aggression, and sleeping; implicated in anxiety disorders
Dopamine	Central nervous system	Involved in movement, attention, mood, and learning; implicated in Parkinson's disease and schizophrenia
Norepinephrine	Central nervous system, autonomic nervous system	Control of alertness and wakefulness, mood, motivation, and directed attention; implicated in bipolar mood disorders
Serotonin	Central nervous system	Regulation of mood, pain, and dreaming; control of eating, sleeping, mood, and arousal; implicated in insomnia and mood disorders
Endorphins	Central nervous system	Pain suppression, pleasurable feelings, appetite, and placebo effects
Adenosine triphosphate	Throughout the nervous system	Involved in memory

Pineal Gland

The *pineal gland* is a small gland in the brain below the corpus callosum and between the cerebral hemispheres. It produces the hormone melatonin, which, under direction from the suprachiasmatic nucleus of the hypothalamus, regulates the sleep–wakefulness cycle. When night falls, the pineal gland produces more melatonin to make us feel less alert. When day breaks, melatonin levels drop, making us feel alert again.

Thyroid and Parathyroid Glands

The *thyroid* and *parathyroid glands* are located in the front part of the neck just below the larynx (voice box). The thyroid is involved in regulating the body's metabolism, the chemical activity of cells that releases energy from nutrients or uses energy to create other substances. The thyroid and parathyroid glands help to regulate calcium in the body.

FIGURE 2.5   Endocrine System

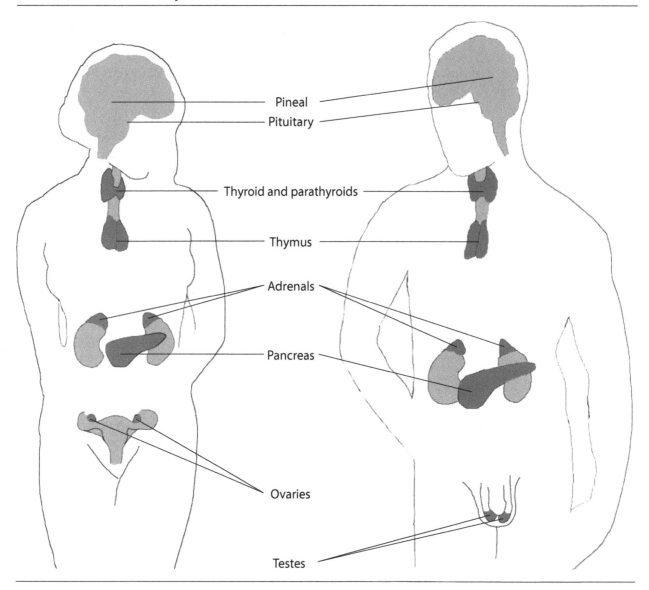

Pineal

Pituitary

Thyroid and parathyroids

Thymus

Adrenals

Pancreas

Ovaries

Testes

↙ Thymus

The *thymus* is in the upper part of the chest, beside the heart. It produces T-lymphocytes, cells that fight infections.

– Adrenal Glands

The *adrenal glands* are located just above the kidneys and are responsible for releasing such hormones as epinephrine, norepinephrine, and corticoids. These hormones are involved in activating stress responses, as well as regulating immune responses, carbohydrate metabolism, and electrolyte balance.

⌐ Pancreas

The pancreas is located near the small intestine and the stomach. It is involved in releasing digestive enzymes (chemicals that break down carbohydrates, fats, proteins, and acids) and insulin and glucagon (hormones that regulate the level of glucose, a sugar in the blood). People with diabetes have too little insulin to break down sugar in the blood, whereas people with hypoglycemia have too much insulin.

─ Gonads

Finally, the *sex glands* are involved in releasing androgens (including testosterone) in males and estrogen and progesterone in females. These hormones make reproduction possible, regulate sexual motivation, and determine secondary sex characteristics, such as facial hair in males and breasts in females.

POINTS TO REMEMBER

This chapter discusses the relationship between psychology and biology. The nervous system consists of the central nervous system and the peripheral nervous system. The spinal cord and the brain comprise the central nervous system. The peripheral nervous system consists of the somatic division and the autonomic division. The autonomic division is itself divided into the sympathetic and parasympathetic divisions. Neurons and neurotransmitters are the basic units of the nervous system and the carriers of its signals. The glands of the endocrine system are a chemical communication network that, through hormones, also stimulate and regulate human behaviour.

KEY TERMS

action potential

amygdala

autonomic nervous system

brain fingerprinting

Broca's area

central nervous system

cerebellum

cerebral cortex

endocrine system

frontal lobe

gland

hippocampus

hormone

hypothalamus

lateralization

left hemisphere

limbic system

medulla

nervous system

neuron

neurotransmitter

occipital lobe

parasympathetic system

parietal lobe

peripheral nervous system

pons

prefrontal cortex

right hemisphere

somatic nervous system

substantia nigra

suprachiasmatic nucleus

sympathetic system

temporal lobe

REFERENCES

Butterfield, F. (1988, March 5). New DNA test suggests Sheppard did not kill his wife. *The New York Times*.

Harrington v. Iowa, 659 NW2d 509 (Iowa 2003).

Iacono, W.G., & D.T. Lykken. (1997). The validity of the lie detector: Two surveys of scientific opinion. *Journal of Applied Psychology, 82*, 426–33.

Levinthal, C.F. (1996). *Drugs, behavior and modern society.* Needham Heights, MA: Allyn and Bacon.

McIlroy, A. (2001, June 9). Science: Neurology. *The Globe and Mail*, p. F7.

Rosenfeld, J.P. (2005). Brain fingerprinting: A critical analysis. *Scientific Review of Mental Health Practice, 4*, 20–37.

Rosenfeld, J.P., M. Soskins, G. Bosh, & A. Ryan. (2004). Simple effective countermeasures to P300-based tests of detection of concealed information. *Psychophysiology, 41*, 205–19.

Royal Canadian Mounted Police (RCMP). (2000, July 5). *Canada opens National DNA Data Bank.* Press release. http://www.rcmp-grc.gc.ca/html/nr-00-10.htm.

Sperry, R. (1984). Consciousness, personal identity and the divided brain. *Neuropsychologia, 22*(6), 661-73.

United States Department of Justice. Federal Bureau of Investigation. (1988, October 13). *The National DNA Index System.* Press release. http://www.fbi.gov/pressrel/pressrel98/dna.htm.

EXERCISES AND REVIEW

Self-Test

Circle the correct answer.

1. Which of the following is the most complex part of the brain?

    a. hindbrain

    b. midbrain

    c. forebrain

    d. all of the above are equally complex

2. The action potential is

    a. the message conducted down an axon

    b. the message conducted up an axon

    c. the best that a person can do in life

    d. none of the above

3. Which of the following is true about chromosomes?

    a. they are thread-like strands of DNA molecules that carry genes

    b. there are 23 pairs of chromosomes in every cell

    c. a and b

    d. none of the above

4. Which of the following is true about split-brain operations?

    a. they destroy a person's personality

    b. they are useless in treating severe cases of epilepsy

    c. they should be banned

    d. none of the above

5. The left hemisphere is

    a. the part of the brain that controls the verbal function

    b. the part of the brain that controls the non-verbal function

    c. lazier than the right hemisphere

    d. totally independent of the right hemisphere

6. Which of the following behaviours is controlled by the hypothalamus?

    a. overeating to the point of obesity

    b. undereating to the point of starvation

    c. drinking

    d. all of the above

7. A police officer stops a car and asks the driver to get out and walk a straight line. The officer suspects the driver has been drinking. The driver shows difficulty getting out of the car and maintaining his balance while walking. Which of the following parts of the hindbrain is likely affected in this case?

    a. cerebellum

    b. pons

    c. limbic system

    d. all of the above

8. A woman walking home alone at night notices she is being followed by a man. She gets goose bumps and her heart starts to pound. Which divisions of the nervous system are working in her?

    a. parasympathetic

    b. sympathetic

    c. somatic

    d. limbic

9. The spinal cord

    a. keeps us walking upright

    b. receives signals from the sense organs and sends signals to the muscles

    c. is a shock absorber for the body

    d. houses the neurons

10. Which of the following is the master gland?

    a. pituitary

    b. ovaries

    c. testes

    d. all of the above

Thinking About Psychology and Law Enforcement

1. What are some possible law enforcement uses of DNA evidence? How can this information help the innocent as well as the guilty? (Hint: Consider not only crimes, but also victims of accidents, natural disasters, and wars.)

2. In 2000, the RCMP opened the National DNA Data Bank, which stores DNA obtained from criminals convicted of violent offences and from crime scenes (RCMP, 2000). In the United States, the FBI has created the National DNA Index System, a similar data bank (US Department of Justice, 1998). Matches among DNA profiles can help to link crime scenes and lead police to possible serial offenders. The RCMP can also share leads with police services across Canada, and the Canadian data bank is matched against the US data bank in case crimes and offenders cross the border.

   Some experts fear that the genetic information might be misused—for example, to identify people with stigmatizing illnesses such as AIDS. Do you think these fears are valid? Why or why not? List the pros and cons of a DNA data bank and the ethical issues involved.

CHAPTER 3

Sensation and Perception

CHAPTER OBJECTIVES

After completing this chapter, you should be able to:

- Understand what is involved in detecting sensory information.
- Describe the structures and functions of the various senses.
- Understand what is involved in perception, or the interpretation of sensory information.

PREVIEW SCENARIO

Blue Line *is Canada's national law enforcement magazine. A close look at the advertisements in the June/July 1999 issue is revealing. Several of the ads involve garments and accessories for law enforcement officers, including Fecheimer Flying Cross shirts and trousers; Elbeco uniforms, turtlenecks and dickies, windshirts, and jackets; Kevlar Protera ballistic protection; R. Nicholls uniforms; Aegis body armour; Michael's holsters, belts, and belt accessories; Kevlar Correctional personal body armour; and Rocky's AlphaForce boots. There are also ads by Nat on Complex Tactical Communication that feature simultaneous multi-radio operation and multi-scan modes operation; by Panasonic featuring the CF-27 Toughbook; by Mega-Tech featuring the roadside screening device Intoxilyzer 400; by Laerdal Medical Canada featuring the automated external defibrillator, HP Heartstream ForeRunner; by Highpoint Security Technologies featuring the Taser TE86, a device that can be used as an alternative to deadly force; and by Maritime Services featuring NightSight, a device that works in daylight or total darkness and is capable of detecting suspects in hiding, recently driven cars, and so on. Finally, two products are featured by* Blue Line: *the Radix RX1 from Frazer Design Consultants, a computer designed for use in harsh environments; and the Jabra EarSet from Omega, a gadget that provides totally hands-free cellphone use. (Blue Line, 1999)*

INTRODUCTION

In carrying out their duties, law enforcement officers not only use their own sensory apparatus (eyes, ears, and so on) but also rely on external sensory and perceptual devices. Technological advancements in sensing and perceiving the world are likely to enhance the varied functions of law enforcement. This chapter discusses the twin processes of sensation and perception.

– SENSATION

sensation
process in which a sensory stimulus is detected and transmitted to the brain for interpretation

stimulus
source of physical energy that elicits a response in the sensory system

perception
process in which a sensory stimulus is sorted out and interpreted by the brain

Sensation is an everyday experience and is intimately related to perception. **Sensation** is the process in which a sensory stimulus is detected and transmitted to the brain for interpretation. A **stimulus** is a source of physical energy that elicits a response in the sensory system. Sensory stimuli take many forms, including visual, auditory, gustatory (taste), olfactory (smell), and tactile. **Perception** is the process in which a sensory stimulus is sorted out and interpreted by the brain. Sensation involves detecting the sounds emanating from the music playing on your iPod, while perception involves experiencing the melodies.

⯈ Sensing the World

THE ABSOLUTE THRESHOLD

absolute threshold
minimum sensory stimulation required for detection

To detect sensory stimuli, a sense organ requires a minimum amount of stimulation. The **absolute threshold** is the minimum sensory stimulation required for detection. Each of the senses has its own absolute threshold. For example, a sound below the absolute threshold is not heard, and a sound above the threshold is heard. The absolute threshold for vision on a dark, clear night is a candle flame 48 km away. Suppose an officer has to decide whether or not a suspect is in a dark room. She has to decide whether she heard or saw the suspect move. The officer's decision is based on detections that are in turn based on the absolute threshold.

THE DIFFERENCE THRESHOLD

difference threshold
smallest detectable difference between two sensory stimuli

A minimum amount of change in stimulation is required for a sense organ to detect a difference in the sensory stimuli. The **difference threshold** is the smallest detectable difference between two sensory stimuli. It is also known as the "just noticeable" difference. As with the absolute threshold, each of the senses has its own difference threshold. Nevertheless, the difference threshold in all cases depends on the intensity of the original sensory stimulus. The more intense the initial sensory stimulus, the more it must be decreased or increased for a difference to be noticed. For example, a brightly lit room requires a greater wattage increase for people to notice a difference than a wattage increase in a dim room.

SIGNAL DETECTION THEORY

signal detection theory
theory that considers detection of sensory stimuli in the context of background noise

The absolute and difference threshold concepts rely only on the properties of the sensory stimuli, thus ignoring important factors other than stimulus strength that may be part of detecting sensory input. The signal detection theory is an approach that focuses on additional factors, such as fatigue, expectation, motivation, and past experience. **Signal detection theory** considers detection of sensory stimuli in the context of background noise—that is, all the other sensory stimuli that are present aside from the target stimulus. For example, two law enforcement officers who are trying to take statements from witnesses to a major traffic accident must screen out the background noise (passing traffic, other people talking, ambulance sirens, and so on) to hear each other for communication. Note that background noise is any stimulus—not only sound—that interferes with signal detection. This "noise" can be a crowd of people blocking your view, a bright light shining directly into your eyes, your physical reaction to stress (pounding heart, racing thoughts), and so on.

Signal detection theory also considers decision making in the detection of a target stimulus and the fact that the decision-making process is imperfect—that is, reporting that a target stimulus is present when it is not, and reporting that a target stimulus is not present when it is. Factors that contribute to errors in judgment include fatigue and expectation. For example, an officer may shoot an innocent person who comes out of a building because the officer is expecting a suspect to appear. Similarly, an officer may accidentally shoot his partner when background noise interferes and the target stimulus (a suspect) is too hard to see, such as in the dark. Finally, an officer can get hurt if she fails to detect a suspect (target stimulus) among a crowd of people (background noise).

SENSORY ADAPTATION

Adaptation is the process of getting used to environmental stimuli or events in life. For example, seasoned law enforcement officers respond differently to hard-core criminals than do novice officers. Similarly, officers do not react with the same intensity to horrific accidents, homicides, and suicides the way they did when they were new recruits. **Sensory adaptation** is the process in which a person becomes less responsive to a sensory stimulus to which he or she is exposed for a prolonged time. A noisy apartment beside a highway seems less noisy after a person has lived in it for some time. Sensory adaptation, however, tends to work less for very strong sensory stimulation, such as the smell of sewage.

sensory adaptation
process in which people become less responsive to a sensory stimulus to which they are exposed for a prolonged time

The Sensory Systems

Controlling muscle movements and regulating the internal environment are among the important functions handled by the brain. The brain relies on information from the sensory systems to do both. A common belief is that the sensory system consists of five separate senses: sight, hearing, smell, taste, and touch. In reality, there are more senses. Table 3.1 summarizes seven known sensory systems and their stimuli, major pathways, and perceptual dimensions. The sensory organs detect stimuli in the environment, and the brain interprets the neural signals from these systems.

CUTANEOUS SENSES: JOYS AND PAINS

Cutaneous, or skin, **senses** involve touch, temperature, and pain.

cutaneous senses
skin senses

Touch

The sense of touch detects pressure against the skin. Because receptor cells of the skin senses are distributed unevenly all over the body, some areas (for example, the fingertips) are more sensitive to touch than other areas (for example, the legs).

TABLE 3.1   Characteristics of Seven Sensory Systems

Sensory System	Stimulus	Major Pathways	Perceptual Dimensions
Cutaneous (skin senses)	Pressure, temperature, tissue damage	Skin, spinal cord, sensory cortex	Pleasure, pain, texture, hot/cold, touch sensations (punch, rub, and so on)
Gustation (taste)	Substances put in mouth	Taste buds, medulla, thalamus, primary gustatory cortex	Bitterness, saltiness, sourness, sweetness, savouriness (flavour)
Audition (hearing)	Sound	Ear, auditory nerve, primary auditory cortex	Pitch, loudness, timbre (tone or quality of sound)
Olfaction (smell)	Odour	Olfactory epithelium, olfactory tract, olfactory cortex	Identification and differentiation of odours; flavour
Vestibular (balance and movement)	Head rotation, movement	Inner ear, spinal cord, cerebellum, temporal cortex	Balance, motion sickness, rotation, dizziness, posture
Kinesthetic (movement, orientation, and posture)	Stretch in skeletal muscles, joints, tendons	Receptors in joints, tendons, and muscles; spinal cord; primary motor cortex	Perception of balance, skilled body movements
Vision	Light	Eyes, retina, optic nerve, thalamus, primary visual cortex	Colour (hue, brightness, saturation), form and depth perception

Temperature

Cutaneous senses detect temperature without direct contact with the skin. Thermo-receptors are involved in detecting decreases or increases in temperature. Thermo-receptors are positioned under the skin to respond to changes in temperature at or near the skin and to help keep the body's temperature at 37 °C.

Pain

The perception of pain is a complex phenomenon that involves more than just a simple response to skin stimulation. Emotional states such as depression and anxiety, negative thoughts, and cultural differences all play an important role in the experience of pain.

gate-control theory
theory that explains the
role of psychological
factors in pain

The **gate-control theory** explains the role of psychological factors in pain. This theory proposes that a "gate" to the parts of the brain that are involved in responding to pain can be opened and closed by particular nerve receptors (Wall & Melzack, 1989). An injury to the body stimulates the nerve receptors, causing the gate to the brain to open and the pain to be experienced. Pain is reduced when another set of nerve receptors is activated, causing the gate to shut.

The gate-control theory is used to explain how acupuncture and gentle rubbing of the skin around an injury effectively reduce pain. In both cases, the relief from pain is attributed to closing the pain gate.

GUSTATION SENSES: BITTER–SWEET WORLD

Gustation is the sense of taste. Substances dissolved in saliva stimulate the taste receptors contained in the papillae (small bumps) of the tongue and produce the basic taste qualities: bitter, salty, sour, sweet, and umami (savoury). Taste is not the same as flavour, which refers to substances tasting good or bad. Gustation, colour, smell, and touch are important partners in processing flavours.

The tongue, palate, pharynx, and larynx are the receptive organs of gustation. They contain close to 10,000 taste buds. Taste buds, or receptors, respond to different taste sensations. The tip of the tongue is most sensitive to sweetness and saltiness, the sides to sourness, and the back to bitterness (Carlson, 1994). Gustatory information is relayed to the brain (taste sensory cortex) by the taste receptors that have formed synapses with dendrites of the sensory neurons. (See Chapter 2 for more information on neurons.)

gustation
sense of taste

AUDITION: WHISPERS IN THE EAR

Sound is produced by an object vibrating and setting air molecules in motion. Sound varies in pitch, loudness, and timbre. Pitch is the perception of the frequency of a sound. A soprano voice is high-pitched; a bass voice is low-pitched. Humans can hear certain frequencies of sounds, but other frequencies fall outside their auditory capacity. Some animals, such as dogs, hear sounds that humans do not. Loudness is the perception of the amplitude of a sound. Prolonged exposure to loud noise is a cause of hearing loss. Timbre is the perceptual quality of sound. Musical instruments playing the same note differ in timbre.

The Auditory Road to the Brain

The outer ear funnels sound to the eardrum, causing the sound vibration to flow to the middle ear and then to the inner ear (see Figure 3.1). The inner ear, which contains the cochlea (from the Greek word *kokhlos*, or land snail) and the sensory receptors of the basilar membrane in the cochlea, translates the sound vibration, or energy, into a neural message for transmission to the brain (Carlson, 1994). The cochlear nerve, a branch of the auditory nerve, transmits the auditory information (electrical impulse) to the primary auditory cortex in the brain. Neurons in the auditory cortex interpret complex stimuli, including detection of pitch, volume, timbre, and the location of sounds.

Hearing Explanations

There are different explanations for the process of hearing. Place theory proposes that different locations in the basilar membrane vibrate in response to different sound frequencies. The place theory accounts well for high-frequency sounds but not for low-frequency sounds.

Frequency theory proposes that the perception of sound is based on the number of times the auditory nerve fires. The frequency theory accounts well for low- and medium-frequency but not for high-frequency sounds. Because the maximum rate of firing of a single neuron is 1,000 times per second, sounds with frequencies exceeding the 1,000-times-per-second limit cannot be signalled to the brain.

The volley theory deals with the single-neuron firing capacity limitation. This theory suggests that properly synchronized volleys, or groups, of neurons can collectively signal to the brain sounds with frequencies higher than 1,000 times per second.

FIGURE 3.1   Structure of the Ear

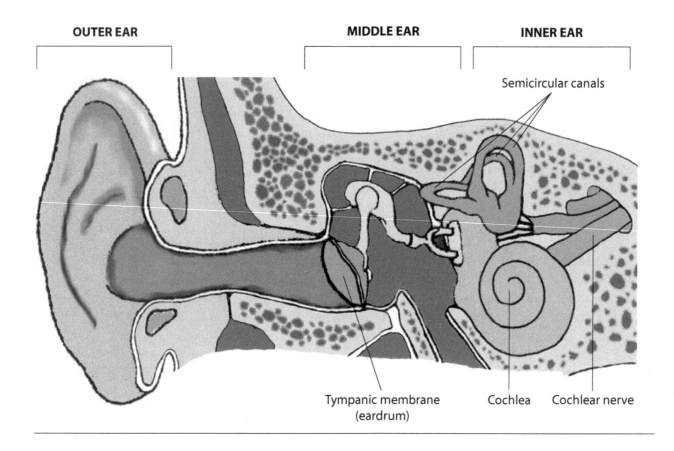

OUTER EAR   **MIDDLE EAR**   **INNER EAR**

Semicircular canals

Tympanic membrane
(eardrum)   Cochlea   Cochlear nerve

Hearing Loss

One in ten people experiences some form of hearing loss. This translates into 3.4 million people in Canada. Major causes of hearing loss include genetic defect, prenatal illness (for example, German measles), meningitis, viruses, medication, stroke, and prolonged exposure to noise (Canadian Hearing Society, n.d.). People with hearing loss can be helped with hearing aids and cochlear implants.

OLFACTION: TO SMELL OR NOT TO SMELL

olfaction
sense of smell

Olfaction is the sense of smell. Odour is produced when the molecules of a substance vaporize (turn into a gas), become airborne, and travel to the olfactory epithelium at the top of the nasal cavity via the nostrils. The olfactory epithelium contains millions of olfactory neurons, the receptor cells for smell. The number of olfactory neurons firing at the same time determines the strength or weakness of a smell stimulus. The olfactory receptors form the olfactory nerve, which relays messages to the olfactory bulb at the base of the brain. Different odours produce different excitatory responses in different parts of the olfactory bulb. The olfactory bulb relays messages via the olfactory tract to the primary olfactory cortex and other parts of the brain (for example, the amygdala). The olfactory system has the capacity to identify not only individual odours (such as coffee) but also mixtures of odours (such as coffee, fried eggs, and bacon). An anosmic person is one who lacks the sense of smell.

VESTIBULAR AND KINESTHETIC SENSES: LOST IN SPACE

The vestibular and kinesthetic senses are involved in movement and orientation in space. The **vestibular senses** provide information about balance and movement. The semicircular canal and the vestibular sacs of the middle ear contain receptors (hair cells) that detect changes in movement and space orientation. The semicircular canals contain fluid to control balance. Balance is maintained by the fluid moving when the body moves. Vestibular information from the receptor cells travels through the vestibular nerve to various parts of the brain, including the cerebellum, spinal cord, medulla, pons, and temporal cortex. These neural pathways control balance, posture, head and eye movements, and motion sickness.

The **kinesthetic senses** provide information about movement, orientation, and posture. Kinesthetic receptors are located in muscles, joints, and tendons and are sensitive to stretches and movements. When you can't walk because your leg is "asleep," the kinesthetic sense is temporarily out of commission.

vestibular senses
senses that provide information about balance and movement

kinesthetic senses
senses that provide information about movement, orientation, and posture

VISION: FOR YOUR EYES ONLY

The Light Stimulus

The eyes detect light, which consists of electromagnetic radiation. Wavelength is the unit of measurement of electromagnetic radiation. Wavelengths represented in the environment include gamma rays, X-rays, ultraviolet rays, infrared rays, and short-wave. The *visible spectrum* is the range of wavelengths that the human eye can see, which is only a very small part of the electromagnetic spectrum. For example, we cannot see infrared and ultraviolet rays.

The Imperfect Camera

Light waves coming from an object travel through the cornea and the pupil, enter the lens, and fall on the retina (Figure 3.2). The retina is the interior lining of the back of the eye, and in it are two types of receptor cells: cones and rods. The rods outnumber the cones 20 to 1. Cones are responsible for daytime vision, visual acuity (clarity and sharpness), and colour vision. Cones do well in the daytime and poorly in very dim light. The central part of the retina is the fovea, which contains only cones and provides for the most acute vision. The colour-blind and poor-acuity rods are responsible for peripheral and night vision. Rods do well in very dim light and poorly in the daytime. They also play a role in dark adaptation, as do cones. Rods and cones are most sensitive to different wavelengths under light and dark conditions, a fact that has an important implication for public safety (Box 3.1).

Dark and Light Adaptation

Dark adaptation is the process in which the ability of the eyes to see in dim light increases. Dark adaptation is important when you move from a brightly lit place (for example, outside a movie theatre on a sunny day) to one that is dark (inside the movie theatre). *Light adaptation* is important for returning back to the sunny outdoors after being in the movie theatre. Light adaptation occurs faster than dark adaptation (about 60 seconds versus about half an hour). Adaptation to the dark is slower because the rods in the eyes take their time to reach their maximum level of adaptation.

FIGURE 3.2   The Eye

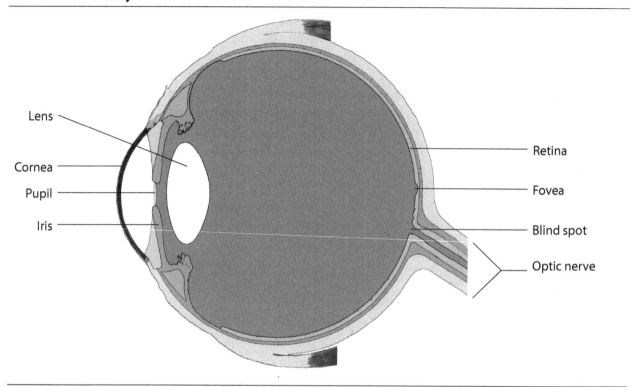

The Visual Road to the Brain

Light energy received by the rods and cones is transformed into neural impulses that are communicated to the brain by a chain of nerve cells, including the optic disc and the optic nerve. The optic disc, which contains no rods and cones and exits the eye through the optic nerve, produces the blind spot. Fortunately, the blind spot does not interfere with people's everyday perception of the world.

The optic nerves from each eye meet at the optic chiasm (*khiasma* is Greek for cross) and split in such a way that the right hemisphere of the brain receives information from the left half of the visual field, and the left hemisphere of the brain receives information from the right half of the visual field (Figure 3.3). The crossover allows visual input from a single eye to be represented in both sides of the brain and also helps with depth perception. The neural impulses carried by the optic nerve reach the thalamus after crossing the optic chiasm. In turn, neural fibres in the thalamus transmit the neural impulses to their final destination, the primary visual cortex in the occipital lobe, for analysis, interpretation, and integration.

Seeing Is Believing

Neurons in the visual cortex are highly specialized in that they respond only to visual stimuli of a certain shape, orientation, movement, texture, depth, and colour (Carlson, 1994). For example, some neurons respond only to horizontal lines and some only to vertical lines. The visual cortex can also integrate information from individual neural systems to transform visual images into a coherent world.

BOX 3.1   What Colour Should Emergency Vehicles Be Painted?

The spectrum of electromagnetic radiation that is visible to humans ranges between 400 and 700 nanometres (a nanometre is one-billionth of a metre). Short lightwaves, those around 400 nm, are seen as blue-violet, while long lightwaves (700 nm) are seen as red. Intermediate wavelengths (between about 500 and 600 nm) are seen as greens and yellows. Cones are most sensitive to wavelengths of about 555 nm, and rods are most sensitive to shorter wavelengths, around 505 nm. Both of these peak sensitivities are in the green–yellow portion of the visible spectrum.

One of the most recognizable cultural icons is the red fire truck. The relative sensitivities of rods means that green–yellow will be easier to detect in dim light or darkness than will short wavelengths (blues) or long wavelengths (reds). Because of this, red fire trucks may be hard to see at night. Evidence suggests this is the case: in one year alone in the United States, there were over 10,000 traffic accidents involving fire trucks. Red trucks are more likely to be involved in accidents than are green–yellow trucks. These accidents have many consequences, including risk of injury to vehicle occupants, costs of vehicle repair, and delays in arriving at a scene. Some jurisdictions have begun to replace red trucks with green–yellow (chartreuse) trucks. In light of the sensitivities of photoreceptors and evidence of vehicle accidents, it may be time to give the red fire truck and other emergency vehicles a fresh coat of paint.

Sources: Karter and Le Blanc (1991); Solomon and King (1995).

Colour Vision and Colour Blindness

Most, but not all, people see the full range of colours. Colour-blind people see a more limited range. The most common version is red–green blindness, followed by yellow–blue blindness, and, in extreme cases, total colour blindness (the inability to perceive any colour). About 8 percent of men and less than 1 percent of women have red–green blindness (Colour Blind Resource Centre, 2000). Many sites on the Internet provide free tests for colour blindness.

Two explanations help in understanding colour blindness. The trichromatic, or three-colour, theory proposes three types of cones, each sensitive to a single colour: the short-wavelength, or "blue," cones; the medium-wavelength, or "green," cones; and the long-wavelength, or "red," cones. In the trichromatic view, colour blindness is the result of irregularities in one or more of the cone types—for example, a person lacking blue cones in the retina sees the world in green and red. However, this theory is limited in that it is unable to explain colours that are combinations of other colours (for example, grey) and the phenomenon of afterimages (described below).

The opponent process theory of colour vision suggests that there are three *paired* receptor cells in the retina: red–green, yellow–blue, and black–white. The first pair is red–green and the second is yellow–blue. The opponent process theory also proposes that each colour in a pair is antagonistic to the other. Thus, a blue object not only stimulates receptors that are sensitive to blue, but also simultaneously inhibits receptors that are sensitive to yellow so that the outcome is perceiving the

FIGURE 3.3   How Visual Images Reach the Brain

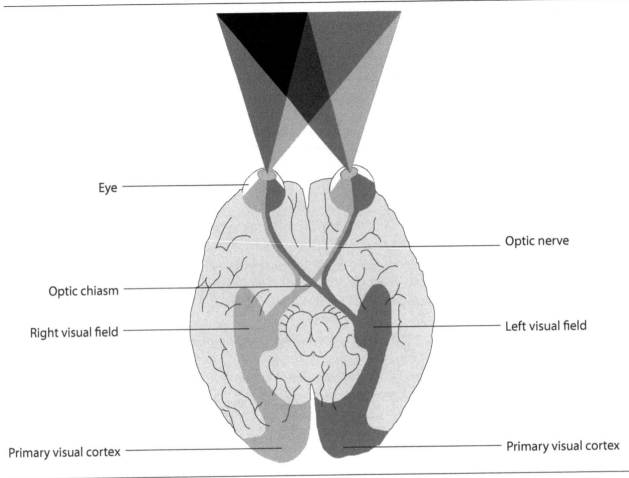

object as blue. The same process works in the case of the red–green and black–white pairings.

This theory accounts well for afterimages. An *afterimage* is the visual sensation that is generated by the brain after the original visual stimulation ends. A visual afterimage can easily be experienced by staring at an object with a particular colour (for example, green) for a minute and then shifting your gaze to a white surface. When you do this, the brain generates a visual sensation of the colour that is opposite to the original object—red, in this case. A modern theory of colour vision, *dual process theory*, synthesizes the trichromatic and opponent process theories; it argues that colour vision is handled by three retinal cone types—red, blue, and green—and by opponent processes located farther along in the visual system (Knoblauch, 2002).

PERCEPTION

Sensation involves the senses detecting sensory information and relaying it to the brain. Recall from the beginning of this chapter that *perception* involves the brain organizing and interpreting the information it receives from the sensory systems. This section discusses perceptual processes, abilities, and illusions, and subliminal and extrasensory perception.

Perceptual Processes

ATTENTION

Attention is the perceptual process of focusing consciousness on particular stimuli or events. Attention is affected by stimulus characteristics and psychological factors. Stimuli that are intense, unusual, coloured, or repeated are more likely to grab your attention than those that do not have these qualities. Psychological factors include interest and bias. For example, law enforcement officers are more likely to attend to stimuli that are related to safety, security, and crime than are average people.

There are two types of attention. **Selective attention** is the perceptual ability to focus on particular stimuli while ignoring all other stimuli. **Divided attention** is the ability to focus on more than one stimulus at a time. The *cocktail party effect* suggests evidence for both types of attention. In the cocktail party effect, a person who is talking to a group of friends in a crowded room while five other conversations are going on in other groups has little trouble focusing on the conversation of his or her group and picking up important bits of information from the other conversations. Divided attention works best on tasks that involve different sensory systems (for example, hearing and vision). Divided attention can be dangerous, however. Driving while using a cellphone, for example, is associated with increased traffic violations, slower reaction times, and lapses in attention (Beede & Kass, 2006).

selective attention
perceptual ability to focus on particular stimuli while ignoring all other stimuli

divided attention
perceptual ability to focus on more than one stimulus at a time

Perceptual Organization

Perception is not passive or random but is an active process in which piecemeal sensory experiences are organized into meaningful wholes to make sense of the world. For example, we see a group of musicians playing a symphony as an orchestra, not as a violin at the front of the stage, a bassoon at the back, and a drum at the side. Basic principles, called the *gestalt laws of organization*, are used in the perceptual organization process. Two of these laws are the figure–ground perception and the grouping principles.

The *figure–ground* principle refers to distinguishing the object (figure) in a sensory field from the background information (ground). For example, in a painting of a tree, the tree is the figure and everything else is the ground. In a high-speed pursuit, the speeding vehicle is the figure; the road, other vehicles, and anything else in the area make up the ground.

Grouping refers to organizing the sensory field on the basis of closure, continuity, proximity, and similarity. Grouping on the basis of *closure* is the tendency to complete sensory stimuli (for example, patterns or forms) that have gaps in them. Grouping on the basis of *continuity* is the tendency to group stimuli (for example, objects) that appear to form a continuous pattern. Grouping on the basis of *proximity* is the tendency to perceive stimuli close to one another as belonging together. Finally, grouping on the basis of *similarity* is the tendency to group together stimuli with similar characteristics.

Perceptual Abilities

Perceptual constancy is the ability to perceive stimuli as unchanging under varying conditions. For example, a person's height is the same whether he or she is standing near you or far from you. Perceptual constancy applies to size, shape, brightness, and colour.

Depth perception is the ability to see visual stimuli in three dimensions and to estimate distance accurately. People use two types of visual cues to see a three-dimensional world. *Binocular depth cues* are those that allow perception of depth and distance with two eyes. The binocular cues that require both eyes are convergence and binocular disparity. In convergence, the eyes turn inward as they focus on nearby visual stimuli. Tension in the converging eye muscles is conveyed to the brain, which uses this information to determine the depth or distance of an object. In binocular disparity, the two eyes register slightly different images of a visual stimulus because the eyes are in slightly different positions (about 6 cm apart). The brain also uses the difference between these images to determine the depth or distance of the object.

A *monocular cue* is depth information that is perceived by one eye. Three monocular cues are interposition, linear perspective, and relative size. In interposition, an object that is partly blocked by another is seen as farther away than the blocking object. In linear perspective, parallel lines (for example, train tracks) appear to converge, or come closer together, as they recede into the distance. In relative size, larger objects are seen as closer than smaller objects.

Perceptual Illusions

Perceptual illusions are sensory stimuli that produce errors in perception. Two examples of visual illusions are the Müller–Lyer illusion and the moon illusion (Figure 3.4). In the Müller–Lyer illusion, two lines of equal length are seen as unequal—the line that has arrows at its ends that point outward is seen as being longer than the line with arrows pointing inward. In the moon illusion, the moon looks bigger when it is on the horizon than when it is high in the sky. Other well-known visual illusions are the Ponzo illusion and the horizontal–vertical illusion, which also make lines of equal length look different.

Explanations for the errors committed in perceptual illusions identify the sensory apparatus, the brain, or culture as the culprits. For example, people who grow up in unindustrialized environments where right angles do not prevail are less susceptible to the Müller–Lyer illusion than people who grow up in right-angled, industrialized environments (cited in Matsumoto, 1994).

Subliminal Perception

subliminal perception
perception of sensory messages without conscious awareness

Limen is another word for threshold, while *subliminal* means below threshold. **Subliminal perception** refers to the perception of sensory messages without conscious awareness. Subliminal perception is a controversial subject because it implies that people's attitudes and behaviours can be affected by below-absolute-threshold stimuli (words, images, sounds, smells) without people being aware of the stimuli. For example, an ad for a soft drink might be flashed on a movie screen so briefly that the audience isn't conscious of it. There is no convincing scientific evidence supporting the ability of subliminal perception to change behaviour. While subliminal perception still has its proponents, the non-believers outnumber the believers.

FIGURE 3.4   Visual Illusions

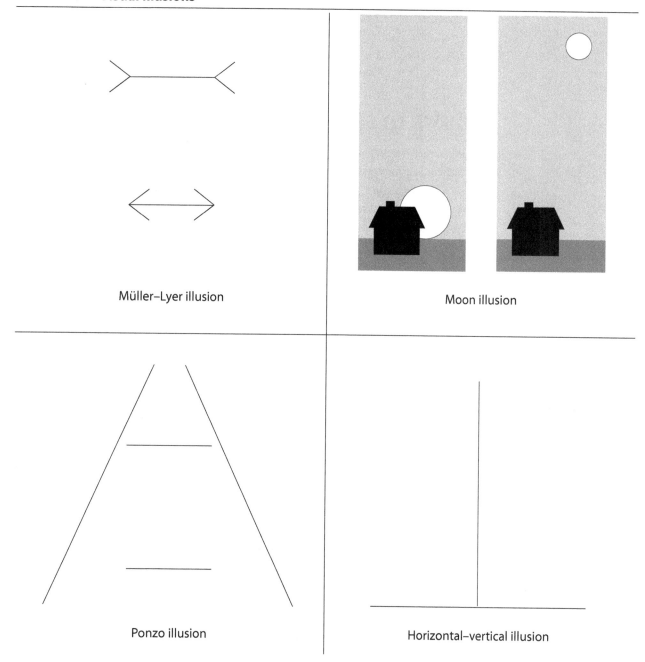

Müller–Lyer illusion

Moon illusion

Ponzo illusion

Horizontal–vertical illusion

Extrasensory Perception

Extrasensory perception (ESP) is perception that relies on means other than the known sensory systems. There are four categories of ESP. Clairvoyance involves extracting information about objects or events without the use of the known senses—for example, "reading" the content of a sealed envelope. Precognition is knowing about an event before it happens. Psychokinesis involves moving objects without touching them. Finally, telepathy is transmitting thought from one person to another.

extrasensory perception
perception that relies on means other than the known sensory systems

ESP is problematic on two counts. First, it violates everything we know about sensation and perception. Second, it is not well supported by scientific evidence. A study on psychological profiling of a closed murder case found that psychics relied on nothing more than social stereotypes in profiling the offender (Kocsis, Irwin, & Hayes, 2000).

POINTS TO REMEMBER

This chapter discusses the intimately related processes of sensation and perception. Sensation is a process that involves the structures and functions of the sensory systems of the skin, gustation (taste), audition (hearing), olfaction (smell), the vestibular sense, and the kinesthetic sense. Perception is the process in which sensory information is sorted out and interpreted by the brain.

KEY TERMS

absolute threshold

cutaneous senses

difference threshold

divided attention

extrasensory perception

gate-control theory

gustation

kinesthetic senses

olfaction

perception

selective attention

sensation

sensory adaptation

signal detection theory

stimulus

subliminal perception

vestibular senses

REFERENCES

Beede, K.E., & S.J. Kass. (2006). Engrossed in conversation: The impact of cell phones on simulated driving performance. *Accident Analysis & Prevention, 38*, 415–21.

Blue Line. (June/July 1999). Various advertisements.

Canadian Hearing Society. (n.d.). *FAQ: What are the statistics on hearing loss?* http://www.chs.ca/programs/marketing/faq50.htm#14.

Carlson, N.R. (1994). *Physiology of behavior* (5th ed.). Needham Heights, MA: Allyn and Bacon.

Colour Blind Resource Centre. (2000). *What is colour blindness?* http://www.colourblind.freeservers.com/Whatis.htm.

Karter, M.J., & P.R. Le Blanc. (1991, November/December). U.S. fire fighter injuries—1990. *National Fire Protection Association Journal, 46,* 43–53.

Knoblauch, K. (2002). Color vision. In H. Pashler & S. Yantis (Eds.), *Stevens' handbook of experimental psychology: Vol. 1. Sensation and perception* (3rd ed.). New York: Wiley.

Kocsis, R.N., H.J. Irwin, & A.F. Hayes. (2000, March). Expertise in psychological profiling: A comparative assessment. *Journal of Interpersonal Violence, 15* (3), 311–31.

Matsumoto, D. (1994). *People: Psychology from a cultural perspective.* Pacific Grove, CA: Brooks/Cole.

Solomon, S.S., & J.G. King. (1995). Influence of color on fire vehicle accidents. *Journal of Safety Research, 26,* 41–48.

Wall, P.D., & R. Melzack (Eds.). (1989). *Textbook of pain* (2nd ed.). New York: Churchill Livingstone.

EXERCISES AND REVIEW

Self-Test

Circle the correct answer.

1. Listening for sounds of a suspect who is thought to be hiding inside an abandoned warehouse, a law enforcement officer depends on his or her

    a. difference threshold

    b. absolute threshold

    c. extrasensory perception

    d. dark adaptation

2. An average wine taster and an expert wine taster likely have different

    a. difference thresholds

    b. absolute thresholds

    c. attention

    d. none of the above

3. In a dimly lit room, our sense of sight depends mainly on

    a. rod vision

    b. cone vision

    c. laser vision

    d. all of the above

4. The scene of a major traffic accident is chaotic with motorists, ambulance personnel, and police. A police officer taking a statement from a witness hears only what the witness is saying. The officer's ability to do this depends on her

   a. divided attention

   b. perceptual organization

   c. selective attention

   d. all of the above

5. Our sense of balance is influenced by

   a. kinesthetic receptors

   b. the middle ear

   c. the visual cortex

   d. all of the above

6. When we are using our vision,

   a. the right hemisphere of the brain receives input from the right half of the visual field

   b. the right hemisphere of the brain receives input from the left hemisphere of the brain

   c. the left hemisphere of the brain receives input from the right half of the visual field

   d. the left hemisphere of the brain receives input from the left half of the visual field

7. Perceptual organization allows us to

   a. perceive the connections among several stimuli

   b. distinguish an object or person from the background

   c. group similar stimuli

   d. all of the above

8. Pain is

   a. a psychological as well as a physical phenomenon

   b. an emotional state

   c. a perceptual illusion

   d. a subliminal perception

9. The parents of two boys who committed suicide sue a rock band for including the message "Do it" in one of its songs. The parents argue that even though the message is embedded in the music, it nevertheless influenced the decision of their boys to commit suicide. On which of the following perceptual phenomena are the parents basing their lawsuit?

   a. perceptual deviance

   b. perceptual illusion

   c. exorcism

   d. subliminal perception

10. Which of the following represents extrasensory perception?

   a. clairvoyance

   b. precognition

   c. telepathy

   d. all of the above

Thinking About Psychology and Law Enforcement

1. What are the implications of sensory impairments (blindness, deafness, and so on) on law enforcement work?

2. What law enforcement functions rely heavily on perception?

3. Should psychics be used in law enforcement to help solve homicides? Why or why not?

CHAPTER 4

States of Consciousness

CHAPTER OBJECTIVES

After completing this chapter, you should be able to:

- Understand the different states of consciousness.
- Describe biological rhythms, sleep, and dreaming.
- Discuss hypnosis and its forensic application.
- Understand drugs and drug-induced altered states of consciousness.

PREVIEW SCENARIO

Elaine Rose Cece and Mary Barbara Taylor were two homeless drifters. They were tried in court and found guilty of second-degree murder for stabbing to death Detective Constable William Hancox, age 32, on the night of August 4, 1998. Hancox was on surveillance duty in a suburban parking lot. Detective Elmer Manuel and Detective Constable Larry Smith were working with Hancox the night he was killed. In a police disciplinary hearing, they were found guilty of misconduct for drinking on the job and neglect of duty at the time of Hancox's slaying. Evidently, Manuel and Smith spent the night of August 4 first at a bar, where they had drinks, and then at another bar, where they ordered drinks moments before learning that Hancox had been stabbed. (Vincent, 2001)

INTRODUCTION

A drug such as alcohol not only alters a person's state of consciousness but also has the potential to ruin the person's quality of life. This chapter describes the concept of consciousness and describes altered states of consciousness due to sleep, hypnosis, and psychoactive drugs.

THE CONCEPT OF CONSCIOUSNESS

Consciousness is a person's state of awareness of his or her external and internal worlds. The external world is the person's surroundings. The internal world includes the experience of the self and personal feelings, perceptions, sensations, and thoughts.

consciousness
people's state of awareness of their external and internal worlds

There are various levels and forms of consciousness. Being wide awake represents a high level of consciousness: a wide-awake person is alert, focused, and able to concentrate, perform mental activities, and carry out required tasks. At the other extreme is unconsciousness: an unconscious person is in a state of total unawareness or coma as a result of injury, disease, poison, or some other damage to the brain. Between alertness and unconsciousness are the altered states of consciousness—changes from a higher state of awareness to a lower or noticeably different level of awareness. Sleep, hypnosis, and psychoactive drugs are all associated with altered states of consciousness.

BIOLOGICAL RHYTHMS

circadian rhythm
daily behavioural or bodily cycle that occurs repeatedly about every 24 hours

Evolution has equipped us with invisible internal clocks that operate in cycles and regulate our daily bodily functions and behaviours. Circadian rhythms are markers of biological clocks. The word "circadian" comes from the Latin *circa*, which means about, and *dies*, which means day. A **circadian rhythm** is a daily behavioural or bodily cycle that occurs repeatedly about every 24 hours (but see more on this below). Biological functions that follow circadian rhythms include blood pressure, body temperature, and the sleep–wakefulness cycle. Circadian rhythms are controlled by interactions between the suprachiasmatic nucleus and the pineal gland (see Chapter 2).

It is interesting to note that the *natural* cycle of humans is approximately 25 hours long, not 24 hours. Natural circadian rhythms are identified by isolating a person completely from environmental cues for time (such as clocks, calendars, night, day, and so on). Isolation experiments show that the human biological clock prefers a 25-hour cycle. We all seem to be guilty of modifying our natural 25-hour rhythm to conform to the prevailing 24-hour schedule. Daylight saving time, change in time zones (as in a transoceanic flight), and shift work are additional factors that disrupt circadian rhythms. The shift work that characterizes law enforcement work can have a negative effect on officers' physical and psychological well-being.

SLEEP AND DREAMING

Sleep—or the lack of it—is important to law enforcement work and to law enforcement officers (Box 4.1). One US study reported that 16 to 20 percent of motor vehicle accidents were sleep-related (Columbus Community Hospital, 1998). On a personal level, an officer is likely to spend one-third of his or her life sleeping. Thus, the officer who lives to be 75 years old will have spent 25 of those years asleep.

As an altered state of consciousness, sleep is a level of awareness that is lower than that of normal waking consciousness. However, sleep is by no means a state of unconsciousness or inactivity. Sleep studies in which brainwaves, blood pressure, breathing rate, eye movement, heart rate, and muscle tension are monitored show that a great deal goes on while we are asleep. Sleep studies also show that there are two major categories of sleep: no-rapid eye movement (NREM, pronounced non-rem) sleep and rapid eye movement (REM) sleep.

BOX 4.1   The Sleepy Officer

Police officers often have to make rapid decisions in uncertain and ambiguous situations, making it crucial to maintain mental alertness. However, many officers work under conditions that may lead to decreased alertness and reduced job performance. Time of day and chronic sleep deprivation are two major culprits for reduced alertness and impaired job performance.

Research indicates that officers working rotating or night shifts experience more frequent sleep disorders than do non–shift workers. In one North American study, nearly 40 percent of police officers whose work schedule overlapped with their usual sleep time were at greater risk of experiencing at least one sleep disorder (including sleep apnea, insomnia, restless leg syndrome, and narcolepsy; see below). Stressful events may also have negative effects on sleep. For example, exposure to traumatic incidents is associated with nightmares.

It might surprise you to know that more police officers die as a result of accidents on the job than assaults. Two factors that influence the risks of on-the-job accidents and injuries are time of day and shift length. Accidents are nearly three times more common among workers on the night shift, and the risk of accidents occurring increases after nine or more hours on duty. The link between sleep and health and job performance has led some police departments in Canada and the United States to impose limits on the number of hours worked per day and per week, and to assess sleep patterns and disorders during annual assessments.

Selected sleep disorders that occur among police officers include:

- *Sleep apnea:* Frequent interruptions in sleep that occur when a person stops breathing, usually because air flow is obstructed for several seconds.

- *Insomnia:* Chronic difficulty getting to sleep or remaining asleep.

- *Restless leg syndrome:* Unpleasant sensations in the legs and the uncontrollable urge to move the legs to gain relief from these feelings.

- *Narcolepsy:* Uncontrollable attacks of sleep, sometimes accompanied by excessive daytime sleepiness, abrupt loss of muscle tone (cataplexy), hallucinations, and episodes of paralysis.

Sources: Barger et al. (2009); Folkard & Lombardi (2006); Garbarino et al. (2002); Neylan et al. (2002); Vila (2008).

No-Rapid Eye Movement (NREM) Sleep

A person who goes to bed with the intent to sleep, lies down, and closes her eyes is likely to move within minutes from a relaxed waking state into NREM sleep. In NREM sleep, rapid eye movements are absent.

NREM sleep consists of four stages (Figure 4.1). Stage 1 is the lightest sleep, in which relatively rapid slow-voltage brainwaves are seen. Stage 2 is a deeper sleep, and is represented by slower, more regular brainwave patterns and periodic sleep

FIGURE 4.1   Stages of Sleep

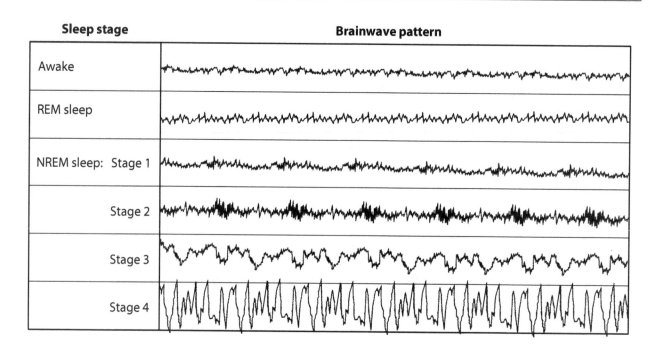

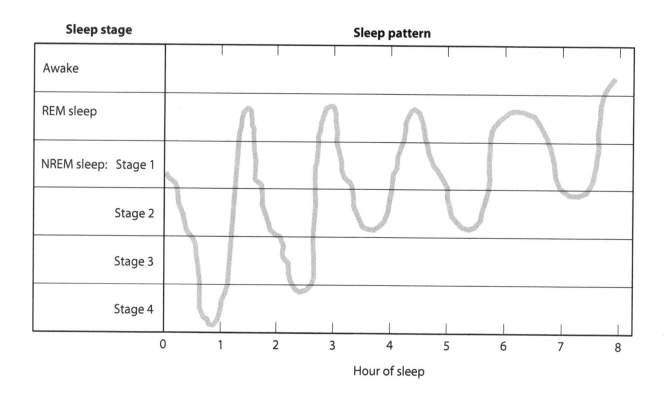

spindles (high-frequency waves). Stage 2 sleepers are harder to wake than stage 1 sleepers. Stage 3 is an even deeper sleep than stage 2 and is represented by large, slow brainwaves called delta waves. Stage 4 is the deepest sleep, represented by even slower and more regular brainwaves than during stage 3. People who wake up during deep sleep (stage 3 or 4) may appear disoriented. They may be confused about the time of day (morning versus night) or the day of the week (weekday versus weekend). Bedwetting, sleepwalking, and sleep talking most often occur in stages 3 and 4.

Rapid Eye Movement (REM) Sleep

At the end of stage 4, the sleeper shows signs of restlessness and starts an upward climb through the NREM stages toward wakefulness. Instead of re-entering stage 1, however, the person goes into REM sleep. In REM sleep, brainwave activity and breathing rate increase, the heart beats faster and irregularly, blood pressure rises, the eyes move back and forth, major muscles (arms, legs, and torso) become paralyzed, males experience erections, females experience lubrication of the vagina, and dreams take place.

Sleep and Circadian Rhythms

People sleep in predictable cycles. In a typical night, a person goes through five 90-minute sleep cycles, sleeping for 7.5 to 8 hours, of which dreaming takes about 1.5 hours. The first two sleep cycles comprise the four stages of NREM sleep and 10 to 15 minutes of REM sleep. The remaining three sleep cycles comprise stage 2 sleep and progressively longer REM sleep (for example, 30 to 40 minutes long). Of course, people show individual differences in their sleep patterns. For example, older people tend to sleep less than younger people. Some people also have sleep problems. Table 4.1 lists common sleep disorders. (See also Box 4.1.)

Dreaming

All humans dream. Some people are good at remembering their dreams while others are not. Dreams are remembered best when the dreamer is awakened as he or she is dreaming. Explanations for the meaning of dreams range from their having no meaning at all to their being the wish fulfillment of our unconscious desires.

HYPNOSIS

Hypnosis is an altered state of consciousness in which a person is highly receptive to suggestion. According to the American Psychological Association's Division of Psychological Hypnosis (2001), hypnosis is a procedure during which the hypnotist suggests that the hypnotized person is experiencing changes in sensations, perceptions, thoughts, or behaviour. The hypnotist gives instructions to imagine or recall pleasant experiences in order to induce relaxation, calmness, and a sense of well-being. Hypnotized people remain aware of who and where they are (unless amnesia is specifically suggested); they usually remember what transpired during hypnosis,

hypnosis
altered state of consciousness in which a person is highly receptive to suggestion

TABLE 4.1   Common Sleep Disorders

Parasomnias	Major Sleep Disorders
Nightmares (frightening dreams)	Insomnia (difficulty falling asleep or remaining asleep)
Somnambulism (sleepwalking)	Narcolepsy (too much daytime sleepiness and sudden REM sleep attack)
Somniloquy (sleep talking)	Sleep apnea (periods when breathing stops during sleep)
Sleep terrors (screaming)	

and although they become more responsive to suggestions, they do not lose control over their behaviour. Most people describe the hypnotic experience as very pleasant.

The success of hypnosis depends on four conditions: (1) comfort and minimal distraction, (2) focused attention or concentration on an image or external object, (3) information on what to expect in the trance-like state (for example, pleasant feelings of relaxation), and (4) the experience of events or feelings predicted by the hypnotist (for example, eyes getting tired, hands getting heavy). Self-hypnosis can be taught as a therapeutic technique.

Most people are susceptible to hypnosis, but a minority (about 10 percent) are consistently non-responsive to a hypnotist's suggestions (Hilgard, 1977). Hypnotized people do not lose consciousness or complete control, and they do not become immoral or turn into supermen or superwomen. Table 4.2 lists some common myths about hypnosis.

Hypnosis is used in medicine, dentistry, and psychiatry. The use of forensic hypnosis in criminal investigations is controversial. Supporters of forensic hypnosis believe that trained hypnosis specialists can help traumatized witnesses remember details of crimes. For example, hypnosis was used in a high-profile 1976 case in which a school bus in California was hijacked (Durbin, 1997). In that case, under hypnosis the bus driver was able to recall the licence plates of the hijackers' cars. However, hypnosis has also been shown to lead to false memories (see Chapter 6) of details that never happened (see, for example, Sheehan, Green, & Truesdale, 1992). Those opposed to forensic hypnosis consider it hocus-pocus and argue that testimony gained under hypnosis is unreliable. The lack of trustworthiness of hypnotically induced memories is due to their susceptibility to be linked with fantasies. Most US states permit the evidence obtained hypnotically from witnesses to be introduced in court. However, some state court systems have imposed constraints on the use of hypnotic evidence because of its questionable reliability (Durbin, 1997).

PSYCHOACTIVE STATES

psychoactive drug
drug that affects
behaviour, feelings,
perceptions, and thoughts

A **psychoactive drug** is one that affects behaviour, feelings, perceptions, and thoughts. Nutrients such as food and water, which also affect normal functioning, are excluded from this definition. Psychoactive drugs can be licit, illicit, and licit–illicit. *Licit drugs* are legal and include alcohol, caffeine, and nicotine. Legal psychoactive drugs may

TABLE 4.2   Common Myths About Hypnosis

Myth 1	Hypnotized people lose consciousness.
Fact 1	Hypnotized people are in an altered state of consciousness—they do not lose awareness or fall asleep; they are awake and alert, and they can hear and respond to the hypnotist's suggestions
Myth 2	Hypnotized people do odd or crazy things, or commit immoral or criminal acts.
Fact 2	Only a stage hypnotist engages his or her subject in buffoonery for entertainment purposes; a professional hypnotist cannot make hypnotized people do anything against their will or commit acts detrimental to themselves or others, including sexual acts.
Myth 3	Hypnotized people lose control and surrender their will to the hypnotist.
Fact 3	The ability of a hypnotist to hypnotize a person rests with the person, not the hypnotist—the person being hypnotized is always in control. A hypnotist guides and develops the hypnotic state; the ability to be hypnotized rests within the subject.
Myth 4	Only weak-willed and feeble-minded people are hypnotizable.
Fact 4	Intelligent people make better candidates for hypnosis. Weak-willed or feeble-minded people are more difficult if not impossible to hypnotize.
Myth 5	Hypnotized people spill all their secrets.
Fact 5	Hypnosis is not a "truth serum"; hypnotized people can still lie or keep their "dirty laundry" secret.
Myth 6	Hypnotized people can get stuck in their hypnotic state.
Fact 6	Hypnotized people are in total control and they can terminate their hypnotic state any time they want (unless they fall asleep, or they are enjoying their state of pleasant relaxation so much that they do not want to be brought out).
Myth 7	Hypnosis weakens the will.
Fact 7	The will of hypnotized people does not change in any way.

Source: Hughes (n.d.).

be properly used, misused, or abused. *Illicit drugs* are illegal and include cocaine, heroin, and LSD. *Licit–illicit drugs* are those that are illegal under the *Criminal Code* (1985) but are made legal to possess, use, grow, and cultivate to individuals suffering from serious, debilitating, or terminal illnesses, such as cancer and AIDS. Marijuana is an example of a licit–illicit psychoactive drug. The Canadian government permits medical use of marijuana by people who must deal with the effects of some diseases and disorders.

Drug Use

Psychoactive drugs may be taken by mouth, injection (hypodermic syringe), inhalation (sniffing or snorting), or absorption through the skin or membranes (for example, through a patch). Three hazards associated with taking drugs are toxicity, addiction, and criminal activity.

TOXICITY

toxicity
physical or psychological harm the quantity of a drug presents to the user

Psychoactive drugs can be toxic. **Toxicity** is the physical or psychological harm the quantity of a drug presents to the user. *Acute toxicity* is immediate harm from ingesting a drug. *Chronic toxicity* is harm caused over a long period of drug use. Repeated use of a drug leads to drug **tolerance**, the diminishing effect of a drug over repeated use. A person who develops tolerance to a drug needs larger and larger doses to get the same effects. Such a person may die accidentally as a result of overdosing on the drug.

tolerance
diminishing effect of a drug over repeated use, necessitating higher doses of the drug

ADDICTION

physical dependence
continued abuse of a drug to avoid unpleasant withdrawal symptoms

Psychoactive drug use can be addictive. An addict is a person who develops physical and psychological dependence on a drug. **Physical dependence** is the continued abuse of a drug to avoid unpleasant withdrawal symptoms. A person who is addicted to alcohol, for example, may continue to drink to avoid the typical alcohol withdrawal symptoms: tremors (shaking), nausea, tachycardia (rapid heart rate), and, in severe cases, delirium, seizures, and visual hallucinations. **Psychological dependence** is a craving for the pleasurable effects of the drug. Addicts may have more difficulty battling their psychological dependence than their physical dependence.

psychological dependence
craving for the pleasurable effects of a drug

CRIMINAL ACTIVITY

pharmacological violence
violence committed under the influence of a particular drug

Drug use is implicated in much crime and violence. In one study, 59 percent of detained arrestees in England and 68 percent in the United States tested positive for one or more drugs (Taylor & Bennett, 1999). There are three aspects to the connection between drug use and violence and criminal activity (Levinthal, 1996). **Pharmacological violence** is violence committed under the influence of a particular drug. Some drugs are more conducive to pharmacological violence than others. Heroin users are less likely to act violently than users of amphetamines (bennies, uppers), cocaine (coke), crack cocaine (crack), and PCP (angel dust). Marijuana users become lethargic and mellow, and heroin users develop a positive state of mind. In contrast, users of bennies, coke, or angel dust may become edgy, paranoid, and prone to violence. Similarly, crack makes users irritable, suspicious, and inclined to lash out at the slightest provocation (Levinthal, 1996).

economically compulsive violence
criminal activity committed for the purpose of supporting a drug habit

Economically compulsive violence is criminal activity—burglary, larceny, robbery, shoplifting, and prostitution—for the purpose of supporting a drug habit. Finally, **systemic violence** is criminal activity and violence that originates from a network of drug trafficking and distribution. For example, disputes over territory may cause violence between two or more drug lords.

systemic violence
violence that originates from a network of drug trafficking and distribution

DRUG-INDUCED ALTERED STATES OF CONSCIOUSNESS

Psychoactive drugs, both legal and illegal, are responsible for a wide variety of altered states of consciousness. The effects of a drug depend on dosage, past experience with the drug, the manner in which it is taken, and the circumstances under which it is taken (for example, place, psychological and emotional stability of drug user, presence of other people, and simultaneous use of other drugs).

The major categories of drugs that produce altered states of consciousness are depressants, stimulants, hallucinogens, and opiates. Psychotropic drugs used in treating psychological disorders are discussed in Chapter 11. Table 4.3 lists drugs that induce altered states of consciousness. The abuse of these psychoactive drugs is not cheap—the total annual cost to the Canadian economy is estimated at $40 billion; that works out to a cost of about $1,300 per Canadian. Abuse of tobacco and alcohol made up 80 percent of the total cost (Canadian Centre on Substance Abuse, 2008).

Depressants

Depressants, or "downers," decrease central nervous system arousal, slow down bodily functions, and impair sensitivity to external sensory stimuli. Depressants include alcohol, barbiturates, minor tranquilizers, and inhalants (glues, solvents, and others).

depressant
drug that decreases central nervous system arousal, slows down bodily functions, and impairs sensitivity to external sensory stimuli

Beer, distilled spirits (for example, gin), and wine are three types of alcoholic beverages. The amount of alcohol in a drinker's blood can be assessed by blood-alcohol concentration (BAC). BAC levels can be estimated from body weight, amount of alcohol consumed, and hours since the start of the first drink. A BAC between 0.05 and 0.10 defines legal drunkenness in many jurisdictions.

Alcohol is not a stimulant. The relaxation and animation a person feels after the first two or three drinks is *not* because alcohol acts as a stimulant but because it depresses the areas of the brain that are normally involved in social inhibition. In other words, alcohol reduces social inhibition (Levinthal, 1996). With increased drinking comes drunkenness—that is, increased reduction of social inhibitions, decreased civility, loss of consciousness, and the possibility of death. An intoxicated person may have slurred speech or be talkative, irritable, or physically violent. Intoxication can also lead to **blackouts** (inability to remember events that occurred during the drinking bout), impaired driving skills, motor vehicle accidents, and diminished sexual behaviour. Chronic use of alcohol is associated with several serious physical consequences, including tolerance (needing more and more alcohol to feel good), liver disease, brain damage, and fetal alcohol syndrome in the babies of alcoholic women. Negative psychological consequences include criminal activity, depression, and family, interpersonal, and work problems.

blackout
inability to remember events that occurred during a drinking bout

Stimulants

Stimulants like caffeine, nicotine, amphetamines, cocaine, and crack are known as "uppers" because they speed up the nervous system. For example, cocaine has the effect of blocking the reuptake process of dopamine, a brain chemical, and to some extent norepinephrine at the synapse (see Chapters 2 and 11 for more details on this process). The blockage allows the neurotransmitters to stimulate the post-synaptic receptors for longer periods and to a greater degree. The psychological effects of cocaine use include bursts in energy (rushing), a sense of well-being, enhanced sexual performance (prolonged erection in men and multiple orgasms in women), and in some instances panic attacks. The euphoria associated with cocaine use is attributed to dopamine's effect on the parts of the brain that control pleasure (Levinthal, 1996).

stimulant
drug that speeds up the central nervous system, makes a person feel rushed or energetic, and increases anxiety

The psychological effects of cocaine wearing off include irritability, depression, and, in some cases, suicidal impulses. Cocaine activates the sympathetic nervous

TABLE 4.3   Psychoactive Drugs That Alter Consciousness

Drugs	Category	Street Name(s)
alcohol	depressant	booze
amphetamines	stimulant	A, bennies, black beauties, cadillacs, speed, uppers, whites
barbiturates	depressant	downers, blues, pink ladies, reds, yellows
cannabis (marijuana, hashish)	hallucinogen	dope, herb, grass, joint, pot, Mary Jane, tea, weed
cocaine, crack cocaine	stimulant	blow, C, coke, crack, doing the line, Peruvian lady, white lady
heroin (white or brown)	opiate	black tar (brown), low, boy, dope, H, junk, stuff
LSD	hallucinogen	acid, electricity, microdot, quasey, white lightning
MDMA	hallucinogen	Adam, clarity, ecstasy, essence, X, XTC
morphine	opiate	Big M, M, dope, unkie
PCP	hallucinogen	angel dust, bad pizza, jet fuel, zombie dust
tobacco (nicotine); caffeine	stimulant	not applicable

system and inhibits the parasympathetic system (see Chapter 2). A cocaine user's heart rate increases, sweating increases, blood vessels constrict, pupils dilate, blood pressure rises, and appetite diminishes. The high-level sympathetic arousal can cause cerebral hemorrhage (bleeding in the brain) and congestive heart failure. Chronic use of cocaine can cause irritability, depression, paranoia, and hallucinations.

Hallucinogens

hallucinogen
drug that is mind-expanding, mind-altering, and perception-distorting

Hallucinogens, also known as psychedelic drugs, alter mental processes and perceptions related to mood, space, and time. They may or may not cause actual hallucinations. Hallucinogens include LSD (acid), mescaline, MDMA (ecstasy), and marijuana.

LSD activates the sympathetic system, initially causing dilation of the pupils, increased heart rate and blood pressure, and slight elevation in body temperature. The LSD user may feel euphoric and restless, and may have bouts of laughing or crying. A psychedelic trip, which may be good or bad, follows and lasts between 10 and 12 hours. A person on an acid trip experiences extreme perceptual distortions (separation of body from mind, visual hallucinations, feeling of timelessness) and intense emotional swings that may include anxiety, depression, euphoria, and panic.

Ecstasy is a hallucinogenic drug that is chemically similar to norepinephrine. It was used in the 1980s by psychiatrists for therapeutic purposes for its presumed ability to enhance empathy. The stimulant and hallucinogenic qualities of this drug made its use popular at raves in the 1990s. Ecstasy is now known to produce extremely high body temperature, cardiovascular problems, jaundice, convulsions, and permanent brain damage (Levinthal, 1996).

Marijuana is extracted from the cannabis plant. A hand-rolled marijuana cigarette is known as a reefer or joint. Even though it is listed as a hallucinogenic drug, marijuana is also known to have stimulant, depressant, and opiate effects. Physiologically, marijuana smoking produces increased heart rate, bloodshot eyes, dry mouth, and thirst. Marijuana's effects on appetite for food and sex depend on cultural beliefs and personal expectations (Levinthal, 1996). Marijuana is believed to be both an appetite suppressant and a producer of the "munchies"—feelings of extreme hunger and cravings for sweets. Psychologically, marijuana smokers report feelings of euphoria, well-being, peacefulness, increased awareness of their surroundings, enhanced visual and auditory perception, increased perception of humour and creativity, slowness of passage of time, drowsiness, sleepiness, and dreaminess. Behaviourally, marijuana smoking impairs a person's speech, memory, and ability to carry out tasks that require attention and concentration (for example, driving).

Opiates

Opiates are drugs (for example, morphine, codeine, and heroin) whose psychoactive ingredients are derived from the sap of the opium poppy. Opiates produce powerful relief from pain and also alter mood, sometimes producing euphoria. These effects occur because opiates stimulate endorphins (our bodies' natural painkillers) and increase dopamine activity. Opiates are highly addictive and carry a high potential for overdose.

opiate
drug that kills pain and alters mood, sometimes producing euphoria

POINTS TO REMEMBER

This chapter describes consciousness and states of consciousness. Circadian rhythms are natural biological cycles that affect bodily functions and behaviours. Sleep is an altered state of consciousness in which there is much brain activity. The sleep cycles include no-rapid eye movement (NREM) and rapid eye movement (REM) sleep and dreaming. Hypnosis is another altered state of consciousness that makes people more receptive to suggestion and makes their memory more accurate. Finally, drug-induced altered states of consciousness, or psychoactive states, are those associated with using depressants, stimulants, and hallucinogens. makes people more receptive to suggestion and makes their memory more accurate. Finally, drug-induced altered states of consciousness, or psychoactive states, are those associated with using depressants, stimulants, hallucinogens, and opiates.

KEY TERMS

blackout	pharmacological violence
circadian rhythm	physical dependence
consciousness	psychoactive drug
depressant	psychological dependence
economically compulsive violence	stimulant
hallucinogen	systemic violence
hypnosis	tolerance
opiate	toxicity

REFERENCES

American Psychological Association. Division of Psychological Hypnosis. (2001). *What is hypnosis?* http://www.apa.org/divisions/div30/hypnosis.html.

Barger, L.K., S.W. Lockley, S.M.W. Rajaratnam, & C.P. Landrigan. (2009). Neurobehavioral, health and safety consequences associated with shift-work in safety-sensitive professions. *Current Neurology and Neuroscience Reports, 9,* 155–64.

Canadian Centre on Substance Abuse. (2008, September 4). *Cost study.* http://www.ccsa.ca/Eng/Priorities/Research/CostStudy/Pages/default.aspx.

Columbus Community Hospital. Regional Sleep Disorder Centre. (1998). *The impact of sleep disorders on the transportation industry.* http://members.tripod.com/~sleephealth.indus3.html.

Criminal Code, RSC 1985, c. C-46, as amended.

Durbin, D.A. (1997, May 30). Assembly passes bill on hypnosis. Associated Press. *Las Vegas Review-Journal.* http:lvrj.com/lvrj_home/1997/May-30-Fri-1997/news/5464739.htm.

Folkard, S., & D.A. Lombardi. (2006). Modeling the impact of the components of long work hours on injuries and accidents. *American Journal of Industrial Medicine, 49,* 953–63.

Garbarino, S., F. De Carli, B. Masialino, S. Squarcia, M.A. Penco, M. Beelke, & F. Ferrilo. (2002). Sleepiness and sleep disorders in shift workers: A study on a group of Italian police officers. *Sleep, 25,* 642–47.

Hilgard, E.R. (1977). *Divided consciousness: Multiple controls in human thought and action.* New York: Wiley.

Hughes, J.C. (n.d.). *Exploding the myths about hypnosis.* http://mind4health. com/m4h_art_myths.shtml.

Levinthal, C.F. (1996). *Drugs, behavior and modern society.* Needham Heights, MA: Allyn and Bacon.

Neylan, T.C., T.J. Metzler, S.R. Best, D.S. Weiss, J.A. Fagan, A. Liberman, C. Rogers, K. Vedantham, A. Brunet, T.L. Lipsey, & C.R. Marmar. (2002). Critical incident exposure and sleep quality in police officers. *Psychosomatic Medicine, 64,* 345–52.

Sheehan, P.W., V. Green, & P. Truesdale. (1992). Influence of rapport on hypnotically induced pseudomemory. *Journal of Abnormal Psychology, 101,* 690–700.

Taylor, B., & T. Bennett. (1999). *Comparing drug use rates of detained arrestees in the United States and England.* Washington, DC: National Institute of Justice.

Vila, B. (2008). Sleep deprivation: What does it mean for public safety officers? *National Institute of Justice Journal, 262,* 26–31.

Vincent, D. (2001, March 31). Officers drank while on the job. *The Toronto Star,* pp. B1, B3.

EXERCISES AND REVIEW

Self-Test

Circle the correct answer.

1. Someone who is asleep is

   a. unconscious

   b. non-conscious

   c. in an altered state of consciousness

   d. in a psychoactive state

2. During REM sleep,

   a. brainwave activity slows down

   b. brainwave activity increases

   c. brainwave activity is unchanged

   d. brainwave activity wakes up the sleeper

3. Under hypnosis, a person can be made to

   a. remember events more accurately

   b. perform ridiculous tasks he or she would not normally do

   c. be more receptive to suggestion

   d. a and c

4. The following are psychoactive drugs:

   a. tobacco

   b. caffeine

   c. nicotine

   d. all of the above

5. Pharmacological violence is criminal activity

   a. committed under the influence of a particular drug

   b. committed under the influence of an illicit drug

   c. committed under the influence of a licit drug

   d. all of the above

6. The drive-by shooting of a competing drug dealer by the "employees" of a drug lord is an example of

   a. systemic violence

   b. pharmacological violence

   c. economically compulsive violence

   d. random violence

7. Drug abuse results in costs to

   a. a country's health-care system

   b. the abuser

   c. a country's criminal justice system, including law enforcement

   d. all of the above

8. If you can't get through the day without several cups of coffee, you may be addicted to caffeine, which is a

   a. depressant

   b. hallucinogen

   c. stimulant

   d. psychotropic drug

9. Toxicity is a measure of a drug's

   a. physical harm to the user

   b. psychological harm to the user

   c. diminishing effect on the user

   d. a and b

10. Which of the following drugs tends to make users most violent?

    a. cocaine

    b. marijuana

    c. alcohol

    d. heroin

Thinking About Psychology and Law Enforcement

1. Should hypnosis be used in interviewing victims and witnesses and to solve murder cases? Explain.

2. Explain the role of law enforcement officers in preventing drug use among teenagers.

3. Should use of a licit–illicit psychoactive drug like marijuana be legalized? Why or why not?

CHAPTER 5

Learning

CHAPTER OBJECTIVES

After completing this chapter, you should be able to:

- Identify three types of learning.

- Describe the processes associated with classical conditioning.

- Explain the processes of operant conditioning.

- Discuss the effects of punishment on behaviour.

- Describe the processes associated with observational learning.

PREVIEW SCENARIO

In 1983, two convicted murderers carried two .22-calibre derringer pistols not for self-protection but to help them escape custody by killing the sheriff's deputies when they were being transported to a court hearing. Evidently, a corrections officer had supplied them with the pistols. Daniel Kohut, also a corrections officer, noticed that one of the prisoners, Richard H., was trying to smuggle something in his shoes, and stepped in to investigate. Kohut was unable to disarm Richard H. because he was punched by the prisoner's cellmate, Louis C. Overpowered, Kohut and another prison employee, Gus Mastros, were taken hostage by Richard H. and Louis C. The hostage ordeal lasted for almost six days. Sixteen years later, Kohut was honoured for his bravery during the incident. He received his medal of valour from the Department of Corrections at age 55. It was recognized that this honour was long overdue. (Simonich, 1999)

LEARNING DEFINED

Treachery and bravery are two of the learned behaviours described in the preview scenario. **Learning** refers to change in behaviour that is relatively permanent and is due to experience rather than to other factors. According to this view of learning, short-term changes in behaviour due to illness, injury, mood fluctuation, fatigue, or lack of effort do not constitute learning. Similarly, permanent changes in behaviour brought about by a brain injury or disease process rather than acquired through experience are not considered learning. Finally, learning is not the same as maturation, which is the unfolding of biologically predetermined patterns of behaviour due simply to the process of growing older. Changes in behaviour that occur as a result of growth and maturation may have nothing to do with learning.

learning
change in behaviour that is relatively permanent and is due to experience

For example, adolescent boys do not *learn* to speak in a deeper voice when they enter puberty; instead, their voices change as a result of physical maturation.

TYPES OF LEARNING

Learning accounts for the development and maintenance of beliefs, emotions, and actions, whether they are appropriate or inappropriate, adaptive (healthy) or maladaptive (unhealthy). Psychologists distinguish among three types of learning: classical conditioning, operant conditioning, and observational learning. This chapter discusses these types of learning and how they apply to law enforcement. The basic elements and essential processes associated with each type of learning are presented in Table 5.1. Note that most learned behaviours involve some combination of the three learning processes described here.

Classical Conditioning

A year ago, Officer Paul stopped a motorist for dangerous driving. When he approached the driver to ask for his licence, the man suddenly pulled out a gun, pointed it at Officer Paul's head, and demanded to be let go. The officer let him go but was able to get his licence plate number. The man was later apprehended and charged. For several months after this incident, every time Officer Paul stopped a motorist his heart would beat wildly, his hands would sweat, and he would feel slightly nauseous. For the past month, although he is still cautious about approaching motorists in their cars, he no longer experiences the earlier physical symptoms. Officer Paul's experience with the traumatic gun event illustrates processes associated with classical conditioning.

BASIC ELEMENTS OF CLASSICAL CONDITIONING

Psychologists distinguish between two types of behavioural response: *respondent behaviour* and *operant behaviour*. Respondent behaviour is the same as classical conditioning. **Classical conditioning** refers to learning in which a neutral stimulus begins to elicit a **reflex**, or involuntary response, when that stimulus becomes associated with another stimulus that naturally evokes the reflexive response. The neutral stimulus is termed "neutral" because it did not elicit this reflex prior to its association with the earlier stimulus.

Ivan P. Pavlov (1849–1936), a Russian physiologist, is the name usually associated with classical conditioning. In fact, classical conditioning is sometimes called Pavlovian conditioning. Pavlov discovered the classical conditioning phenomenon accidentally when he noticed that his laboratory dogs responded (salivated) not only to the ingestion of food (as they should) but also to the mere sight of food or the sound of the footsteps of his assistant who normally brought in the food. Pavlov realized that the dogs were responding reflexively to stimuli in the environment not just on the basis of biological need (hunger) but also on the basis of learning.

To test this observation, Pavlov conducted a series of experiments on respondent behaviour. In a well-known study, he attached a tube to the salivary gland of a dog so that he could measure the amount of saliva the dog produced. Pavlov then

classical conditioning
learning in which a stimulus begins to elicit a reflexive response when that stimulus becomes associated with another stimulus that naturally evokes the reflexive response

reflex
involuntary response to a particular stimulus

TABLE 5.1   Basic Elements and Essential Processes of Learning in Psychology

Type of Learning	Elements	Processes
Classical conditioning	• Respondent behaviour • Unconditioned stimulus • Unconditioned response • Conditioned stimulus • Conditioned response	• Acquisition • Stimulus generalization • Stimulus discrimination • Extinction • Spontaneous recovery • Higher-order conditioning
Operant conditioning	• Operant behaviour • Consequence	• Acquisition • Extinction • Schedules of reinforcement • Generalization • Discrimination • Shaping • Superstitious behaviour • Punishment
Observational learning	• Observer • Model	• Acquisition • Vicarious reinforcement • Self-reinforcement

sounded a tone using a tuning fork and, just a few seconds later, presented the dog with meat powder. He repeated the tone/meat powder routine a number of times. Initially, the dog salivated only in response to the meat powder. However, the dog soon began to salivate at the sound of the tuning fork. In fact, the dog continued to salivate at the sound even when the meat powder was removed from the experiment. This finding demonstrated that classical conditioning had occurred: the dog was responding not just on the basis of a biological need, but had learned to respond to a previously neutral stimulus, in this case, the tone.

The basic elements of classical conditioning are as follows (see also Figure 5.1):

- Unconditioned stimulus: A stimulus to which a person responds reflexively—for example, food, a puff of air in the eye, or touching a hot stove burner.

- Unconditioned response: A respondent behaviour, or automatic response, that is evoked by the unconditioned stimulus and does not require previous training. Examples include salivating when one smells food, blinking when a puff of air hits the eye, or withdrawing one's hand from a hot stove burner.

- Conditioned stimulus: A previously neutral stimulus to which a person learns to respond after it becomes associated with an unconditioned stimulus—for example, bells, buzzers, and lights, or, in Pavlov's experiment, the sound of the tuning fork.

- Conditioned response: A respondent behaviour, the response that is evoked by the conditioned stimulus—for example, the dog's salivating at the sound of the tuning fork.

CLASSICAL CONDITIONING PROCESSES

Six processes are associated with classical conditioning.

Acquisition: A New Association

In Pavlov's experiment, the dog's learning to respond to the tone represents the *acquisition* process of classical conditioning. Note that classical conditioning does not involve learning a new behaviour, but rather involves associating a new stimulus with an existing involuntary or reflexive response. Classical conditioning accounts for many human emotional reactions. For example, after several run-ins with the police, teenagers' hearts may start beating faster when a police car with its red light and siren on pulls up behind them.

Stimulus Generalization: All the Same

Pavlov observed that his dogs often salivated not only at the sound of the tuning fork but also at sounds that were similar, such as a bell or buzzer. This phenomenon is called **stimulus generalization**. In our earlier example, for several months Officer Paul became anxious whenever he had to stop a motorist, even if the situation and the driver did not resemble those from the gun incident. The greater the similarity between two stimuli, the greater the likelihood of stimulus generalization. The less similar the new stimulus to the original stimulus, the weaker the conditioned response to the new stimulus. In fact, when the new stimulus is sufficiently different from the original stimulus, the conditioned response may not occur at all. Such behaviour is the result of stimulus discrimination.

stimulus generalization
responding to a stimulus that is similar to the original unconditioned stimulus

Stimulus Discrimination: All Not the Same

In classical conditioning, **stimulus discrimination** refers to the tendency to distinguish between similar stimuli and to restrict response to the original stimulus. In Officer Paul's case, becoming anxious only when approaching male drivers but not female drivers illustrates stimulus discrimination.

stimulus discrimination
responding only to the original stimulus

Extinction: Out of Sight, Out of Mind

A conditioned response may come to be inhibited if conditions that were present during acquisition change. When the unconditioned stimulus is no longer present, the learned response may weaken. In Pavlov's classic experiment, salivation diminished when dogs received several additional trials in which the sound of the tuning fork was presented by itself, no longer paired with the meat powder. The weakening of a conditioned response is called **extinction**. In Officer Paul's case, stopping several motorists without being physically threatened gradually led to a reduction in anx-

extinction
weakening and eventual disappearance of the conditioned response

FIGURE 5.1 The Classical Conditioning Model

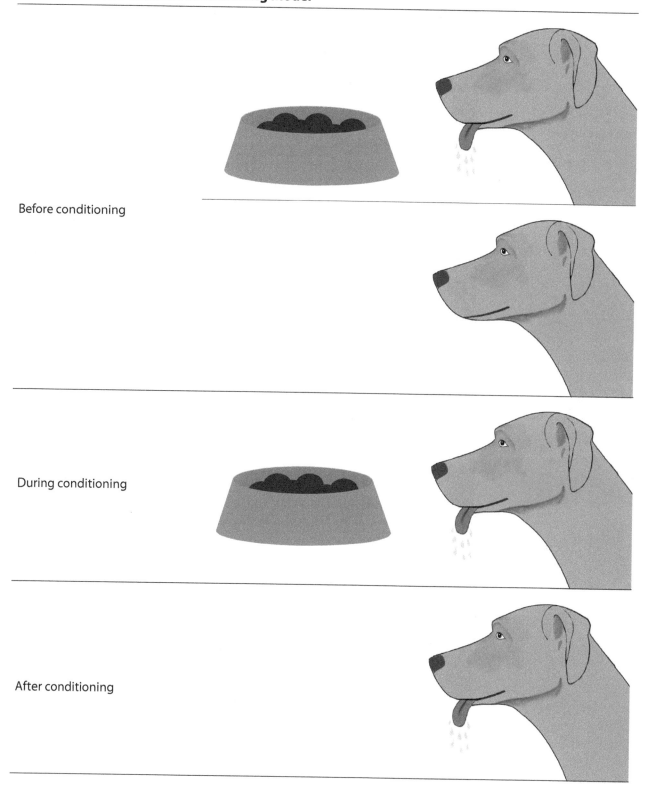

Before conditioning

During conditioning

After conditioning

iety, illustrating extinction in another context. Extinction does not mean that the association between the conditioned stimulus and the conditioned response is forgotten or erased—it simply means that the conditioned response is gradually weakened or suppressed.

Spontaneous Recovery: Gone but Not Forgotten

spontaneous recovery
re-emergence of an
extinguished response

Spontaneous recovery is concrete evidence that conditioned responses are inhibited or suppressed through the process of extinction rather than permanently lost. **Spontaneous recovery** refers to the classical conditioning process in which the extinguished conditioned response reappears following a rest period (say, a week after the conditioned response is extinguished). However, the response is weaker and lasts a shorter time than the original conditioned response. Because of the nature of the spontaneously recovered response, it can be extinguished more quickly than before.

Spontaneous recovery accounts for a variety of human experiences, including relapse into alcohol and drug addictions. Even though cocaine addicts may be "cured" of their addiction following treatment—that is, they may be "clean" for a long time—their craving for the drug may, over time, resurface at the sight of stimuli previously associated with drug use, such as a cocaine pipe. It is for this reason that former addicts and alcoholics may need "booster" sessions to combat spontaneous recovery and help them stay clean.

Higher-Order Conditioning: Chaining of Hearts

Higher-order conditioning is the process in which a neutral stimulus that is paired repeatedly with an existing conditioned stimulus elicits the conditioned response all by itself. Note that in this case, the existing conditioned stimulus *functions* as an unconditioned stimulus. Higher-order conditioning may account for the development and maintenance of feelings and attitudes, both positive (likes) and negative (dislikes), toward stimuli. This process may explain some people's prejudice against members of various cultures (for example, associating black people with laziness, or gay and lesbian people with immorality) or those with physical or mental handicaps. Similarly, a member of a motorcycle gang may react with intense dislike not only at the sight of a police officer but also at merely hearing the word *police*.

CONDITIONING, DRUGS, AND DEATH

**conditioned
compensatory response**
physiological changes that
counteract a drug effect
and that result from the
association of a drug effect
with environmental cues

It is common to assume that instances of drug overdose result from the administration of a larger-than-normal quantity of drugs. However, this is not always the case; some overdoses occur when the drug user administers the usual amount, *but does so in an unusual environment* (see, for example, Siegel, 1983; Gerevich et al., 2005). Chapter 4 introduced the concept of drug tolerance—the progressively weaker effect felt as a result of repeatedly taking a drug. When a drug is administered, the internal physiological environment of the user changes in complex ways. In one scenario, the effect of the drug triggers an unconditioned physiological change that opposes the drug effect. The drug effect is thus an unconditioned stimulus that elicits a reflexive compensatory response. If a drug user tends to use a drug in a particular location (say, the basement of his home), the cues (sights, smells, and sounds) of the room become associated with the drug effect, and may end up eliciting a **conditioned compensatory response**. The implication is that the familiar

BOX 5.1   The Use of Animals in Law Enforcement

Law enforcement often requires detection of substances that may occur in minute quantities or in dangerous conditions, as well as surveillance of vast areas. These realities create significant demands on officers and agencies. The unique physical and sensory capabilities of some animal species make them well suited to assist alongside human agents in many contexts.

Historically, animal applications in law enforcement largely have been limited to the use of horses for transportation, and dogs for drug detection, search and rescue, and apprehension of suspects. Yet, associative learning abilities occur in species of all shapes and sizes, ranging from insects to large mammals, and many such animals are increasingly being trained to serve in other policing functions. Consider the following examples.

Researchers at the Los Alamos National Laboratory have made use of bees' well-developed sense of smell by training honeybees and wasps to detect the scent of ingredients commonly found in bombs, as well as the drugs cocaine and methamphetamine. Using a simple conditioning approach, trainers expose bees to a particular odour and then give them a sugar-water reward. Bees quickly learn to extend their proboscis (bees' version of a tongue) in response to the odour. Hives of trained bees could be used in airports or suspected drug havens. Bees will "tell" agents if target odours are present by sticking out their "tongues"!

Concerns that public water supplies may be susceptible to acts of terrorism and the enormous range of possible contaminants have led to the use of bluegill fish to monitor water supplies. In one system, eight bluegill fish swim freely in tanks while a computer analyzes their behaviour. If six or more fish show behavioural abnormalities, the computer alerts a technician, who then checks the tank for contaminants. After a period in the tank, the fish are removed and rewarded for their efforts with a meal of shrimp.

Sources: Boisvert and Sherry (2006); Macuda and Timney (1999); Mott (2006).

room cues elicit physiological responses that lessen the drug effect. Therefore, tolerance may occur as a result of conditioning. If the user takes the same amount of drug in a new setting that lacks the familiar conditioned stimuli, no compensatory response is elicited, and the usual dosage may pack a lethal punch—an apparent "overdose" (Siegel, 1983; Gerevich et al., 2005).

Operant Conditioning

Operant conditioning is the second basic type of learning in psychology. **Operant conditioning** involves changing the probability of an existing voluntary behaviour and learning an entirely new behaviour. Operant conditioning principles (such as positive reinforcement and shaping) are used in many aspects of law enforcement, including police K9 training (Box 5.1).

B.F. Skinner (1904–1990) is the name most associated with operant conditioning. An American psychologist, Skinner recognized the importance of classical con-

operant conditioning
changing the probability of an existing voluntary behaviour and learning an entirely new behaviour

operant
behaviour emitted
voluntarily

ditioning but believed that most human behaviour involves freely *emitted* responses. Skinner referred to behaviour emitted voluntarily as an **operant**. The term implies an active rather than a passive subject (as in classical conditioning) who "operates" on his or her environment, controlling the environment and being controlled by it.

BASIC ELEMENTS OF OPERANT CONDITIONING

consequence
event or stimulus that
follows an operant and
determines its future
probability

The two basic elements of operant conditioning are an *operant* and a *consequence.* Again, an operant is a voluntary response. A **consequence** is an event or a stimulus that follows an operant and determines its future probability. For maximum effectiveness, a consequence should immediately follow an emitted behaviour. This is not what happened in the case of Daniel Kohut, the corrections officer in the preview scenario. His operant (heroic act) was consequenced 16 years after it was emitted. A consequence that is far removed from the behaviour is unlikely to affect the probability of that behaviour recurring, or it may affect the wrong behaviour, an unintended one.

There are two types of consequences: positive or pleasant, and negative or unpleasant. A positive consequence strengthens or increases the probability of the behaviour it follows. If Ms. Singh, an introductory psychology instructor, tells a joke in the classroom (an operant) and all of her students laugh or smile (a positive consequence), she will be more likely to tell jokes in class in the future. A negative or unpleasant consequence decreases the likelihood of a behaviour recurring in the future. If after telling a joke Ms. Singh's students walk out on her (a negative consequence), she will be less likely to tell jokes in class, at least in the immediate future.

OPERANT CONDITIONING PROCESSES

The eight processes associated with operant conditioning follow.

Acquisition: Promoting the Good, the Bad, and the Ugly

In operant conditioning, acquisition is the learning of a new behaviour (good, bad, or ugly) or the strengthening of an existing response. New behaviours are learned and existing behaviours are strengthened through positive and negative reinforcement.

positive reinforcement
process in which a positive
consequence follows a
behaviour and increases
the probability of the
behaviour being repeated

Positive reinforcement is the process in which a positive consequence follows a behaviour and increases the probability of the behaviour's repetition. Rewarding prisoners for good behaviour is likely to increase good behaviour. Praising a new recruit for keeping cool in a stressful situation is likely to strengthen this behaviour. For positive reinforcement to be effective in "stamping in" a particular behaviour, the reinforcing stimulus has to be meaningful for the person receiving the reward.

negative reinforcement
process in which a
response that terminates
an unpleasant stimulus
increases the probability of
the behaviour being
repeated

Negative reinforcement is the process in which a response that terminates an unpleasant stimulus increases the probability of the behaviour's repetition. An individual who takes a painkiller to get rid of a headache today is likely to take the same painkiller again tomorrow for another headache. The behaviour of taking the painkiller is "stamped in" because it terminates the existing aversive condition—pain, in this case.

Negative reinforcement consists of two major forms of learning: escape and avoidance. *Escape conditioning* involves learning a response to end an existing aversive condition or situation. Children who pull their hands away from a hot stove burner are exhibiting escape conditioning.

Avoidance conditioning involves learning a response that allows the person to evade an aversive condition or situation. A troubled teenager who runs away from a police officer who is about to apprehend him is exhibiting avoidance conditioning. Similarly, a woman in an abusive marriage who runs out of the house when she picks up signals that her husband is getting dangerously angry is exhibiting avoidance conditioning.

It is important to recognize that both escape conditioning and avoidance conditioning are not synonymous with punishment. As described below, punishment is an aversive stimulus that follows a response and *decreases* its probability.

Extinction: Losing the Good, the Bad, and the Ugly

In operant conditioning, *extinction* is the process in which a behaviour is weakened or stops altogether because it is not followed by a reinforcer or a reward. A law enforcement officer who leaves voicemail messages for her boss that are not returned will soon stop leaving voicemail messages. Another officer who "cries wolf" all the time, calling his co-workers for emergency help in non-emergency situations, will fail to get their help in a real emergency.

Schedules of Reinforcement: When Will It Happen?

There are two ways to reinforce a particular behaviour: continuous reinforcement and intermittent (or partial) reinforcement. **Continuous reinforcement** is reinforcing or rewarding a behaviour every time it is emitted. Continuous reinforcement is the most effective approach to learning a new behaviour.

However, in real life, behaviour is not reinforced every time it occurs—instead, rewards tend to be intermittent. **Intermittent reinforcement** refers to the process of rewarding some but not all emitted responses. An officer is unlikely to receive praise from her boss for every responsible act she performs on the job, for example. Intermittent reinforcement is effective in maintaining a newly learned behaviour rather than acquiring one.

continuous reinforcement
reinforcement of all responses

intermittent reinforcement
reinforcement of some but not all responses

Generalization: Acting the Same

In operant conditioning, *generalization* is the process in which a behaviour that is reinforced positively or negatively in one stimulus situation is extended to similar stimulus situations. Ten-year-old Ashley is rewarded for having good manners at home, and soon has good manners in a variety of social situations outside the home. In another example, after she is sexually assaulted by a stranger, Semareh feels shame and hostility toward all men rather than just toward her assailant. Similarly, following a single frightening experience with a black person, Constable Mario stereotypes all black people as bad, and avoids social contact with them.

Discrimination: Acting Differently

Discrimination is the opposite of generalization. In operant conditioning, it is the process in which reinforcement occurs in the presence of a stimulus, and non-reinforcement occurs in the presence of other stimuli. The stimulus that signals that a certain response is likely to be reinforced, ignored, or punished is called the *discriminative stimulus*. This stimulus enables the person to anticipate the probable outcome associated with a particular response in a particular situation. A prisoner is more likely to behave herself when a prison guard is around and more likely to create havoc when none is around. Similarly, a wise law enforcement officer asks for a raise when his supervisor is in a good mood rather than when she is in a bad mood.

Discrimination allows the learning of appropriate behaviours in everyday life situations. Law enforcement officers develop the skill of discriminating between situations that are dangerous and those that are not. Drivers who get traffic tickets for failing to stop at red lights hopefully learn the easy lesson of responding differently to red and green traffic lights to avoid having to pay fines and possibly losing their driver's licence.

Shaping: A Step at a Time

shaping
process in which a complex behaviour is learned when only those responses that successively approximate the desired behaviour are reinforced

Shaping is the process in which a complex behaviour is learned when only those responses that successively approximate the desired behaviour are reinforced. Skinner used the successive approximation process to shape a chopping motion in Erich Fromm, a psychoanalyst who was giving a lecture that annoyed Skinner. Fromm gestured a lot while he talked. Skinner looked directly at him whenever Fromm lifted his hand, and nodded and smiled whenever Fromm brought his hand down. Within five minutes, Fromm was chopping the air so vigorously that his wristwatch kept slipping down (Skinner, 1983, pp. 150–51).

Superstitious Behaviour: Lucky Charms

Superstitious behaviour presumes a connection between a response and a positive or an aversive consequence. Samantha is a regular bingo player. On one occasion, she won the jackpot after touching a Smurf doll she was carrying in her purse. Samantha associated carrying the Smurf with winning the jackpot. From then on, Samantha made sure to touch her "lucky" Smurf every time she played bingo.

Punishment: Unpleasant Penalties

punishment
application of an aversive stimulus or withdrawal of a pleasant stimulus to decrease the probability of a response

Punishment refers to the application of an aversive stimulus or withdrawal of a pleasant stimulus to decrease the probability of a response. Prisoners may lose privileges, such as daily time outdoors, as punishment (withdrawal of a pleasant stimulus) for, say, behaving violently. Some may face time in isolation as punishment (application of an aversive stimulus) to reduce their violent behaviour.

Note that punishment is different from negative reinforcement. Punishment *decreases* the likelihood of a behaviour occurring in the future, while negative reinforcement *increases* the likelihood of a behaviour occurring in the future by removing an existing aversive stimulus.

Finally, punishment and negative or positive reinforcement may operate in the same situation. For example, Officer Linh handcuffs an agitated and verbally abusive suspect. In this situation, the suspect's behaviour is being punished (his verbal abuse is consequenced by an aversive stimulus, being handcuffed) and is thus likely to diminish. Officer Linh's behaviour—handcuffing the suspect—has thus terminated an unpleasant stimulus. This negative reinforcement will make her more likely to handcuff verbally abusive suspects in the future.

Punishment has the advantage of effectively *suppressing* a behaviour when it follows the behaviour immediately. However, it does not eliminate a behaviour, nor does it teach a new behaviour. Punishment also has known side effects, including fear of the punisher, hostility, and aggression. A prison environment that is too harsh, particularly where punishment is perceived by the prisoners as unjust, is likely to foster the potentially destructive forces of humiliation, resentment, fear, and even revolt. Punishment for the purpose of breaking a prisoner's spirit may help to control that prisoner, but it is also a powerful force for provoking rebellion and revenge in others. Punishment has an obvious connection to law enforcement through the use of criminal sentences. Its use in this context is subject to many factors that influence its effectiveness. Punishment may be administered intermittently rather than continuously, or at low levels. Punishment for criminal behaviour may also provide a criminal with her only significant source of attention. In this case, punishment would be a discriminative stimulus that signals positive reinforcement.

Observational Learning

Both classical and operant conditioning emphasize individual experience. However, much of our learning occurs as a result of watching others behave—**observational learning**. By observing others we can learn how to perform a particular behaviour, as well as the consequences that can result when that behaviour occurs.

observational learning
learning by observing

Consider the following example. Constable Arsinée is the shooting instructor for new recruits. Before having them practise, she first teaches them through example. She demonstrates how to load the gun, hold it steady, take aim at the target, and fire. Then she instructs the recruits to repeat what she has just demonstrated. Constable Arsinée is using observational learning in teaching the recruits the new behaviours.

Observational learning requires an *observer* and a *model*. The **observer** is the person who learns by observing and imitating the model. The **model** is the person who demonstrates the behaviour to be learned. In the example above, the new recruits are the observers and Constable Arsinée is the model. Parents, spouses, law enforcement officers, teachers, judges, and police chiefs are all powerful models in the communities they live in and beyond. Fellow prisoners are also powerful models for one another. Prisoners may learn through observing peers being prosocial (cooperative, friendly) or antisocial (aggressive, obnoxious).

observer
person who learns by observing and imitating a model

model
person who demonstrates a behaviour to be learned by an observer

OBSERVATIONAL LEARNING PROCESSES

Three processes are associated with observational learning.

Acquisition: Learning by Seeing

Learning by observing is far from a "monkey see, monkey do" process. Rather, it involves four processes: attention, retention, motor reproduction, and motivation (Bandura, 1977). These processes are presented in Figure 5.2.

- Attention: Attention refers to the extent to which the observer is likely to pay heed to the model. A police officer who is sleeping while her instructor is demonstrating the use of firearms is unlikely to learn any of the demonstrated information or skills. An effective model is one who is able to capture the attention of the observer to maximize the learning process. Similarly, an effective observer is one who is in a physical and psychological state that makes him or her capable of maximizing the ability to pay attention to the model. Attention to a model is also affected by the model's characteristics, including his or her status, competence, power, age, sex, attractiveness, and culture or ethnicity. People are more likely to be influenced by models who are similar to rather than different from them.

- Retention: Retention refers to the extent to which the observer is likely to remember the behaviour that is modelled. Simply put, no memory means no learning. Retention can be maximized by the manner in which the modelled behaviour is presented or by the observer's use of good retention strategies. Strategies that are known to be effective in storing and retrieving information include using imagery, rehearsing, organizing, and using retrieval cues (see Chapter 6).

- Motor reproduction: This refers to the observer's physical capacity to reproduce the model's behaviour correctly. The more complex the modelled behaviour and the less physically skilled the observer, the poorer the outcome of learning.

- Motivation: Motivation refers to the observer's translating the learned behaviour into action. Reinforcement is not necessary for observational learning to occur, but an observer may choose not to display the learned behaviour unless he or she receives some incentive or reward. Similarly, an observer is unlikely to display a learned behaviour when punishment is the likely outcome for doing so.

Vicarious Reinforcement: (Dis)Inhibition

Observational learning can have two behavioural influences: direct external consequences, as in operant conditioning, or observation of consequences resulting from the behaviour of a model. In other words, the observer's thoughts, feelings, and actions are likely to be influenced by the consequences arising from the model's thoughts, feelings, and actions. This is known as *vicarious consequence*, where an observer witnesses an external outcome of a model's behaviour. **Vicarious positive reinforcement** occurs when an observer's behaviour increases as a result of observing positive reinforcement of the model's behaviour. An observer is more likely to imitate a model who is rewarded. For example, Staff Sergeant Gamal volunteers free time to the Police Ethnic and Cultural Exchange program after learning that Staff Sergeant Taline has been praised by the chief for her volunteer work with the program. **Vicarious punishment** occurs when an observer's behaviour is reduced as a result of observing punishment of the model's behaviour. An observer is less likely to imitate a model who is punished. For example, in a meeting, Constable Margit decides not to speak her mind after observing Constable Tomas being ostracized by the inspector for expressing views about the management of the police services.

vicarious positive reinforcement
occurs when an observer's behaviour increases as a result of observing the positive reinforcement of the model's behaviour

vicarious punishment
occurs when an observer's behaviour is reduced as a result of observing the punishment of the model's behaviour

Self-Reinforcement: Outcomes Imposed on Self

Human feelings, thoughts, and actions are influenced not only by external consequences and consequences observed in models, but also by self-imposed consequences. People evaluate their own behaviours and reward or punish themselves. For example, in performing his duties, Officer Xinyin does not need his supervisor to be around. He treats offenders with dignity for his own satisfaction rather than just for the satisfaction of his superiors. Officer Xinyin praises himself frequently for

FIGURE 5.2   Four Processes Associated with Acquisition in Observational Learning

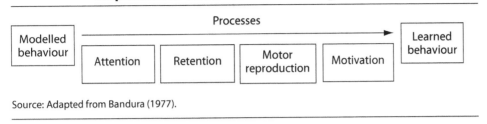

Source: Adapted from Bandura (1977).

doing his best at work. On the other hand, he also criticizes himself when he doesn't live up to his own expectations. Officer Xinyin relies more on internal self-regulated consequences—self-satisfaction, self-pride, self-dissatisfaction, self-criticism, and self-guilt—for his behaviour than on external consequences.

POINTS TO REMEMBER

All three major types of learning—classical conditioning, operant conditioning, and observational learning—may be involved in acquiring a behaviour. In classical conditioning, a person makes a new association between a stimulus and an involuntary response. Classical conditioning contributes to our understanding of likes and dislikes and negative emotions such as fear and phobia. In operant conditioning, consequences either increase or decrease the probability of the behaviours they follow. Operant conditioning contributes to our understanding of voluntary behaviours and the ease or difficulty with which they can be eliminated. Observational learning—learning by example—contributes to our understanding of internal and external influences on human thoughts, feelings, and actions.

KEY TERMS

classical conditioning

conditioned compensatory response

consequence

continuous reinforcement

extinction

intermittent reinforcement

learning

model

negative reinforcement

observational learning

observer

operant

operant conditioning

positive reinforcement

punishment

reflex

shaping

spontaneous recovery

stimulus discrimination

stimulus generalization

vicarious positive reinforcement

vicarious punishment

REFERENCES

Bandura, A. (1977). *Social-learning theory.* Englewood Cliffs, NJ: Prentice Hall.

Boisvert, M.J., & D.F. Sherry. (2006). Interval timing by an invertebrate, the bumble bee *Bombus impatiens. Current Biology, 16,* 1636–40.

Gerevich, J., E. Bacskai, L. Farkas, & Z. Danics. (2005). A case report: Pavolian conditioning as a risk factor of heroin "overdose" death. *Harm Reduction Journal, 2,* 11.

Macuda, T., & B. Timney. (1999). Luminance and chromatic discrimination in the horse (*Equus caballus*). *Behavioral Processes, 41,* 301–7.

Mott, M. (2006). Bluegill fish monitor water supplies for terrorist attacks. *National Geographic News.* http://news.nationalgeographic.com/news/2006/09/060928-bluegill-fish.html.

Siegel, S. (1983). Classical conditioning, drug tolerance, and drug dependence. In Y. Israel, F.B. Glaser, H. Kalant, R.E. Popham, W. Schmidt, & R.G. Smart (Eds.), *Research advances in alcohol and drug problems: Vol. 7.* New York: Plenum.

Simonich, M. (1999, May 7). *Former corrections officer honored for bravery for being hostage in 1983.* http://www.post-gazette.com/regionstate/19990507kohut7.asp.

Skinner, B.F. (1983). *A matter of consequences.* New York: Knopf.

EXERCISES AND REVIEW

Self-Test

Circle the correct answer.

1. As a child, Officer Andrew heard his parents repeatedly use the words "dirty," "lazy," and "stupid" in reference to non-white people. Which of the following most likely explains Officer Andrew's stereotypical attitudes toward non-whites?

   a. higher-order conditioning

   b. generalization

   c. spontaneous recovery

   d. spontaneous discovery

2. When Josée reacts with fear only when her father starts pacing around the house, pacing has become a(n) _____ for fear.

   a. unconditioned stimulus

   b. discriminative stimulus

   c. conditioned response

   d. unconditioned response

3. A corrections officer considers all prisoners "hopeless cases." This view is an example of

    a. positive reinforcement

    b. punishment

    c. generalization

    d. extinction

4. Antonio enjoys his law enforcement courses but continues to be fearful of tests and tends to "play sick" on test days. He is unlikely to overcome his test anxiety because he uses _____ as a way of coping with negative emotions.

    a. avoidance

    b. escape

    c. negative reinforcement

    d. punishment

5. Inspector Aram responds to the demands of police in 54 Division by finally giving in and doing what they want. His behaviour is being controlled by

    a. punishment

    b. negative reinforcement

    c. positive reinforcement

    d. stupidity

6. In the case above, the behaviour of the police in 54 Division is being controlled by

    a. punishment

    b. generalization

    c. positive reinforcement

    d. manipulation

7. Which of the following is likely to make observational learning less effective?

    a. daydreaming during a use-of-force training session

    b. listening to a presentation on shoplifting in a quiet lecture room

    c. attending firearms training

    d. participating in a hostage-taking dramatization

8. Officer Verinder observes his partner using excessive force on an apprehended suspect and getting pleasure from it. Officer Verinder is

   a. more likely to use excessive force

   b. less likely to use excessive force

   c. not likely to be influenced at all by his partner's behaviour

   d. likely to beat up his partner

9. A prisoner who witnesses another prisoner break a rule and get away with it may

   a. develop the belief that rules can be broken in this correctional institution

   b. decide to break a rule too

   c. more strongly believe that rules are made to be broken

   d. all of the above

10. A child who observes his mother act in fear at the sight of a dog in the street is likely to develop a fear of

    a. his mother

    b. dogs

    c. streets

    d. none of the above

Thinking About Psychology and Law Enforcement

1. Identify the schedules of reinforcement in the following examples:

   a. a police officer receives a promotion for apprehending a specific number of criminals

   b. a prisoner attempts to escape from prison every three months

   c. a person plays a slot machine at a casino

   d. a security officer works an eight-hour shift

   e. a prison guard makes rounds at different times of the day, averaging about two-hour intervals

2. Deterrence is the oldest criminal justice model. Its two components are specific deterrence and general deterrence. The goal of specific deterrence is to prevent a future crime from being committed by the individual who is caught and punished. The goal of general deterrence is to prevent members of society from contemplating committing a crime.

   How might the three types of learning help in understanding deterrence generally and its two components particularly?

3. B.F. Skinner believed that North American society is a punishing society. For example, police punish drivers by stopping them when they are speeding or breaking traffic rules, and ignore them when they are complying with the law. Should society generally, and the criminal justice system particularly, shift from a punishing mode to a rewarding mode to increase the number of law-abiding citizens? Explain.

CHAPTER 6

Memory, Intelligence, and Problem Solving

CHAPTER OBJECTIVES

After completing this chapter, you should be able to:

- Identify the major divisions of memory.
- Describe the processes associated with encoding, storing, and retrieving information.
- Explain the evidence that memory is reconstructive and prone to distortions.
- Discuss the factors that affect eyewitness memory.
- Explain why "recovered" memories are controversial.
- Describe the components of intelligence and requirements of intelligence tests.
- Discuss the major methods of solving problems.

PREVIEW SCENARIO

In 1984, a man broke into Jennifer Thompson's apartment and raped her. Determined to remember her assailant, she spent every moment of this traumatic and agonizing event studying his face. She memorized his hairline, his eyes, the shape of his nose; she looked for unique scars or tattoos that would identify him. That same day following her attack she went to the police department. She helped create a composite sketch of her attacker based on her memory of his facial features. Then, a few days later, she identified the culprit from a photo line-up and chose him again in a live lineup. In 1985, Ronald Cotton was convicted of rape and burglary. In 1986, Cotton was sentenced to life in prison.

One year later, the case was retried. During that trial, Bobby Poole, another inmate, was called to testify. Poole had boasted in prison that he, not Cotton, had committed the rape. When Poole appeared in court, Jennifer Thompson was asked if she had ever seen him before.

She answered that she had never seen him in her life. As a result, Ronald Cotton was returned to prison. Then, in 1995, a DNA test was run on evidence collected from the assault. Jennifer Thompson was soon informed that Bobby Poole was the rapist, and Ronald Cotton was exonerated after serving 11 years in prison. (Thompson, 2000)

INTRODUCTION

Memory plays a central role in police work. Officers often must rely on eyewitness memory to identify details of a crime and the identity of a culprit. Investigators have to sort out the details of criminal events by combining remembered information with new information gathered after the crime occurs. When officers testify in court, they too must retrieve memories pertaining to the details of a particular case, often months or years after the event occurred.

REMEMBERING: A FRAMEWORK

memory
the processes involved in the acquisition, storage, and retrieval of information

Memory refers to the processes involved in the acquisition, storage, and retrieval of information. It is often conceptualized as a set of interactions among three distinct systems (Atkinson & Shiffrin, 1968). **Sensory memory** stores information from the sensory subsystems—vision, hearing, olfaction, and so on—for a very brief period (from a fraction of a second to a few seconds, depending on the sensory subsystem).

sensory memory
information from the bodily senses, stored for a brief time

You probably can recall waving sparklers through the air when you were young and delighting in the trailing flash of light that followed the sparkler as it moved. That trailing light is a *visual sensory memory*. Visual sensory memories are short-lived, lasting only a fraction of a second.

Because sensory memories fade so quickly, most do not persist in the memory system. However, when we use selective attention, some of the contents of sensory memory enter our short-term or working, memory. **Short-term memory** (STM) holds the contents of your current awareness (that is, whatever you are thinking about right now) for about 20 seconds. STM can hold between five and nine pieces of information at a time. George Miller (1956) described the capacity of STM as the "magical number seven, plus or minus two." STM is limited in both its capacity and its duration, but strategies can be employed to extend these limits. One strategy to extend the duration of STM is to actively rehearse the information you are trying to remember. **Rehearsal** helps to keep active the contents of memory, but it's not foolproof, as you've likely discovered if someone has interrupted you while you tried to repeat a phone number to yourself until you reached a phone.

short-term (working) memory
recently acquired information stored in limited capacity

rehearsal
repetition of information to keep it active in short-term memory

Try to remember this string of letters by reading them once and then jotting down as many of them in order as you possibly can:

NFLDTGIFSOSFBICFLRCMPNY

You probably found this a difficult task. There are 23 letters in this string, far beyond the capacity of short-term memory. But what would happen if you arranged these 23 pieces of information into larger, more meaningful *chunks*, as follows:

NFLD TGIF SOS FBI CFL RCMP NY

chunking
grouping individual pieces of information into larger, meaningful units to aid memory

Now you have to remember only seven units of information. Grouping individual pieces of information into larger, meaningful units is called **chunking**. Chunking is an effective way of getting around the limited capacity of STM.

long-term memory
the store of long-lasting, relatively permanent memories

In addition to holding information from sensory memory, STM also holds information retrieved from **long-term memory** (LTM), our store of long-lasting, relatively permanent memories. LTM appears to have no limits on capacity or duration.

Memories stored here can last a lifetime, and new information can be added to LTM across the lifespan, even into old age. LTM is analogous to a warehouse that stores the full set of knowledge you have acquired.

Encoding

Can you accurately draw the heads side of a coin from memory? Most people cannot, despite having encountered coins on thousands of occasions over their lifetime. This example demonstrates that not all of the information we are exposed to makes its way into long-term memory. **Encoding** is the transformation of information into a form that can be stored in memory. Selective attention is necessary in order for information or events to be encoded successfully. For example, if you witness a mugging, you may try to remember the culprit by creating an image of this person in your mind. Organizing information in meaningful ways, imagery, and rehearsal are all strategies that help encode information in memory.

encoding
transformation of information into a form that can be stored in memory

Storage

Different types of information reside in different subsystems of long-term memory. **Declarative memory** (sometimes called *explicit memory*) stores factual knowledge and has two subtypes. Knowledge that is general and impersonal in nature is called **semantic memory**. Knowing that a Taser is a weapon that uses electrical current to disrupt muscle control represents a semantic memory. Remembering the legal blood alcohol limit in a particular jurisdiction would also represent semantic memory. **Episodic memory** refers to one's knowledge of personal experiences. Episodic memories involve remembering *when*, *where*, and *what* one did during a particular episode in one's life. Episodic memories permit a sort of reliving of an experience. An eyewitness remembering the last moments of a victim's life would be drawing upon episodic memory.

declarative memory
a person's store of long-term factual knowledge

semantic memory
long-term knowledge that is general and impersonal in nature

episodic memory
long-term knowledge of one's personal experiences

Non-declarative memory (often called *procedural* or *implicit memory*) stores knowledge that is not easily expressed or verbalized, such as skills and actions. The skills and knowledge required to ride a bicycle or play a musical instrument are stored as procedural memories. Skills like these are performed by experienced individuals with little or no conscious effort. Classically conditioned responses can also be considered procedural memories. Officer Paul's conditioned fear (see Chapter 5) associated with stopping motorists is one such example.

non-declarative memory
a person's store of knowledge not easily expressed or verbalized, such as skills and actions

ARE THESE MEMORY SYSTEMS REALLY DIFFERENT?

The most compelling evidence that there really are distinct types of memory comes from cases where individuals have suffered injuries to the brain that have left one or more systems impaired while sparing other systems. Consider, the case of Clive Wearing. In 1985, Wearing, a musicologist and classically trained pianist, suffered an infection that left him with the world's worst known case of amnesia (Sacks, 2007). Wearing was left unable to store new long-term memories; if he is asked a question, he often forgets what the question was by the end of the sentence. This inability to store new long-term memories is called **anterograde amnesia**. He has also been left with severe **retrograde amnesia**, an inability to remember virtually anything that occurred before the infection. Tragically, he has lost most memories

anterograde amnesia
the inability to store new long-term memories

retrograde amnesia
the inability to remember anything before the event that resulted in loss of memory

of his own personal past (episodic memory). He is able to remember facts, such as the capital of England or the names of famous composers, indicating that his semantic memory was unaffected. Procedural memory was also spared, enabling Wearing to play the piano, write, prepare coffee, and so on. Cases such as Wearing's demonstrate that memory is not a single entity; rather, it is composed of different categories or subsystems. These subsystems are shown in Figure 6.1.

Retrieval

retrieval cue
a stimulus that triggers a forgotten long-term memory

Information stored in long-term memory can be recalled into short-term memory. A **retrieval cue** is a stimulus that activates a long-term memory and facilitates its transfer to short-term memory. The more cues that are available, the more easily a memory is retrieved. For example, Peter witnessed a stabbing at a nightclub, but was having trouble recalling some details about the criminal, until an officer asked if the assailant said anything before the attack. This question acted as a retrieval cue, and helped Peter recall that the perpetrator shouted the victim's name just before the attack, indicating that the victim and the culprit knew each other.

encoding-specificity principle
the rule that memories are more easily recalled in environmental conditions that match those experienced during encoding

Memory is enhanced when retrieval cues are present that were also present at the time the information was encoded. Memories are often more easily recalled when the environmental conditions present during retrieval match those present during encoding. This is known as the **encoding-specificity principle** (Tulving & Thomson, 1973). This principle is often exploited in cognitive interviews (see Chapter 1, Box 1.1). A witness might be asked to mentally reconstruct an image of a crime scene, or be physically taken to the scene, in order to assist in memory retrieval. Christianson and Nilsson (1989) describe a case of "hysterical amnesia" in which a woman out jogging was accosted, beaten, and raped. Immediately after the assault she could not recall what had happened. When she returned to the scene of the crime with police, she became anxious and highly emotional. Soon after, while jogging, her memory of the event returned. One form of the encoding-specificity principle is *context-dependent memory*: memories are usually more easily recalled when the person is in the same physical environment that he or she was in during encoding. The other is *state-dependent memory*, whereby memory is enhanced when the person's psychological state is the same during retrieval as it was during encoding. The victim's ability to remember the assault might have involved both context-dependent (returning to the scene of the crime) and state-dependent (emotional arousal) effects.

MEMORY: THE DARK SIDE OF THE MIND

The mind's retrieval of distant events in what seem to be vivid and detailed recollections may suggest that memory functions like a camera, faithfully recording details of events and experiences as they happen. Research, however, does not support this conclusion. Instead, memory is fragile and prone to distortions and errors. As you will soon see, memories are reconstructions, in which people combine pieces of stored information with other knowledge, including their expectations and biases.

FIGURE 6.1   Divisions of Long-Term Memory

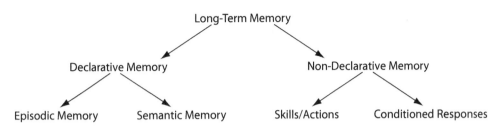

Memory researcher Daniel Schacter (2001) describes the fragility of memory by identifying several common errors of memory. When memory fails, it tends to do so in predictable ways. **Errors of omission** occur when a person is unable to retrieve a piece of information. An example is the so-called tip of the tongue phenomenon, wherein a person knows something but just can't quite bring it to mind. **Errors of commission** occur when people recall unwanted or inaccurate information. For example, a police psychiatrist might question an individual and, as a result of the questioning, the individual may come to believe that he or she was the victim of abuse, when no abuse actually occurred. This *suggestibility* is an example of an error of commission.

The reconstructive nature of memory has many implications for police work. This is perhaps most true in two areas: eyewitness memory and so-called recovered memories.

errors of omission
information that cannot be retrieved by short-term memory

errors of commission
the recall of inaccurate or unwanted information

Eyewitness Memory

Inaccurate eyewitness identifications account for more cases of wrongful conviction than all other causes combined (Wells & Bradfield, 1998). As the case of Jennifer Thompson illustrates, eyewitness memory is prone to error. Distortions of recall, along with additional factors such as bias, may influence which details of a crime are encoded in memory as well as how these details are retrieved.

STRESS

Stress can affect what information gets encoded in memory by focusing the person's attention on a narrow range of stimuli or events. An eyewitness to a crime in which a weapon was used may attend primarily to the weapon and fail to encode other aspects of the crime (see, for example, Kramer, Buckhout, & Eugenio, 1989). This **weapon focus** may cause the witness to remember the weapon very well but to forget other important details of the crime. Stress may also affect police officers' memory (see Box 6.1).

weapon focus
impairment of a witness's recall due to distraction caused by the perpetrator's use of a weapon

SOURCE CONFUSION

Many errors in eyewitness memory are caused by a phenomenon called **source confusion**. Here, a witness remembers something but forgets where he encountered it. This might occur, for instance, in cases of *unconscious transference*, where a witness

source confusion
flawed recall due to previous exposure to similar stimuli

BOX 6.1   Stress and Memory Among Police Officers

Stress affects memory. It disrupts brain structures that are involved in consolidating information into long-term memory. It may also bias attention toward threatening stimuli, causing other stimuli to be poorly remembered (as in the case of weapon focus). The effects of stress on witness memory have received considerable attention. But what are the effects of stressful events on police officers' memories? It might be predicted that experienced officers would be relatively immune to the effects of stress, given that they are more practised in dealing with it than members of the general population. On the other hand, repeated exposure to stressors can lead to significant disruptions or distortions of memory.

These questions were examined in a study in which police officers walked into a fake crime scene, were given several minutes to study it, and were asked to remember as many details as possible. In the most stressful condition, each officer completed a training-style session in which individuals entered a house they had reason to believe contained armed, hostile people (represented as mechanical targets that moved from behind cover to aim at the officer). In less stressful conditions, officers watched a videotape of an officer clearing the house. The officer in the video had to clear the house and could shoot a handgun if necessary. Experimenters planted a number of objects in the house so that memory for these objects could be tested after the stressful event. Some officers answered questions about the events immediately after clearing the house or watching the video. All officers were also questioned 12 weeks later.

Officers in the most stressful condition showed enhanced memory for armed people but poorer memory for unarmed people and objects compared with subjects in less stressful conditions. This finding reflects weapon focus, or, in this case, threat focus. Officers who were asked questions immediately after the session showed improved memory 12 weeks later. The opportunity to ask questions immediately after the event represents an opportunity to rehearse the events; this rehearsal seems to have helped officers commit details to long-term memory.

Results of this study have implications for some professional duties required of police officers. For example, the writing of police reports following events may be a real-world form of rehearsal and may function to enhance memory for details of events.

Source: Beehr et al. (2004).

photo bias
source confusion
produced by familiarity
with an often-viewed
image

to a crime identifies one of the other bystanders as the culprit. The witness recognizes the bystander but errs in remembering why she looks familiar. Another example of source confusion, **photo bias**, can occur when police repeatedly use an individual's picture in photo lineups. A witness's repeated exposure to a photo makes the face seem more familiar. Witnesses may later incorrectly identify the often-seen face as the culprit's, based on this heightened sense of familiarity.

THE MISINFORMATION EFFECT

Another source of memory distortion occurs when inaccurate or misleading information is given to witnesses after a crime occurs. Such information may be incorporated into the memory of what happened, or it may bias a witness's judgment about the circumstances of a crime. Such **misinformation effects** have been described in clever experiments investigating eyewitness memory. In one example (Loftus & Palmer, 1974), students were shown video footage of a car accident and later asked to judge how fast the cars were moving. Each of several groups was asked the question, "How fast were the cars going when they _____ each other?" The missing words were manipulated among the groups, so that one group's question read "smashed into," while another group's read "contacted." Although all students had seen the same footage, their judgment was affected by the way the question was worded. For example, the group whose question read "smashed into" judged the cars to be moving significantly faster than did the group whose question read "contacted."

misinformation effect
distortion of a witness's memory after receiving misleading information

LINEUPS

The way in which a person is asked to remember a piece of information or an event can influence what he or she remembers. For example, a test question asking you to define "eyewitness memory" provides no retrieval cues other than the concept itself. Asking a question in this way is known as a *recall* test. Imagine, instead, that you were given a *recognition* test in which you were asked to identify which of several definitions provides the best explanation of eyewitness memory. You might find this test easier because there is more information available on which to base a judgment.

A police lineup is akin to a recognition test. In a **lineup** a suspect, or a photo of a suspect, appears among other individuals who are known to be innocent. These innocent individuals are called *distractors*. Sometimes a lineup is created so that an innocent suspect appears among distractors, but the actual culprit is absent.

In practice, a lineup may proceed in two different ways (Wells & Olson, 2003). In a **simultaneous lineup** the suspect and the distractors appear at the same time in front of the witness. This is the most common procedure. Less common is a **sequential lineup**, in which one member of the lineup is presented at a time, in a sequence, until the last member has been presented to the witness. The type of lineup used may influence witness responses. Wells (1993) argues that a simultaneous lineup leads a witness to compare all members of the lineup against one another, encouraging the witness to pick whomever looks most like his or her memory of the culprit. A sequential lineup, on the other hand, may encourage an identification based primarily on the witness's memory of the culprit and less on the relative similarities and differences among the members of the lineup. Some research indicates that sequential lineups reduce the occurrence of mistaken identifications (see, for example, Steblay et al., 2001). However, sequential lineups have also been associated with lower rates of identification in lineups in which the culprit is present.

lineup
a recognition test in which a suspect appears among others known to be innocent

simultaneous lineup
a lineup in which the suspect and distractors appear before a witness at the same time

sequential lineup
a lineup in which members are presented to the witness one at a time

WITNESS AGE

The age of an eyewitness influences identifications depending on how a lineup is arranged (Wells & Olson, 2003). When a culprit is present in a lineup, young children and the elderly identify the culprit with similar accuracy as young adults.

However, when the culprit is absent from a lineup, young children and the elderly are more likely to make a false identification than are young adults.

Another concern around witness age is the greater susceptibility of children to suggestibility. For example, in one study (Bruck et al., 1995), several young children who had been examined by a doctor but had *not* undergone a routine genital exam, when later asked to demonstrate on a doll how the doctor touched their genitals, provided demonstrations of genital touching on the doll. Children may be more prone to answer questions in a way that supports the interviewer's question.

Recovered Memories

One of the most hotly debated topics in psychology is whether painful memories of abuse can be repressed for years but then suddenly be recovered and remembered accurately. Freud argued that traumatic episodes of abuse might be repressed, or blocked from consciousness, and buried in one's unconscious mind (see Chapter 8). Given the preceding discussion on distortions and reconstructions in memory, and given the enormous impact that allegations of prior abuse have on both the alleged victim and perpetrator, psychologists have been examining this issue carefully.

One major problem in interpreting a claim of past abuse is that many times no material or corroborating evidence exists to support the claim. It is impossible to determine whether a person "forgot" abuse when the question of whether abuse ever occurred is unclear. One way of shedding light on this problem is to find individuals who were admitted to abuse centres in the past and ask them about their current recollections of the abuse. Williams (1994) reported that 38 percent of a sample of 129 women who had been admitted to sexual abuse clinics more than 15 years earlier claimed to have no memory of the abuse. These data suggest that a substantial minority of victims of abuse may have trouble remembering traumatic episodes.

Complicating the issue are findings that some cases of apparent forgetfulness may not be forgetting at all. Consider cases in which the abuse was not forgotten. Schooler (1994) reports cases in which individuals reported abuse to their spouses years before "recovering" the memory of the abuse. In these cases, the victims were shocked to learn that they had known about the abuse and had reported it. This phenomenon has been termed the "forgot-it-all-along" effect, in which individuals underestimate their prior recall of a trauma and therefore falsely believe they repressed the memory. The implication of the forgot-it-all-along effect is that the absence of memory for a prior event does not necessarily mean the event has been forgotten.

Traumatic events may be encoded in memory differently than non-traumatic events. Traumatic events involve high levels of stress and emotion. High levels of stress have been shown to disrupt the functioning of brain structures responsible for binding together in memory the many different components of an experience (Sapolsky, 1996). This finding suggests that when abuse occurs, the event may not be encoded in a manner that facilitates retrieval, perhaps making the memory more susceptible to reconstruction or distortion.

Another major concern in the recovered memory controversy is whether false memories of abuse can be created during therapy or caused by certain investigative techniques. It is unethical to plant false memories of abuse in individuals. However, false memories of mundane stimuli or events have been implanted during laboratory experiments. One classic approach to examining false memories in the laboratory involves presenting subjects with a list of words to remember. All words in a list are associated with a single word that is not presented. For example, one list might contain several words all related to *sweet* (candy, sugar, taste, tooth, chocolate, pie, and so on), but the word *sweet* is not included in the list. Subjects are then given tests of recall and recognition. In the recall test they are asked to freely recall as many words from the list as they can. In the recognition test they are presented with a set of words that includes words from the list, an associated word (called the *lure*) that is absent from the original list (in this case, *sweet*), and other words that did not appear in the original list. A common finding is that people frequently falsely recall the lure, demonstrating a sort of illusory memory.

Clancy et al. (2002) used this experimental approach to examine subjects who claimed to have recovered memories of a traumatic event that is unlikely to have actually occurred: abduction by aliens. One group consisted of subjects who believed themselves to have been abducted by aliens but who had no memories of the abduction. Another group contained people who had recovered memories of an alien abduction, while the third (control) group denied ever having been abducted by aliens. The fascinating result was that the two groups that reported alien abduction were more likely than the control group to show false recall and recognition of lure words. One implication of this finding is that some individuals may be especially prone to the implantation of false memories. Clancy et al. (2002) suggest that the false memories exhibited by the subjects in their experiment may reflect source confusion. For example, they may have seen movies depicting alien abduction during their childhood but then came to believe, falsely, that these abductions actually took place because they forgot the source of the event (that is, a movie).

INTELLIGENCE

Intelligence is the ability to acquire knowledge, to reason and solve problems effectively, and to deal effectively with one's environment. Psychologists have been debating the very nature of intelligence since the early 1900s. Some argue that intelligence refers to a single, generalized ability that exerts itself across various contexts. This notion of **general intelligence** suggests that if a person is bright in one area she will also tend to be bright in other areas. Others propose that independent types of intelligence have evolved and each is adapted to function in a particular domain. In one **multiple intelligence** theory (Gardner, 2000), humans are equipped with eight types of intelligence:

- *linguistic* intelligence (reflecting language skills)

- *logical/mathematical* intelligence (math and quantitative reasoning skills)

- *visuospatial* intelligence (spatial reasoning, navigational skills)

- *musical* intelligence (ability to understand components of music and to produce music)

- *body-kinesthetic* intelligence (ability to manipulate and control body movements)

- *interpersonal* intelligence (ability to understand and relate to others)

general intelligence
the view of intelligence as a single, generalized ability that applies in all situations

multiple intelligence
the view of intelligence as a variety of independent abilities of greater or lesser effectiveness

- *intrapersonal* intelligence (ability to understand one's own emotions and behaviours)

- *naturalistic* intelligence (ability to understand the natural world and other living organisms)

According to this perspective, a person might be highly intelligent in one domain but less intelligent in others.

Intelligence Tests

The most commonly used intelligence tests administered to individuals are those created by David Wechsler. Among these tests are the *Wechsler Adult Intelligence Scale* (now in its fourth edition, abbreviated WAIS), the *Wechsler Intelligence Scale for Children* (WISC), and the *Wechsler Preschool and Primary Scale of Intelligence* (WPPSI). These tests contain a set of verbal and performance (non-verbal) subtests. An individual receives three intelligence quotient (IQ) scores—an overall IQ score, a verbal IQ score, and a performance IQ score. Group tests are those administered to large groups of people at the same time. *Achievement tests* measure what a person already knows. *Aptitude tests* measure a person's ability to solve novel problems that might indicate particular abilities for future learning and performance.

Most police departments administer some type of intelligence test to applicants. One such test, the *Police Analytical Thinking Inventory* (PATI), assesses mathematical skills as well as deductive and inductive reasoning. Mathematical skills are required when police perform quantitative operations to determine rates of travel, stopping distance, travel time, and so on. **Deductive reasoning** means taking a set of general principles or findings to reach a conclusion about a specific case. This skill is required when police must draw conclusions about the relevance or meaning of specific pieces of evidence. **Inductive reasoning** involves starting with specific facts and figuring out how they fit together, another requirement of investigative work.

Any psychological test must meet certain basic scientific standards. A test must show **reliability**, which means that the measurements obtained from it are consistent. For example, when a person is retested on the same test, the scores obtained should be consistent with those obtained on previous occasions. **Validity** means that the test is actually measuring what it is supposed to measure. One indication of validity would be strong correlations between scores on an intelligence test and performance in school. Tests must be administered in standardized conditions with standardized instructions given to test-takers. Another important aspect of **standardization** is the establishment of *norms* that provide a way to interpret individual test scores. When a test is developed it is given to large samples of individuals. The average IQ for a particular population is 100; approximately 50 percent of all scores in a population fall between 90 and 110.

Intelligence: Nature *and* Nurture

Intelligence, like any other trait, is the result of complex interactions between genetic and environmental factors. If intelligence were strictly genetically determined, we would expect identical twins (who are genetically identical) to have identical IQ scores. Correlations of IQ scores for identical twins, although strong, are rarely a

deductive reasoning
application of general principles or findings to reach a specific conclusion

inductive reasoning
analysis of specific facts to arrive at a conclusion

reliability
consistency in test results when administered to the same individuals on different occasions

validity
the degree to which a test measures what it purports to measure

standardization
the establishment of norms to guide administration of tests and interpretation of their scores

match. The correlation drops when identical twins are raised in separate environments. Most estimates for the relative influence of genes and environmental factors suggest that genetic factors probably account for 50 to 70 percent of the differences in IQ among people (Bouchard et al., 1990; Plomin, 1997). Clearly, however, both environmental and genetic factors contribute to intelligence.

PROBLEM SOLVING

In solving problems, people may take one of two approaches. One method of solving a problem is strategic planning. Here a person *interprets* or *frames the problem* to be solved. Upon an initial examination of a crime scene with deceased spouses and no evidence of other fingerprints or weapons, an investigator may decide that one or both partners were somehow responsible for the deaths. After framing a problem, the next step is to *generate possible explanations*. In this case, the investigator might suspect that one spouse killed the other and then committed suicide. The investigator then *tests an explanation*. To do this, she may consider a coroner's conclusions about the time of death for both deceased. If the results of such a test do not support her hypothesis, she must *re-evaluate the explanations*, and possibly generate new ones. If the coroner's report indicates both individuals died at the same time and both showed evidence of a poisonous substance in their system, the investigator may consider a new explanation, such as joint suicide.

Another approach to solving problems is to rely on shortcuts that can be applied to special kinds of problems in order to save time. A police officer may need to estimate how much time it will take to reach a destination, given a known distance and speed. Using a mathematical formula—Distance/Speed = Time—provides a solution to this problem. Formulas are one example of shortcuts that can guarantee a correct solution to a particular problem.

POINTS TO REMEMBER

Memory is not a simple phenomenon. It comprises sensory as well as short-term and long-term subsystems. Long-term memory too comprises distinct divisions, including declarative and non-declarative forms. Memory does not preserve events and experiences in perfect form, as a camera might. Instead, memories are reconstructed from fragments of remembered information; these reconstructions are susceptible to distortions and errors. For example, some victims of abuse may experience "recovered" memories after a period of apparent forgetfulness. However, such memories are controversial.

Proponents of general intelligence suggest that intelligence is a single, general ability that manifests itself in many different contexts. Others argue that humans possess several distinct forms of intelligence that are specific to particular contexts. Intelligence tests must meet specific scientific standards to be useful in measuring IQ.

Problem solving may involve careful planning and analysis, although shortcut rules may be effective for solving particular kinds of problems.

KEY TERMS

anterograde amnesia	non-declarative memory
chunking	photo bias
declarative memory	rehearsal
deductive reasoning	reliability
encoding	retrieval cue
encoding-specificity principle	retrograde amnesia
episodic memory	semantic memory
errors of commission	sensory memory
errors of omission	sequential lineup
general intelligence	short-term (working) memory
inductive reasoning	simultaneous lineup
lineup	source confusion
long-term memory	standardization
memory	validity
misinformation effect	weapon focus
multiple intelligence	

REFERENCES

Atkinson, R.C., & R.M. Shiffrin. (1968). Human memory: A proposed system and its control processes. In W.K. Spence & J.T. Spence (Eds.), *The psychology of learning and motivation: Vol. 2. Advances in learning and theory*. New York: Academic Press.

Beehr, T.A., L. Ivanitskaya, K. Glaser, D. Erofeev, & K. Canali. (2004). Working in a violent environment: The accuracy of police officers' reports about shooting incidents. *Journal of Occupational and Organizational Psychology, 77*, 217–35.

Bouchard, T.J., D.T. Lykken, M. McGue, N.L. Segal, & A. Tellegen. (1990, October 12). Sources of human psychological differences: The Minnesota study of twins reared apart. *Science, 250* (4978): 223–28.

Bruck, M., S.J. Ceci, E. Francoeur, & A. Renick. (1995). Anatomically detailed dolls do not facilitate preschoolers' reports of a pediatric examination involving genital touching. *Journal of Experimental Psychology: Applied, 1*, 95–109.

Christianson, S.A., & L.G. Nilsson. (1989). Hysterical amnesia: A case of aversively motivated isolation of memory. In T. Archer & L.G. Nilsson (Eds.), *Aversion, avoidance, and anxiety: Perspectives on aversively motivated behavior*. New Jersey: Erlbaum and Associates.

Clancy, S.A., R.J. McNally, D.L. Schacter, M.F. Lenzenweger, & R.K. Pitman. (2002). Memory distortion in people reporting abduction by aliens. *Journal of Abnormal Psychology, 111*, 455–61.

Gardner, H. (2000). *Multiple intelligences: The theory in practice.* New York: Basic Books.

Kramer, T.H., R. Buckhout, & P. Eugenio. (1989). Weapon focus, arousal, and eyewitness memory: Attention must be paid. *Applied Cognitive Psychology, 14*, 167–84.

Loftus, E.F., & J.C. Palmer. (1974). Reconstruction of automobile destruction: An example of the interaction between language and memory. *Journal of Verbal Learning and Verbal Behavior, 13*, 585–89.

Miller, G.A. (1956). The magical number seven, plus or minus two: Some limits on our capacity for processing information. *Psychological Review, 63*, 81–97.

Plomin, R. (1997). *Behavioral genetics.* New York: St. Martin's.

Sacks, O. (2007, September 24). The abyss. *The New Yorker.* http://www.newyorker.com/reporting/2007/09/24/070924fa_fact_sacks.

Sapolsky, R.M. (1996). Why stress is bad for your brain. *Science, 273*, 749–50.

Schacter, D.L. (2001). *The seven sins of memory: How the mind forgets and remembers.* New York: Houghton-Mifflin.

Schooler, J.W. (1994). Seeking the core: The issues and evidence surrounding recovered accounts of sexual trauma. *Consciousness and Cognition, 3*, 452–69.

Steblay, N., J. Dysart, S. Fulero, & R.C.L. Lindsay. (2001). Eyewitness accuracy rates in sequential and simultaneous lineup presentations: A meta-analytic comparison. *Law and Human Behavior, 25*, 459–73.

Thompson, J. (2000, June 18). I was certain, but I was wrong. *The New York Times.* http://www.truthinjustice.org/positive_id.htm.

Tulving, E., & D.M. Thomson. (1973). Encoding specificity and retrieval processes in episodic memory. *Psychological Review, 80*, 359–80.

Wells, G.L. (1993). What do we know about eyewitness identification? *American Psychologist, 48*, 553–71.

Wells, G.L., & A.L. Bradfield, A.L. (1998). "Good, you identified the suspect": Feedback to witnesses distorts their reports of the witnessing experience. *Journal of Applied Psychology, 83*, 360–76.

Wells, G.L., & E.A. Olson. (2003). Eyewitness testimony. *Annual Review of Psychology, 54*, 277–95.

Williams, L.M. (1994). Recall of childhood trauma: A prospective study of women's memories of childhood abuse. *Journal of Consulting and Clinical Psychology, 62*, 1182–86.

EXERCISES AND REVIEW

Self-Test

Circle the correct answer.

1. Performing often-practised skills, such as tying one's shoe laces, involves

    a. semantic memory

    b. episodic memory

    c. declarative memory

    d. procedural memory

2. _____ refers to the processing involved in remembering information.

    a. encoding

    b. explicit memory

    c. retrieval

    d. storage

3. An inability to store new memories is called

    a. retrograde amnesia

    b. anterograde amnesia

    c. false memory

    d. illusory memory

4. Karla witnesses an armed robbery. Soon after, she remembers the gun used in the robbery, but forgets whether the robbers were male or female. This demonstrates

    a. weapon focus

    b. the gun-retrieval effect

    c. context-dependent memory

    d. a misinformation effect

5. Research indicates that elderly eyewitnesses are _____ to misidentify a suspect from a lineup if the suspect is _____.

    a. less likely than children; present

    b. less likely than young adults; absent

    c. more likely than children; present

    d. more likely than young adults; absent

6. Subjects' recollection of a lure in memory research indicates that

    a. retrieval processes are unusually accurate and free from bias

    b. encoding occurred properly

    c. childhood abuse likely occurred

    d. false memory implantation has occurred

7. Which of the following is *not* one of Gardner's specific intelligences:

    a. linguistic intelligence

    b. interpersonal intelligence

    c. dynamic intelligence

    d. naturalistic intelligence

8. Inductive reasoning involves

    a. thinking "on your feet" to solve problems quickly

    b. using specific facts to reach a general conclusion

    c. applying a general principle to a specific case

    d. strategies such as chunking and rehearsal

9. Several police departments in Manitoba began using a new intelligence test to screen job applicants, but found that applicants' scores on the test were not strongly related to their college or university marks. This suggests the new test likely suffers from poor _____.

    a. validity

    b. reliability

    c. standardization

    d. all of the above

10. The first step in solving a new problem is

    a. guessing at a solution

    b. solving an equation

    c. framing the problem

    d. determining why the problem exists in the first place

Thinking About Psychology and Law Enforcement

1. Identify the types of memory used in the following examples:

   a. an officer quickly draws his Taser and fires a cartridge at a suspect resisting arrest, without thinking about how to do this

   b. an officer explains to her daughter how a Taser works

   c. an officer recalls the first time she used a Taser on a suspect

   d. a suspect fleeing a police officer tries to figure out which of two escape routes is best

   e. for a second after a gun is shot, a bystander can still hear the sound of the gunshot

2. Police dramas are commonly shown on television. These shows often show details of crimes in vivid detail. Do you think that exposure to these scenes may lead to source confusion for individuals who witness actual crimes in real life? If so, give examples of how this might occur.

3. Have you or someone you know served on a jury? In this role, did any of the factors influencing memory discussed in this chapter influence your (or their) evaluation of testimony or witnesses? If so, how?

CHAPTER 7

Motivation and Emotion

CHAPTER OBJECTIVES

After completing this chapter, you should be able to:

- Define the concepts of motivation and emotion.
- Explain what motivates people to do what they do.
- Describe the role of biological and social needs in motivation.
- Understand emotions and their functions.
- Evaluate the use of microexpressions in detecting deception.

PREVIEW SCENARIO

Corruption in law enforcement has always been a problem. An investigation identified two types of corrupt police officers: Meat Eaters and Grass Eaters.

Meat Eaters are law enforcement officers who aggressively misuse their law enforcement power for personal gain. These officers demand bribes, threaten legal action, and cooperate with criminals. Grass Eaters, on the other hand, are law enforcement officers who do not actively seek out bribes but accept bribes that are offered to them. Most corrupt law enforcement officers are Grass Eaters rather than Meat Eaters. (Wood, 1996)

INTRODUCTION

The preview scenario describes corruption in law enforcement. However, it fails to explain the *why* of this corruption—that is, what motivates some law enforcement officers to choose a path of corruption in their careers and others to become neither Meat Eaters nor Grass Eaters. Because emotions play a part in motivation, this chapter discusses the related topics of motivation and emotion.

MOTIVATION

motivation
force behind human
behaviour that explains
why people do what they
do

The word *motivation* comes from the Latin *movere*, which means to move. **Motivation** is the force behind human behaviour—it explains why people do what they do. When a law enforcement officer stops a speeding motorist and asks why the person was going so fast, the officer is asking for the motorist's motivation. A behaviour is motivated when it is energized, directed, and sustained to satisfy biological or psychological needs.

Theories of Motivation

In studying motivation, psychologists have tried to answer the following questions:

- What motivates people to pursue a goal?

- Why do people pursue some goals and not others?

- What determines how much effort and determination people will put into pursuing a goal?

Motivation theories tend to see motives as being biological, stimulus-based, or social. Some of the major theories follow.

INSTINCT THEORIES

instinct
inborn rather than learned
pattern of behaviour

The instinct theories of motivation are biological explanations. They suggest that instincts motivate people from within to act in certain ways. An **instinct** is an inborn rather than a learned pattern of behaviour that motivates individuals. Aggression, curiosity, and reproduction are examples of instincts.

For example, an instinct theorist is likely to offer the aggression instinct as an explanation for gang fights. Similarly, an instinct theorist is likely to explain sexual behaviour as a response motivated by the instinct to reproduce.

The instinct theories fell out of favour in the 1920s for their exclusive reliance on the biology of motivation. It became obvious that many instincts were needed to explain human behaviour. In fact, instincts seemed only to describe behaviour rather than to explain it. Many instinct theories suffer from circular logic, in which the explanation for the phenomenon is taken to be the phenomenon itself. This is illustrated with the following dialogue:

Person A: Why do people show aggression?
Instinct theorist: Because there is an instinct for aggression.
Person A: But how do you know it is an instinct?
Instinct theorist: Because people are aggressive.

DRIVE REDUCTION THEORY

need
biological requirement
that demands satisfaction

drive
internal state of tension
that motivates a behaviour
that satisfies a need

Drive reduction theory suggests that people are always motivated to reduce internal tension. The theory relies on three main concepts: need, drive, and homeostasis.

A **need** is a biological requirement that demands satisfaction—for example, the need for food motivates the behaviour of eating. A need gives rise to a drive. A **drive** is an internal state of tension that motivates a behaviour that satisfies the need. Primary drives satisfy biological needs such as hunger, thirst, and sleepiness. A hungry

FIGURE 7.1   Yerkes–Dodson Law

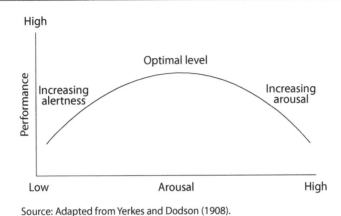

Source: Adapted from Yerkes and Dodson (1908).

officer is in a state of tension because of the biological need for food. The officer's hunger drive motivates him to seek food to reduce the primary drive of hunger and satisfy the biological need for food. Secondary drives are learned or acquired, and include fear, anxiety, and desire for achievement, among many others.

The drive reduction theory offers homeostasis as the reason for the officer's efforts to seek food. **Homeostasis** is the tendency of the body to maintain an internal balanced state. Any disturbance in the internal balance gives rise to a drive to restore the balance.

A major problem with the drive reduction theory is that it fails to explain the behaviour of people who are motivated to increase their internal state of tension rather than to decrease it.

homeostasis
tendency of the body to maintain an internal balanced state

AROUSAL THEORY

Arousal theory helps to explain why people sometimes increase their internal state of tension. This approach suggests that people are motivated to maintain an optimal level of arousal. **Arousal** is a state of physical and mental stimulation. When arousal is below the optimal level, people seek stimulation to bring it up to its optimal level. Bored teenagers are likely in a state of arousal that is below the optimal level. To increase their level of arousal, teenagers may do exciting things such as commit vandalism or go on joy rides.

arousal
state of physical and mental stimulation

When arousal exceeds the optimal level, people seek to reduce stimulation to bring it down to its optimal level. Police officers who go to a bar for a drink after witnessing the stabbing of one of their fellow officers are reducing their heightened level of stimulation to an optimal level.

The *Yerkes–Dodson law* (1908) states that people perform best when their arousal level is moderate. When their arousal level is too low, people are bored and unmotivated. When their arousal level is too high, people feel stressed and anxious (Figure 7.1). The ideal level depends on the person and the situation. Simple, boring tasks require a high level of arousal to motivate people to do them (think about how you have to force yourself to take out the garbage because the task doesn't interest or engage you). Complex, fun tasks require a low level of arousal to motivate people to do them (think about how you can easily concentrate on playing a new video game because it captures your interest and attention).

The arousal theory suggests that people differ in the level of stimulation they tolerate. Some people thrive on constant stimulation, while others prefer a relatively low level of arousal. Law enforcement officers may be in the category of people who are sensation-seekers. Law enforcement work provides a high degree of stimulation in the forms of unpredictability, risk, and voluntary entry into dangerous situations. Officers seem to love the thrill of this work.

INCENTIVE THEORY

This approach suggests that people are motivated by external factors rather than just internal needs. For example, even if you just had a big breakfast, you may decide to accept an invitation from a friend to go out for a doughnut. Similarly, many people have had the experience of ordering an enticing dessert despite having eaten past the point of being full. The technical term for an external factor is incentive. An **incentive** is an external stimulus or event that is positive or negative and that motivates behaviour. Salaries and benefits are positive incentives for choosing law enforcement as a career. Demotions or terminations of employment are negative incentives for staying sober on the job or acting ethically.

incentive
external stimulus or event that is positive or negative and that motivates behaviour

COGNITIVE THEORY

This approach gives thoughts, expectations, and perceptions important roles in motivation. For example, a person who is considering law enforcement as a career and is taking a police foundations course will be more motivated to study if she believes that there will be a payoff to her studying, such as a good grade or graduation with distinction.

The cognitive approach differentiates extrinsic motivation from intrinsic motivation. **Extrinsic motivation** is doing things to gain tangible rewards or to avoid undesirable consequences. An officer who does the minimum requirements of his job to continue to draw his salary and avoid being fired is extrinsically motivated. **Intrinsic motivation** is doing things because they are enjoyable to do. An officer who teaches a five-day forensic anthropology course in a forest with a team of coroners and university faculty for the sheer enjoyment of teaching students and being in a forest is intrinsically motivated. There are no strings attached or expectations of rewards for his teaching. Intrinsically motivated people are hard workers, do high-quality work, and tend to persevere in what they do. Interestingly, a person's intrinsic motivation may diminish if he or she is given external rewards (for example, praise for a job well done).

extrinsic motivation
doing things to gain tangible rewards or to avoid undesirable consequences

intrinsic motivation
doing things because they are enjoyable to do

HIERARCHY OF NEEDS THEORY

Abraham Maslow (1970) proposed a hierarchical order to the various human needs or motives (Figure 7.2). He placed the physiological, or lower-order, needs (food, water, sleep, and so on) at the base of the hierarchy and the need for self-actualization, or highest-order need (the need to realize one's full potential) at the top. Maslow suggested that lower-order needs have to be satisfied before higher-level needs emerge and can be satisfied.

FIGURE 7.2   Maslow's Hierarchy of Needs

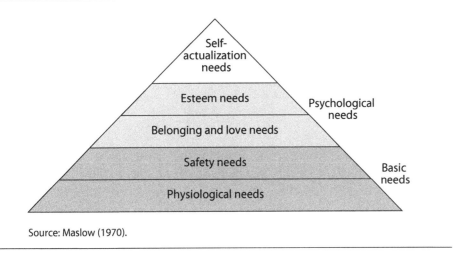

Source: Maslow (1970).

The **hierarchy of needs** approach to motivation is popular even though the specific ordering of the needs is not well validated by research. It is possible that hierarchies of needs do exist but that the order of the needs is different for different people.

Basic Needs

Physiological needs (food, water, sleep, shelter, sex, and so on) and *safety needs* (safety and security) are basic needs. People who are homeless or who live in poverty and are constantly hungry, for example, are concerned about finding shelter and food, not about reaching their full potential. Their motivation to satisfy these needs may be strong enough that they ignore safety or other needs, such as taking shelter in an abandoned building that is dangerously close to collapse, or stealing food or money and risking being caught.

Safety needs include the needs for structure and for freedom from fear and anxiety. Most people need to feel that the world is a fairly predictable place and that they are physically safe, and they are motivated to avoid situations that will put them in danger. Safety needs help to explain why the majority of people obey the law and recognize the need for government (no matter how much they complain about politicians!).

Psychological Needs

Belonging and love and *esteem needs* are psychological needs, but they also have an important social, or affiliation, aspect. We all need to feel loved, to feel like part of a family or other group, and to feel that we belong. Our need for affiliation motivates us to seek personal relationships, friendships, marriage, and so on. This sense of belonging to a community is one reason law enforcement officers often enjoy friendships with other officers—they enjoy not only the friendships for friendship's sake, but also the sense of being with "their own."

People who are unable to fill their belonging and love needs often feel lonely and alienated. This sense of being apart from the rest of the world can lower people's motivation to avoid hurting others, for example. Not hurting people who are im-

hierarchy of needs
Maslow's model of motivation that presents human needs in hierarchical order from lower-order needs to higher-order needs

portant to us is a way of making sure we maintain the relationships that fill our affiliation needs.

Esteem needs are both internal and external. People need self-esteem, which comes from feeling competent, from achieving, and from excelling at something. They also need to feel they are well regarded and have the respect of others. For some people, the needs for social status, prestige, and even power are important esteem needs.

Self-Actualization Needs

Self-actualization is reaching one's full potential. Having filled all the other categories of needs, this is the stage at which people feel they are using their talents and are able to enjoy happiness, fulfillment, creativity, humour, and all the other arguably non-essential things that make life worth living. The characteristics of self-actualized people are described in Chapter 8.

Primary Drives

Three basic biological drives are hunger, thirst, and sex.

HUNGER

Food is critical for personal survival. *Hunger* and eating are more complex than the presumed simple chain of events of feeling hungry, getting food, eating food, and stopping when you feel full. It is now accepted that hunger is influenced by both internal cues and external cues.

The three biological actors involved in hunger are the hypothalamus, the stomach and intestines, and the blood. As mentioned in Chapter 2, the hypothalamus regulates the behaviour of eating—that is, feeling hungry and feeling full. Stimulation of the feeding centre of the hypothalamus gives rise to eating, and stimulation of the satiety centre causes eating to stop.

Stomach signals also affect hunger. The stomach signals hunger via its contractions. People feel hungry and eat when their stomach growls or when they experience hunger pangs. Stomach and intestinal distention also signal the brain to stop hunger. In addition, hormones, such as cholecystokinin (CCK), are released while a person is eating and send a signal to the brain to stop eating.

However, stomach signals are not the only agents that affect hunger. People may still experience hunger even in the absence of stomach signals. For example, people whose stomachs have been surgically removed continue to experience hunger pangs.

Blood glucose (sugar) affects hunger. The blood signals hunger or satiety by the level of glucose it contains. A signal of a low level of glucose in the blood prompts the sugar receptors in the brain to stimulate the feeling of hunger. The hormone insulin causes hunger because it lowers blood sugar. Conversely, a signal of a high level of glucose in the blood prompts the sugar receptors in the brain to inhibit the feeling of hunger.

The hypothalamus, stomach, and blood are not the only actors in hunger. Actors outside the body, called external cues, play a powerful role in influencing the behaviour of eating. The appearance, sight, and smell of appetizing food and the company of other people are all external cues that stimulate appetite and motivate people to eat.

THIRST

Fluid, like food, is critical for personal survival. People who are thirsty experience a dry mouth and can only do without fluids for four or five days. The perception of *thirst* arises from a loss of fluids from the body. Thirst is triggered by the loss of fluid either from the body tissues or from inside the body cells. Bleeding, diarrhea, hot weather, physical exercise, and vomiting all cause water discharge from the body tissues. Alcohol also contributes to the loss of fluid from the body tissues. Therefore, consuming alcohol to quench one's thirst on a hot day is not such a good idea.

Water from inside the body cells is lost when people eat salty food and the salt level exceeds its threshold. The ingestion of the excess salt disturbs the balance of salt and water in the blood and in the outside tissues of the body cells. Because salt has trouble entering the cells easily, the body cells allow some of their own water to seep through and restore the salt–water imbalance. Dehydration of the body cells stimulates thirst and motivates the thirsty individual to increase the water volume by drinking.

SEX

Sex is not critical for personal survival. Nobody dies from not having sex. However, the sexual drive is needed for the survival of humanity. As a primary drive, sex represents a complex network of internal and external factors.

On the internal biological side, the internal sex organs (ovaries and testes), the pituitary gland, the hypothalamus, and the limbic system are involved. The ovaries in females and the testes in males secrete hormones. The main female sex hormones are estrogens, while the main male sex hormones are androgens. Both hormones, however, are contained in the bodies of females and males. Sex drive in females and males is influenced by androgen fluctuations. High levels of testosterone (a key androgen) increase sexual activity in both sexes, and the influence is as strong in females as it is in males. Estrogen fluctuations do not seem to influence the sex drive of women.

The pituitary gland keeps tabs on the secretion of the sex hormones. It sends signals to the ovaries and testes to release hormones as needed. It also communicates with the hypothalamus to maintain an optimal level of sex hormones in the body.

The hypothalamus works with the pituitary gland to regulate sexual behaviour. Hypothalamus stimulation gives rise to sexual activity—for example, 20 ejaculations in 1 hour in males whose hypothalamus was electrically stimulated (Santrock, 2005, p. 439). Surgical removal of the hypothalamus causes sexual inhibition. The limbic system is involved in sexual behaviour in that its stimulation causes orgasm in females and erection in males.

The internal sex organs, pituitary gland, hypothalamus, and limbic system are not the only key players in sexual motivation. *Pheromones* are also implicated in the desire for sex. Pheromones are odorous substances or chemicals that serve as powerful attractants when released by animals. Pheromones are working when a male animal knows that the time is right for romance from a substance in the urine of an ovulating female animal, or "when all the male cats in a neighbourhood know that a female cat is in heat" (Santrock, 2005, p. 441).

The role of pheromones in human sexual attraction is less clear. Pheromones in humans are believed to be in the glands at the base of the hair follicles, especially in the armpits and the genital region. It is presumed that these glands produce as yet unidentified chemicals, the odours of which attract members of the opposite sex. Perfume companies are developing fragrances isolated from male and female sweat and marketing them as sexual pheromones.

Pheromones are being touted for their aphrodisiac value as well. An *aphrodisiac* is a substance that is thought to increase sexual desire or to improve sexual prowess and performance. The list of presumed aphrodisiacs is limitless: they include animal genitalia, drugs and alcohol, fruits and nuts, perfumes, spices, vegetables (Johan's Guide to Aphrodisiacs, 2000), and other products such as soap bars. At present, aphrodisiacs are presumed rather than genuine. As Nordenberg (1996) of the US Food and Drug Administration states, "[T]he reputed sexual effects of so-called aphrodisiacs are based in folklore, not fact."

The availability of and attraction to a partner are important external influences on sexual behaviour. Men and women are selective in their attraction to partners. People may be attracted to same-sex partners as in gay and lesbian relationships, opposite-sex partners as in heterosexual relationships, and opposite-and-same-sex partners as in bisexuality. Factors that influence partner selection include partner personality, physical beauty, occupation, and social status.

An external factor that affects sex drive is erotic materials. Sexual stimuli in the form of reading material, pictures, and films can increase sexual arousal in those who are receptive or positively inclined to such stimulation. Sexually aroused individuals are more likely to engage in sexual activity after exposure to erotic material.

Social Motivation

Three drives that have a social rather than a biological basis are achievement, affiliation, and power. The home environment plays a significant role in the development and expression of social motives. Even though a person may have all three drives, one of them tends to dominate a person's overall behaviour.

NEED FOR ACHIEVEMENT

The need for achievement is the social motive to excel. People can be low achievers or high achievers. Those with a low need for achievement are driven by the fear of failure rather than by an expectation of success. Low achievers tend to set goals that are either very low or exceedingly high, and avoid those that are intermediate. In contrast, high achievers set goals that they find challenging and that they can attain, and attribute their successes to their own abilities and efforts.

NEED FOR AFFILIATION

The need for affiliation is the social motive to build and keep relationships with others. People with a high need for affiliation value their friends, want to spend time with them, and are sensitive to their rejection. The "blue wall"—insulation of law enforcement officers from others in society—motivates officers to befriend their own.

NEED FOR POWER

The need for power is the social motive to influence and control others. People with a high need for power want to be seen as powerful and may seek professions that meet their drive for control and influence. People who choose law enforcement as a career may be people with a high need for power. Authority is a key characteristic of law enforcement. Law enforcement officers are "constantly expected to respond with an aura of authority to bring order to a situation in disarray, to take control in the face of threatening, deviant behaviour" (Sewell, 1985, pp. 175–76).

EMOTION

Emotion is the experience of having pleasant or unpleasant feelings. Happiness is an example of a pleasant emotion, and fear is an example of an unpleasant emotion. Emotion is related to motivation in that feelings motivate people to act, just as needs and drives do.

emotion
experience of pleasant or unpleasant feelings

Components of Emotion

Emotions have three components: physiological, cognitive, and behavioural. The physiological component is the internal bodily changes that accompany an emotion. Examples include the heart beating fast, sweating, and having a dry mouth. The cognitive component is the thoughts that accompany an emotion. Negative thinking contributes to unpleasant emotions, while positive thinking contributes to pleasant emotions. The behavioural component is the outward expression of an emotion. Examples include body posture, tone of voice, and facial expression. The meaning of facial expressions is universal—people around the world express anger, disgust, fear, happiness, sadness, and surprise in the same ways. Interestingly, even people who have been blind since birth produce the same facial expressions—such as smiling when they are happy—that seeing people do. Law enforcement officers serving and protecting people of diversity should have no trouble recognizing people's emotional states from their facial expressions, although in some contexts facial expressions may disguise true emotions.

Theories of Emotion

Emotions can be both responses and motivators of behaviour. That is, do we run because we are afraid, or are we afraid because we run? Theories of emotion explain the sequence of events involved in experiencing pleasant and unpleasant feelings. Figure 7.3 summarizes these theories.

JAMES–LANGE THEORY

The approach to emotion developed separately by William James (1884) and Carl Lange (1885) considers the experience of emotion a result of bodily arousal to an external situation. In this counterintuitive view, physiological responses to a situation occur first and give rise to pleasant or unpleasant feelings. For example, a protester outside the Summit of the Americas sees a gas-masked and heavily padded

FIGURE 7.3   Theories of Emotion

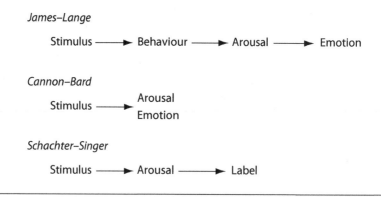

riot officer, runs, and experiences fear on sensing the bodily arousal caused by his running. Although this sequence of events sounds improbable, some research suggests that smiling can make you feel happy, while frowning can make you feel sad. Still, in the traditional view, the protester sees the riot officer, becomes fearful, and then runs.

There are three major limitations to the James–Lange theory. The first is the one described above—that emotions are experienced before bodily arousal is noticed. Second, this theory presumes that unique bodily changes cause unique emotional experiences. The reality is that there are known limitations to the range of physiological changes that the body can produce. Thus, many emotions are caused by similar bodily arousal. Conversely, every emotion is not produced by a different pattern of physiological change. Third, bodily arousal does not always give rise to emotions. A jogger may not experience any specific emotion after a long run, for example.

CANNON–BARD THEORY

Walter Cannon (1927) pointed out that people often feel an emotion before they react physically. Philip Bard (1929), one of Cannon's students, refined this theory. The Cannon–Bard theory suggests that bodily arousal and the feeling of emotions occur at the same time. A person's perception of an emotion-arousing situation activates the thalamus (see Chapter 2), which in turn sends two simultaneous signals, one to the sympathetic nervous system and the other to the cerebral cortex. The sympathetic nervous system produces the state of arousal at the same time that the cerebral cortex produces the experience of emotion.

For example, a riot officer who feels angry and battles with a protester does not feel angry because she strikes the protester—the strike does not cause the anger. The riot officer feels anger at about the same time that she battles the protester.

SCHACHTER–SINGER THEORY

The cognitive labelling theory of Stanley Schachter and Jerome Singer (1962) suggests that feeling emotion involves bodily arousal to a situation and labelling or interpreting the physical reactions so that they are appropriate to the situation. For example, the riot officer in the previous example notices her muscles getting tense, her face getting red, and her teeth clenching. She immediately tries to make sense of these physical changes, reasoning that there must be some explanation for them. She considers the situation she is in and recognizes that protesters are taunting her and her fellow officers, calling them names, and throwing stones and bottles at them. She interprets her bodily arousal as anger. "Anger" is the label the officer uses to explain her physical response, a response that seems appropriate to the situation.

Expressing Emotions

The development and expression of emotions are influenced by developmental and socio-cultural factors. The ability to communicate distress in response to pain, and to express disgust, interest, a neonatal smile (a spontaneous form of smiling for no apparent reason), and a startled response are present at birth. The emotional expressions of distress, neonatal smile, and startled response that appear in the first few weeks after birth are precursors of the emotions of sadness and surprise and of the social smile rather than expressions of inner feelings (Izard, 1994). The social smile emerges at the age of four to six weeks, and anger, surprise, and sadness at three to four months. Fear emerges at five to seven months, shame and shyness at six to eight months, and contempt and guilt at two years.

The expression of emotions in all cultures is based on display rules. **Display rules** are principles that are followed for expressing emotions—that is, what, how, when, and where emotions should be expressed. For example, when a law enforcement officer is killed in the line of duty, officers from all over the country often gather for the funeral in a powerful display of emotion and solidarity (Sewell, 1985). Display rules, which are often unwritten, are learned from childhood and vary across cultures. For example, male-to-male greetings in the form of hugging and kissing are uncommon in North American and European cultures but very common in Middle Eastern cultures.

> **display rules**
> principles followed by different cultures for expressing emotion—what, how, when, and where emotions should be expressed

Expressing emotions serves the purpose of conveying not only feelings but also needs and intentions. Communication of feelings, needs, and intentions is not always truthful because people may lie or try to cover them up. Truth is important for law enforcement officers who investigate crimes and interview eyewitnesses and suspects. An ability to detect deceit is therefore fundamental. Officers are "motivated to get the actual perpetrator and not be misled to pursue the innocent" (Wells et al., 2000). Some evidence indicates that training and motivation in judging deception on the basis of people's demeanour can improve the ability to accurately detect the kinds of lies routinely encountered in law enforcement settings. However, other evidence suggests this is not always the case (Box 7.1).

POINTS TO REMEMBER

This chapter discusses the two related topics of motivation and emotion. In addition to elucidating the concepts of primary drives and social motives, explanations for motivation generally and for specific motives and needs are described. Finally, the nature of emotions, the experience of emotion, and the expression of emotion are considered.

BOX 7.1   Would You Lie to Me?

Expressing emotions serves the purpose of conveying not only feelings but also needs and intentions. Communication of feelings, needs, and intentions is not always truthful because people may lie or try to cover them up. Truth is important for law enforcement officers who investigate crimes and interview eyewitnesses and suspects. An ability to detect deceit is therefore fundamental. The problem, however, is that most people are very good at deceiving others: research indicates that observers do not do much better than chance (that is, guessing) when judging whether they are being lied to. In one study, police officers did no better than chance when assessing the honesty of individuals interviewed about missing relatives.

Facial expressions of emotion are complex indeed. First, different emotions are conveyed by the unique patterns of activity in several muscles in the upper and lower parts of the face. Second, facial expressions of emotion can be manipulated in several ways. A criminal might *simulate* an expression of sadness with no genuine emotion in order to appease members of a parole board. It may be possible to *mask* a genuinely felt emotion with an expression that corresponds to a different emotion (for example, smiling to cover up actual sadness). Lastly, a person may conceal a true emotion by adopting a neutral expression, thereby *neutralizing* his or her genuine feelings.

One aspect of emotional expression that has received much attention is microexpressions, uncontrollable changes in facial expression that last only a fraction of a second and which reflect a genuine emotion leaking out before being manipulated by the deceiver. Psychologist Paul Ekman suggests that microexpressions are shown by everyone trying to conceal their true feelings and that training may help detect them. In response to terrorist activity at home and abroad, large-scale training programs are being implemented in North America to improve security officials' ability to detect deception by identifying microexpressions.

Evidence suggests that training may indeed help officers identify cases of deception. Research from Dalhousie University indicates that many facial "slips" may last up to a second or longer, several times longer than a typical microexpression. On the other hand, it was found that microexpressions often involve only one half of the face (the upper or lower face) rather than the entire face. This finding suggests that training programs that attempt to identify full-face expressions may be less effective than those that target specific parts of the face.

Sources: Bond and DePaulo (2006); Ekman, O'Sullivan, and Frank (1999); Porter and ten Brinke (2008); Vrij and Mann (2001).

KEY TERMS

arousal	homeostasis
display rules	incentive
drive	instinct
emotion	intrinsic motivation
extrinsic motivation	motivation
hierarchy of needs	need

REFERENCES

Bard, P. (1929). The neurohumoral basis of emotional reactions. In C.A. Murchison (Ed.), *Foundations of experimental psychology* (pp. 449–87). Worcester, MA: Clark University Press.

Bond, C.F. Jr., & B.M. DePaulo. (2006). Accuracy of deception judgments. *Personality and Social Psychology Review, 10,* 214–34.

Cannon, W. (1927). The James–Lange theory of emotions: A critical examination and an alternative theory. *American Journal of Psychology, 39,* 106–12.

Ekman, P., M. O'Sullivan, & M.G. Frank. (1999, May). A few can catch a liar. *Psychological Science, 10* (3), 263–66.

Izard, C.E. (1994). Innate and universal facial expressions: Evidence from developmental and cross-cultural research. *Psychological Bulletin, 115,* 288–99.

James, W. (1884). What is an emotion? *Mind, 9,* 188–205.

Johan's Guide to Aphrodisiacs. (2000, August 15). *All you need to know about aphrodisiacs.* http://www.santesson.com/aphrodis/aphrhome.htm.

Lange, C.G. (1885). The mechanism of the emotions. Benjamin Rand (Trans.). First appeared in B. Rand (Ed.), (1912), *The classical psychologists* (pp. 672–84). Boston: Houghton Mifflin.

Maslow, A. (1970). *Motivation and personality* (2nd ed.). New York: Harper & Row.

Nordenberg, T. (1996, January–February). Looking for a libido lift? The facts about aphrodisiacs. *FDA Consumer Magazine.* http://www.fda.gov/fdac/features/196_love.html.

Porter, S., & L. ten Brinke. (2008). Reading between the lies: Identifying concealed and falsified emotions in universal facial expressions. *Psychological Science, 19,* 508–14.

Santrock, J.W. (2005). *Psychology* (7th ed.). New York: McGraw-Hill.

Schachter, S., & J.E. Singer. (1962). Cognitive, social, and physiological determinants of emotional state. *Psychological Review, 69,* 379–99.

Sewell, J. (1985). *Police: Urban policing in Canada.* Toronto: James Lorimer.

Vrij, A., & S. Mann. (2001). Telling and detecting lies in a high-stake situation: The case of a convicted murderer. *Applied Cognitive Psychology, 15,* 187–203.

Wells, G.L., R.S. Malpass, R.C.L. Lindsay, R.P. Fisher, J.W. Turtle, & S.M. Fulero. (2000, June). From the lab to the police station: A successful application of eyewitness research. *American Psychologist, 55* (6), 581–98.

Wood, D. (1996). *Issues in policing.* Lecture notes. University of Alaska, Anchorage. http://local.uaa.alaska.edu/~afdsw/police3.html.

Yerkes, R.M., & J.D. Dodson. (1908). The relation of strength of stimulus to rapidity of habit-formation. *Journal of Comparative Neurology and Psychology, 18,* 459–82.

EXERCISES AND REVIEW

Self-Test

Circle the correct answer.

1. Which of the following is true about instincts?

    a. they improve with practice

    b. they are unlearned

    c. they are inborn

    d. all of the above

2. Officer Shani is an enthusiastic mountain climber. Which of the following motivation theories best explains her behaviour?

    a. instinct theory

    b. drive reduction theory

    c. arousal theory

    d. hierarchy of needs theory

3. Which of the following represents a need for safety and security?

    a. saving money in the bank

    b. buying life insurance

    c. wanting protection from mayhem in the streets

    d. all of the above

4. Which of the following internal factors is involved in hunger?

    a. blood

    b. pheromones

    c. aphrodisiacs

    d. none of the above

5. Which of the following is suggested to be most characteristic of law enforcement officers?

   a. need for power

   b. need for achievement

   c. need for affiliation

   d. need for a quiet life

6. An officer makes an anonymous donation to a local youth drug rehabilitation program. Which of the following best explains the officer's behaviour?

   a. intrinsic motivation

   b. extrinsic motivation

   c. esteem needs

   d. none of the above

7. Which of the following is true about emotions?

   a. they are independent of motivation

   b. they motivate behaviour

   c. they are extremely difficult to detect

   d. none of the above

8. Which of the following emotions is (are) expressed with a universal facial expression?

   a. anger

   b. sadness

   c. disgust

   d. all of the above

9. Which of the following explains "We feel sorry because we cry"?

   a. James–Lange theory

   b. Cannon–Bard theory

   c. Schachter–Singer theory

   d. Maslow's hierarchy of needs

10. Which of the following is true about detecting people who are lying about their emotions?

   a. they can be detected only by a select group of law enforcement officers

   b. they can be detected by trained and motivated law enforcement officers in routine encounters with such individuals

   c. they are so smart it is useless to try to detect their lies

   d. none of the above

Thinking About Psychology and Law Enforcement

1. Using the motivation theories discussed in this chapter, explain why some law enforcement officers might accept bribes or otherwise act unethically.

2. Does law enforcement work have more intrinsic rewards or extrinsic rewards? Explain.

CHAPTER 8

Personality and Human Development

CHAPTER OBJECTIVES

After completing this chapter, you should be able to:

- Explain the concept of personality.

- Appreciate the differences among the psychoanalytic, neopsychoanalytic, humanistic, trait, social–cognitive, and interdependent self perspectives on personality.

- Describe human developmental stages and processes.

PREVIEW SCENARIO

Crystal T. was a 17-year-old high school student from Conway, a tiny community in South Carolina. She played piano at her church and planned to go to college. Crystal was well liked and was described as pleasant and sociable.

One morning Crystal's body was found in a roadside ditch. She had been stabbed 35 times, her throat had been cut, and a knife had been driven through her skull after she was dead. Her high school ring was the only clue to her identity. An autopsy confirmed that she had been raped. A sample of the suspect's semen was recovered from the girl's body.

Crystal's murder stunned the tiny community. People demanded answers from the police, who looked immediately for help as they had never handled a crime of this magnitude. Captain David Caldwell, a profiler with the South Carolina Law Enforcement Division, was called in for assistance. Profilers are a select group of professionals trained to probe the criminal mind. They are brought in to investigate the toughest cases of abuse and criminal behaviour. In contrast to the police tradition of looking for physical evidence, profilers use their knowledge of personality and of the past behaviours of people who have committed criminal acts to help them profile a suspect.

When Captain Caldwell arrived at the scene, he tried to imagine what the victim first heard and saw, and when she first realized that she was in trouble. He noticed that Crystal's body was in the ditch rather than hidden. He hypothesized that this was a sign of disorganization on the part of the killer, reasoning that it would take an organized killer no more than a few minutes to hide the body in such a way that it would never be found. Caldwell also believed that the killer did not think he would be suspected of the killing, or he would have taken a few extra minutes to hide the body.

Beginning with the school parking lot where Crystal's car was found, Caldwell retraced her last hour. He considered the possibility that the suspect could have been a stranger who saw the girl in the parking lot waiting for a friend, and who came out of his car and whisked her away. Caldwell considered it more probable that Crystal met someone she knew, moved the car to the parking lot, and left it there. He believed that whomever Crystal had met there, she had to feel comfortable talking to him or had to feel that there was nothing to fear when she left with him.

Based on his knowledge of similar cases, Caldwell profiled Crystal's killer as a white male in his early 20s; a strong individual possibly working in construction; a friend of the victim, living within an 8 km radius; a person with a history of trouble with teachers, friends, and especially law enforcement; and someone with a psychosexual maladjustment.

Based on Caldwell's profile and the use of DNA testing, police were able to obtain a confession from John R., a friend of Crystal's family. John was white, male, 19 years old, worked in construction, lived 5 km away from the victim's home, and had a history of exposing himself and making threatening obscene phone calls to women. John had been a pallbearer at Crystal's funeral. (Highroad Films, 1996)

INTRODUCTION

personality
unique and stable patterns of thoughts, feelings, and behaviours characteristic of an individual

Personality refers to the unique and stable patterns of thoughts, feelings, and behaviours characteristic of an individual. The word is derived from the Latin *persona*, which means mask. Personality suggests a degree of consistency and internal causality in the physical, mental, emotional, and social characteristics of an individual. Although people share universal human characteristics, no two individuals have the same personality. Psychologists and profilers use personality theories to identify and describe the main features of personality, explain how personality develops, and account for individual differences.

This chapter first discusses six approaches to the study of personality—psychoanalytic, neopsychoanalytic, humanistic, trait, social–cognitive, and interdependent self—followed by a description of the stages and processes inherent in human development.

PERSONALITY THEORIES

Psychoanalytic Perspective

psychoanalysis
the first comprehensive personality theory that emphasized unconscious motives in human behaviour

Sigmund Freud (1856–1939) was the father of **psychoanalysis**, the first comprehensive personality theory in psychology. He initially described personality in terms of three levels: conscious, preconscious, and unconscious (Freud, 1940/1949).

The *conscious* level is like the tip of an iceberg, the part that is above the surface of the ocean. It represents all thoughts, fantasies, feelings, sensations, perceptions, and memories that are in a person's awareness.

The *preconscious* level falls between the conscious and the unconscious. It represents material that is not conscious at present but can be readily brought into awareness with the passage of time or with a bit of effort. The preconscious is like a bridge between the conscious and the unconscious. The "tip of the tongue" phenomenon exemplifies the preconscious. An officer may not readily remember the name of a suspect he apprehended earlier, but suddenly remembers it a minute later.

The *unconscious* level is like the huge unseen mass of an iceberg below the surface of the ocean. It contains painful childhood experiences and instinctual drives and impulses that are hidden from conscious awareness. Instinctual drives are infantile wishes, desires, needs, and demands. Dreams, slips of the tongue or hand, and fantasies are disguised clues to the unconscious. A therapist is required to uncover the disguised material and help a person understand its meaning.

Freud later described three personality structures: the id, the ego, and the superego. The id is totally unconscious, whereas the ego and the superego operate at all three levels of consciousness. These structures do not exist in actual physical terms.

In Latin, *id* means "it." The id represents the immature and grumpy child of personality. It is instinctual and primitive. Its primitive drives relate to hunger, sex, aggression, and irrational impulses. The id drives are replenished or fuelled by the libido. The *libido* is the sexual energy that underlies biological urges. The id operates on the **pleasure principle**, the essence of which is the immediate gratification of needs. The id wants what it wants right away.

pleasure principle
immediate gratification of needs

The *ego* has the tough job of mediation and relies on the **reality principle**. This principle dictates an approach that balances the needs of the id and the superego against the needs of society. The ego performs its mediation through the rational functions of thinking, problem solving, and decision making.

reality principle
balances the needs of the id and the superego against the needs of society

The *superego* is the rigid and punitive master that represents societal morality. The superego develops as a result of rewards for socially sanctioned ("right") behaviours and punishment for behaviours that are considered wrong or immoral. Over time, society's moral values are internalized—that is, people rely less on external consequences for right or wrong behaviours.

ANXIETY: DEFENCE MECHANISMS FIGHT THE BATTLE

Painful childhood experiences (such as incest) and instinctual drives that surface to conscious awareness cause conflict, turmoil, and anxiety. *Anxiety* is a feeling of fear and apprehension without conscious awareness of its source. It serves the function of a fire alarm, alerting the ego of any threat or impending danger, and prompting it to take action. The ego uses several coping strategies or **defence mechanisms** to ward off anxiety:

defence mechanism
coping strategy that wards off anxiety

- Denial: Refusing to accept or acknowledge threatening information. For example, a woman "knows" her husband is having an affair with another woman but continues to behave as if the affair does not exist.

- Displacement: Using a substitute object or person as a target for negative thoughts, feelings, and actions. For example, a law enforcement officer is angry with his boss but instead of expressing his feelings to her he yells at his children when he gets home.

- Identification: Internalizing the attributes of another person. For example, prisoners who are beaten by corrections officers may act like them with other prisoners.

- Intellectualization: Using an intellectual rather than a behavioural or emotional approach to dealing with conflict. For example, an officer who is having serious conflicts with her supervisor becomes philosophical about her situation rather than making an effort to improve it.

- Projection: Attributing one's unwanted thoughts, feelings, and impulses to someone else. For example, a man who deep down feels hatred toward women because of the way his mother treated him as a child comes to feel that all the women in the world hate him. Projection allows the expression of an emotion or impulse, but in a way that the ego cannot recognize, therefore reducing anxiety.

- Rationalization: Offering a lame excuse or false but plausible explanation for an unacceptable thought or action. For example, a man who asks a woman for a date and is turned down reasons that she did not deserve him anyway.

- Reaction formation: Repressing an impulse and expressing its very opposite. For example, an officer who hates gays and lesbians becomes overly ingratiating toward them.

- Regression: Retreating to an earlier stage of development to cope with conflict. For example, a husband who is having severe marital problems starts chasing other women.

- Repression: Warding off or pushing back into the unconscious unpleasant thoughts, feelings, impulses, and memories. For example, a person may "forget" that he was once beaten viciously by his father.

- Sublimation: Rechannelling sexual or aggressive energy into more socially acceptable forms of behaviour. For example, a teenager plays heavy metal music as a channel for his aggressive drives.

PSYCHOSEXUAL STAGES

Freud proposed four psychosexual stages and one dormant period in the development of personality. Psychosexual conflicts arise from frustration or overindulgence, and cause fixation. *Frustration* means thwarting the expression of needs or failing to gratify them optimally. *Overindulgence* is excessive gratification of a need. **Fixation** is the process of "getting stuck" at a particular stage of development.

fixation
process of "getting stuck" at a particular stage of development

Oral Stage

The oral stage lasts from birth to the "terrible twos." This stage has an oral incorporative phase and an oral aggressive phase. The oral incorporative phase involves the pleasurable stimulation of the mouth. Frustration of or overindulgence in "taking in" behaviour (sucking, swallowing) leads to fixation. As adults, oral incorporative people show either preoccupation with oral activities (smoking, drinking, eating, and kissing), or excessive concern with oral activities and an overly optimistic, trusting, and dependent personality. A person who "swallows" anything anybody tells her was likely overindulged orally as an infant.

The oral aggressive phase involves the painful experience of teething. Aggressive behaviours such as biting, chewing, and spitting become important ways of coping with conflict. As adults, oral aggressive people are sarcastic, making "biting" remarks, and are argumentative, sadistic toward others, and prone to excessive hostility, aggression, and pessimism.

Anal Stage

The shift in the child's interest from the oral end to the other end signals entry into the anal stage at about age two until about age three. The most dramatic event in this stage is the parental demand for bowel and bladder control. Children resort to two strategies to cope with the trauma of toilet training: retaining the feces or defecating at forbidden times and places. Children who resort to "holding in" grow up to be anal retentive personalities: obstinate, stingy, orderly, punctual, and excessively clean. Children who do their thing whenever and wherever they wish grow up to be anal aggressive personalities: cruel, destructive, disorderly, and hostile.

Phallic Stage

The phallic stage lasts from age three to age five. The most dramatic conflict in this stage is the **Oedipus complex** for boys and the *Electra complex* for girls. Basically, the child develops unconscious incestuous desires for the parent of the opposite sex and murderous wishes to get rid of, replace, or kill the parent of the same sex. A son also develops castration anxiety, the fear that he is going to lose his penis; a daughter develops penis envy, the wish to have that which she seems to have lost.

Oedipus complex
boy's unconscious incestuous desires for his mother and murderous wishes to get rid of his father

Parental attitudes and reactions to the child's incestuous fantasies, sexual overtures, and specific fears are critical for the successful resolution of the Oedipus and Electra complexes. The boy ultimately resolves the conflict by giving up on his wish to go to bed with mommy and deciding to become more like daddy. Freud was not specific about the resolution of the Electra complex in girls. Children who fail to resolve their conflicts develop a phallic personality. A man who has the phallic personality is narcissistic, vain, brash, and preoccupied with asserting his masculinity through repeated sexual conquests. A woman with the phallic personality exaggerates her femininity, uses her charms to seduce and conquer men, and then dumps them.

Latency Period

The latency period lasts from age six to puberty. This period is a break for the child (and the child's parents) and a time for sublimation. **Sublimation** refers to a child's efforts to channel sexual energy into non-sexual activities. The child sublimates the sexual instinct in school activities, hobbies, and sports, and in the establishment of same-sex relationships.

sublimation
child's efforts to channel sexual energy into non-sexual activities

Genital Stage

The genital stage, from puberty on, is the final stage of personality development. People who survive the preceding stages without fixation and who mature physically lead a normal (as opposed to neurotic) life with heterosexual interests.

The Neopsychoanalytic Perspective

neopsychoanalytic perspective
personality theory that stresses social and cultural rather than sexual influences in personality development

The **neopsychoanalytic perspective** was developed during Freud's lifetime and continued after his death, and represents a revolt against his emphasis on instincts and his overly pessimistic view of humankind. The neopsychoanalytic approach paints a more optimistic view of human nature and stresses social and cultural rather than sexual influences in the development of personality. Finally, the neopsychoanalytic concern with conscious and rational processes has contributed to the emergence of self or ego psychology.

Nevertheless, neopsychoanalytic theorists do not all think alike. Carl Jung, Erik Erikson, Alfred Adler, and Karen Danielson Horney each developed unique views on the basis of their own personal stories or experiences in life.

CARL JUNG: EGO, PERSONAL UNCONSCIOUS, AND COLLECTIVE UNCONSCIOUS

Carl Jung (1875–1961) developed his own model of the levels of personality: the ego, the personal unconscious, and the collective unconscious.

The *ego* in Jungian theory is the conscious part of personality. It serves the "executive" function of personality by assuming responsibility for activities of daily living. The *personal unconscious* is the part of personality that contains conscious feelings, perceptions, and thoughts and unconscious memories, wishes, and impulses. The **collective unconscious** is the evolutionary reservoir for the universal experiences of humanity. The collective unconscious accounts for intercultural similarities in religious beliefs, dreams, symbols, and myths.

collective unconscious
evolutionary reservoir for the universal experiences of humanity

ERIK ERIKSON: THE EIGHT AGES OF MAN

Erik Erikson's (1902–1994) most original and important theoretical contribution is his discussion of the eight "ages," or stages, of psychosocial development (Hjelle & Ziegler, 1981), which are summarized in Table 8.1.

Erikson believed that a crisis or conflict is associated with each stage—for example, to trust or not to trust. A crisis at a particular stage needs to be resolved to enable a person to move to the next stage of development.

ALFRED ADLER: INFERIORITY AND SUPERIORITY COMPLEXES

inferiority complex
inability to solve life's problems

Alfred Adler (1870–1937) believed that inferiority feelings are universal childhood experiences and are necessary for personal growth and development (Ansbacher & Ansbacher, 1956). Individuals who fail to overcome their inferiority feelings develop an **inferiority complex**, "an inability to solve life's problems" (Orgler, 1963, p. 63). Physical defect or disability, child pampering, or child neglect can cause an inferiority complex. Individuals with an inferiority complex may overcompensate and develop a *superiority complex* by becoming boastful, arrogant, vain, egocentric, and sarcastic.

KAREN DANIELSON HORNEY: MOVING TOWARD, AGAINST, AND AWAY

basic anxiety
pervasive feeling of isolation, loneliness, and helplessness in a hostile world

Karen Horney (pronounced "Hornay," 1885–1952) believed that basic anxiety was at the core of psychological ill health (Horney, 1926/1967). **Basic anxiety** is a per-

TABLE 8.1   Erikson's Eight Stages of Psychosocial Development

Stage	Age	Coping	Positive Outcome
Oral–sensory	Birth–1	Trust–mistrust	Trusting of oneself and others
Muscular–anal	1–3	Autonomy–doubt	The strength/will to be oneself
Locomotor–genital	3–5	Initiative–guilt	Development of superego
Latency	6–11	Industry–inferiority	Development of sense of competence
Adolescence	12–18	Identity–role confusion	Development of proper ego identity (knowing who you are)
Young adulthood	18–35	Intimacy–isolation	Development of friendships and intimate sexual relationships
Adulthood	35–55	Generativity–stagnation	Sense of contribution to humanity
Maturity	55+	Ego integrity–despair	Sense of fulfillment and life satisfaction

Source: Adapted from Erikson (1963).

vasive feeling of isolation, loneliness, and helplessness in a hostile world. It develops as a result of parental neglect to meet a child's needs for satisfaction and security. Satisfaction refers to physical needs (food, water, sleep). Security refers to feelings of safety and freedom from fear. Neglected children repress their anger and hostility toward their parents rather than expressing their true feelings because of helplessness, fear of punishment, potential loss of parental love, and guilt. The repressed hostility persists as basic anxiety.

Horney identified three personality profiles for coping with basic anxiety. The *compliant personality* uses the "moving toward people" coping strategy: weakness, helplessness, and constant pursuit of love, protection, and acceptance from others. The *aggressive personality* uses the "moving against people" coping strategy: strength, power, superiority, toughness, and a domineering and controlling manner. The *detached personality* uses the "moving away from people" coping strategy: emotional distance from other people, aloofness, self-sufficiency, and protection of personal privacy.

People who rely exclusively on one of the three coping strategies are neurotic. People who are flexible and use all three strategies as they see fit are normal.

The Humanistic Perspective

Humanistic psychology emphasizes the goodness of human nature and people's potential for growth and actualization (maturity, self-fulfillment, and healthy psychological growth). Humanistic psychologists argue that the study of abnormality can yield only an abnormal psychology. They suggest that normal and supernormal (exceptional) individuals should also be of interest to the psychology of personality.

humanistic psychology personality theory that emphasizes the goodness of human nature and people's potential for growth and actualization

Abraham Maslow and Carl Rogers are the two psychologists most associated with the humanistic perspective.

ABRAHAM MASLOW: FROM SURVIVING TO BEING

Abraham Maslow (1908–1970) is best known for his theory of motivation (discussed in Chapter 7) and his work on the self-actualizing person (Maslow, 1970). Maslow believed that people are born with positive qualities, but he also acknowledged the existence of the bad and the evil. Similarly, he believed in the importance of childhood experiences in personality development but rejected the view of people as forever being pawns or victims of early childhood. Finally, he believed that there is more potential to humanity than is realized, and that all that is required is an environment conducive to unleashing the human potential. He characterized self-actualizing people as follows:

- efficient perception of reality—ability to perceive others correctly and efficiently, being "with it";

- acceptance of self, others, and nature—respect for one's self and the world;

- spontaneity, simplicity, and naturalness—possible unconventionality and absence of artificiality;

- problem-centredness—commitment to tasks undertaken, living to work rather than working to live;

- autonomy—personal and life satisfaction not dependent on others or the physical environment;

- freshness of appreciation—capacity to appreciate ordinary life events with a sense of awe and pleasure;

- peak or mystic experiences—moments of intense excitement and tension as well as of relaxation and bliss;

- social interest—deep feelings of kinship with humanity;

- interpersonal relations—capacity to form deep and close personal relationships with others;

- democratic character structure—free from prejudice and ability to respect all people;

- differentiation between means and ends—well-developed moral and ethical standards;

- creativity; and

- resistance to enculturation—ability to make decisions even if they are at odds with popular opinion.

CARL ROGERS: FROM INCONGRUENCE TO CONGRUENCE

Carl Rogers (1902–1987) worked with delinquent children. He found that factors internal to delinquents, such as self-understanding or self-insight, were better predictors of delinquent behaviour than factors external to delinquents, such as family environment and social and educational background. Rogers believed that everyone has a sense of self as distinct from the rest of the world and that everyone has a need for positive regard. People's **self-concepts** are the views that they develop about themselves—who they are, who they think they should be, and who they might like to be. The self strives for consistency. A person with an inconsistent or incongruent self is a troubled individual (see below).

Positive regard is the pervasive need for acceptance, love, and approval from significant people in one's life. People whose needs for positive regard are met experience self-growth. A social climate of unconditional positive regard contributes to self-growth. **Unconditional positive regard** refers to the process in which individuals are accepted, loved, and respected for what they are, independent of their behaviour. *Conditional positive regard*, or *conditions of worth*, has the opposite effect in that it hinders growth. **Conditional positive regard** refers to people's belief that they are worthy of love, acceptance, and respect only when they think, feel, and act as others want them to.

People who must deny certain experiences, thoughts, feelings, and beliefs and suppress their true feelings and thoughts for fear of criticism and disapproval are in a state of incongruence. **Incongruence** is a state of discrepancy between the self-concept and aspects of the individual's experience. The more incongruence, the more likely are self-estrangement and feelings of anxiety. Incongruence between self and experience is a yardstick for normalcy. Healthy people are those who allow themselves to experience all aspects of the self rather than succumb to distortion, denial, or censure. They have the freedom to achieve personal growth and self-actualization.

The Trait Perspective

The **trait perspective** defines personality in terms of traits or internal dispositions. A **trait** is a relatively stable and consistent personal feature. Traits are used to describe, explain, and predict personality. Trait theorists avoid classifying individuals into discrete categories. Rather, they view traits as existing on a continuum ranging from very low to very high. For example, Officer Sarah may possess some amount of aggression, but Officer Ali may be even more aggressive.

RAYMOND CATTELL: SURFACE AND SOURCE TRAITS

Raymond Cattell (1905–1998) classified traits into two types: common and unique. A *common trait* is a personality feature that characterizes all people to some degree. Examples of common traits are intelligence and introversion. Heredity and culture influence the expression of common traits. A *unique trait* is a personality feature that characterizes a single or a few individuals. Unique traits tend to be represented in people's interests and attitudes—for example, a passion for collecting rare species of butterflies.

Cattell also distinguished between surface traits and source traits. *Surface traits* are those that seem to an observer to go together. You have probably met people who are curt, unfriendly, argumentative, and belligerent, and thus have observed people with the surface trait of hostility. Surface traits are limited in that they represent perceptions of behaviour rather than explanations for behaviour.

self-concept
view that people develop about themselves

positive regard
pervasive need for acceptance, love, and approval from significant people in one's life

unconditional positive regard
process in which individuals are accepted, loved, and respected for what they are, independent of their behaviour

conditional positive regard
people's belief that they are worthy of love, acceptance, and respect only when they think, feel, and act as others want them to

incongruence
state of discrepancy between the self-concept and aspects of an individual's experience

trait perspective
personality theory that defines personality in terms of traits or internal dispositions

trait
relatively stable and consistent personal feature

As the label implies, *source traits* are the basic elements of personality that give it coherence and explain behaviour. Dominance–submission is an example of a source trait. Cattell identified 16 source traits of personality on the basis of more than two decades of research.

HANS J. EYSENCK: PSYCHOTICISM, NEUROTICISM, INTROVERSION–EXTRAVERSION

psychoticism
personality dimension that differentiates between normal people and those who are psychotic

neuroticism
personality dimension that differentiates between normal people and those who are neurotic

introversion
personality of shyness, quietness, self-control, introspection, and inhibition

extraversion
personality of sociability, exuberance, impulsivity, and craving for excitement

Hans J. Eysenck (1916–1997) identified three underlying personality dimensions: psychoticism, neuroticism, and introversion–extraversion. **Psychoticism** differentiates normal people from psychotic people. Psychotic people are those who have lost touch with reality. People with a high level of **neuroticism** tend to be emotionally unstable, easily aroused, and chronic worriers, and they frequently complain of anxieties and bodily aches. In contrast, normal people tend to be emotionally stable, reliable, calm, and even-tempered. **Introversion** refers to the personality characterized by shyness, quietness, self-control, introspection, and inhibition. **Extraversion** refers to the personality characterized by sociability, exuberance, impulsivity, and craving for excitement. In contrast to introverts, extraverts show a greater tolerance for pain, lower levels of physical arousal, greater need to seek out stimulation, more resistance to conditioning (see Chapter 5), and more responsiveness to rewards than to punishment.

PAUL COSTA AND ROBERT MCCRAE: THE BIG FIVE PERSONALITY DIMENSIONS

five-factor theory
trait model that suggests that personality can be explained using five broad dimensions: neuroticism, extraversion, openness to experience, consciousness, and agreeableness

Paul Costa and Robert McCrae's five-factor theory (Costa & McCrae, 1992) is the most widely discussed trait model in contemporary personality psychology, and is supported by studies in many languages and cultures and across different age groups. This theory—also known as the Big Five approach—is used in selecting law enforcement officers. The **five-factor theory** suggests that personality can be explained using five broad dimensions:

- *Neuroticism* is a proneness to psychological distress and unhealthy coping responses. High scorers on this personality dimension tend to be anxious, emotional, and insecure, and they feel inadequate and tend to worry. Low scorers on this dimension tend to be easygoing, calm, hardy, relaxed, secure, and self-satisfied.

- *Extraversion* is the personality dimension that assesses interpersonal interaction, activity level, need for stimulation, and capacity for joy. High scorers on extraversion tend to be active, affectionate, assertive, fun-loving, outgoing, person-oriented, sociable, and talkative. Low scorers on the extraversion dimension tend to be aloof, quiet, reserved, retiring, and task-oriented.

- *Openness to experience* is the personality dimension that assesses the disposition to seek and appreciate experience and to tolerate and explore the unfamiliar. High scorers on this dimension tend to be broad-minded, creative, cultured, curious, imaginative, and untraditional. Low scorers on this dimension tend to be conventional and concrete-minded, and to have narrow interests.

- *Consciousness* is the personality dimension that taps into an individual's degree of organization. High scorers on this dimension tend to be ambitious, dependable, hard-working, organized, persevering, punctual, self-disciplined, and thorough. Low scorers on this dimension tend to be aimless, careless, sloppy, and unreliable.

- *Agreeableness* is the personality dimension that assesses the quality of interpersonal orientation. High scorers on this dimension tend to be forgiving, good-natured, gullible, helpful, soft-hearted, and straightforward. Low scorers on this dimension tend to be aggressive, argumentative, cynical, uncooperative, and vindictive.

THE TRAIT APPROACH AND THE LAW ENFORCEMENT PERSONALITY

There is no universally accepted description of law enforcement officers. Considerable care needs to be taken in researching and describing the "typical" law enforcement personality to ensure no negative or positive bias exists. One description sees the law enforcement personality as dogmatic, authoritarian, suspicious, racist, hostile, insecure, conservative, and cynical (Wood, 1996). This is inconsistent with descriptions of this personality as competent, honest, professional, and psychologically stable (MacDonald, 1999); self-disciplined, socially bold, extroverted, emotionally tough, and low in anxiety (Lorr & Strack, 1994); and tough-minded, practical, self-assured, conservative, composed, relaxed, considerate, self-controlled, and less inhibited than the average person (Hofer, 1995).

The Social–Cognitive Perspective

The social–cognitive perspective is an extension of B.F. Skinner's behavioural approach, discussed in Chapter 5. First, the **social–cognitive approach** emphasizes the importance of both social–environmental and cognitive factors in understanding personality and human behaviour. It stresses the role of social learning through observation rather than through unconscious processes or personality traits and maintains that virtually all forms of behaviour are learned in a social context. According to this perspective, cognitions influence the learning-by-example process. People are not as machine-like as behaviourists suggest, but rather make deliberate, conscious, and informed decisions to behave like others (Ansbacher & Ansbacher, 1989). Second, the social–cognitive approach relies on basic and applied research to understand personality and to extend social–cognitive principles to the clinical setting. This section discusses the theoretical contributions of Albert Bandura to the social–cognitive perspective.

social–cognitive approach
personality theory that emphasizes the importance of social–environmental and cognitive factors in understanding personality and human behaviour

ALBERT BANDURA: SELF-CONTROL, RECIPROCAL DETERMINISM, SELF-EFFICACY, AND COLLECTIVE EFFICACY

Albert Bandura advanced four concepts that are significant to understanding personality: self-control, reciprocal determinism, self-efficacy, and collective efficacy.

Self-Control

self-control
people's ability to regulate their own behaviour

Self-control refers to people's ability to regulate their own behaviour. Officer Cliff feels proud of his ability to relate to prisoners and of his personal efforts toward their rehabilitation. His behaviour at work exemplifies the concept of self-control. First, his behaviour does not depend on external rewards, such as salary. Second, Officer Cliff has consciously committed himself to excellence. Finally, he has established his own system of rewards and punishments in meeting his self-imposed performance standards at work.

The three stages of self-control are self-observation, self-evaluation, and self-reinforcement (Bandura, 1977). *Self-observation* is people's capacity to view their own behaviour as it occurs. *Self-evaluation* is setting standards of behaviour and monitoring adherence to those standards. Finally, *self-reinforcement* is responding to the outcomes of self-evaluation—that is, rewarding behaviours that have positive outcomes and punishing behaviours that have negative outcomes. Officer Cliff rewards himself on days when he lives up to his own expectations, and feels guilty on days when he doesn't.

Reciprocal Determinism

reciprocal determinism
belief in interaction of behavioural, cognitive, and environmental influences

Reciprocal determinism is the belief in the interaction of behavioural, cognitive, and environmental influences. People both affect and are affected by their environment.

Self-Efficacy

self-efficacy
people's beliefs about their ability to exercise control over events that affect their lives

Self-efficacy refers to people's beliefs about their ability to exercise control over events that affect their lives (Bandura, 1989). Self-efficacy is an important cognitive factor in personality. Bandura distinguishes between efficacy expectations and outcome expectations. *Efficacy expectations* are people's feelings of confidence that they are able to cope with particular situations in their lives. Officer Renée's strong belief in her ability to handle crisis situations exemplifies efficacy expectations. *Outcome expectations* are people's beliefs that their actions will result in particular outcomes. Officer Renée's confidence that her actions will result in defusing a crisis exemplifies her outcome expectations.

Collective Efficacy

collective efficacy
a group's shared beliefs about their competency

Collective efficacy refers to a group's shared beliefs about their group's competency (Bandura, 1989). A group's collective efficacy is important in influencing group potency and group performance (Stajkovic, Lee, & Nyberg, 2009).

The Interdependent Self Perspective

The psychoanalytic, neopsychoanalytic, humanistic, trait, and social–cognitive personality theories view individuals as striving for autonomy, independence, and self-fulfillment, and deriving self-esteem from personal accomplishments. As such, they present an ethnocentric Western picture of human personality. In non-Western cultures such as those of Japan, India, South America, Central America, and the Middle East, personality is more likely to be shaped into an interdependent self that strives for connectedness with family, kin, and in-groups, values group harmony, cohesion, and cooperation, and derives self-worth from relatedness (Markus & Kitayama, 1991). Similarly, individuals from collectivist cultural groups in Canada such as Hispanics and Asians are more likely to construe the self as interdependent rather than independent. Consequently, the families and communities from these cultural groups are more likely to be adversely affected when one of their own has an altercation with the law or a personal issue with law enforcement.

HUMAN DEVELOPMENT

Psychologists study the way human personality develops from the embryo stage into old age, focusing on genetic and environmental factors that contribute to intelligence, morality, well-being, and quality of life. The consensus is that both genetic predisposition (inborn temperament) and environmental factors (such as parenting styles) shape people's social, emotional, cognitive, and personality development. (See Box 8.1.)

Identity and Social Development

Identity refers to people's understanding of themselves as discrete, separate entities. All children form a personal identity and a social identity based on their group affiliation, such as family and ethnicity, beginning in early childhood through a process called "identification," in which they attempt to look, act, and feel like other people in their social environment (Phinney & Ong, 2007; Kazarian & Boyadjian, 2008). An important aspect of the development of personal identity is the discovery of maleness and femaleness and the roles associated with them. According to Kohlberg (1966), children acquire their sex roles in three stages. In the basic *sex-role identity* stage (2–3.5 years), children label themselves as either boys or girls but believe their sex can change. In the *sex-role stability* stage (3.5–4.5 years), children are aware that sex is stable over time—that is, boys grow to be men and girls grow to be women. In the *sex-role constancy* stage (4.5–7 years and upward), children recognize that their sex remains the same independent of time or situation, such as dress change or outward appearance.

identity
people's understanding of themselves as discrete entities

Identity formation has been most extensively described by Erik Erikson in his theory of developmental stages. According to Erikson, identity formation begins in childhood but gains prominence during adolescence. Adolescents who experience temporary instability and confusion over their identity yet resolve their identity crisis achieve an integrated and a stable adult identity.

Canadian developmental psychologist James Marcia's (1966) model of identity formation refines and extends Erikson's work on identity. In addition to proposing that identity involves the adoption of a sexual orientation, a set of values and ideals, and a vocational direction, Marcia described four identity statuses, or common ways in which adolescents deal with the challenge of identity formation.

- Identity achievement: Attained by those who experience, confront, and resolve their identity crisis.

- Identity foreclosure: The status of those who do not experience an identity crisis but make identity commitments that conform to the expectations of others (such as parents) without questioning them or investigating alternatives.

> ### BOX 8.1   Is There a Police Personality?
>
> What is a police personality, and how does it develop? These two questions have been the subject of considerable debate. Two opposing views, the predispositional view and the occupational–socialization view, have dominated the debate over the development and formation of the police personality.
>
> The *predispositional model* suggests a pre-existing police personality that predisposes certain individuals to police work. The *occupational-socialization model* suggests that police personality is made or shaped on the job. Of course, there is a third viable theory, which views police personality as a combination of predisposition and on-the-job experience.
>
> The debate over the definition of police personality has focused on the core personality, characteristics, attributes, or qualities of police officers. Anecdotal definitions of the police personality abound and include such descriptors as *macho, brave, authoritarian, cynical, aggressive, suspicious, solidaristic, conservative, alienated*, and *bigoted*. Popular culture is also conflicted on what police officers are like and how they behave (for example, compare the Mel Gibson type in *Lethal Weapon* with the Denzel Washington type in *Training Day*).
>
> A review of studies on police personality shows that police departments rigorously attempt to screen out individuals who exhibit such personality traits as impulsivity, hostility, undue aggression, lack of autonomy, immaturity, anti-social tendencies, potential for alcohol/drug abuse, emotional lability, social introversion, paranoia, and psychoses. For this reason, most cadets enter the police force with highly similar personality traits. What happens to these officers during the course of their careers continues to shape them. Ultimately, it is job-related experience that seems to form the "police personality."
>
> Source: Twersky-Glasner (2005).

- ■ Identity diffusion: The situation of those who may or may not have experienced an identity crisis but who have not made a commitment, or appear to have given up any attempt to make commitments, needed for developing a clear sense of identity.

- ■ Identity moratorium: The status of those who are experiencing an identity crisis, have not yet made a decision, yet are trying to "find themselves"; they appear to be moving forward toward identity formation and commitment.

Cognitive Development

While Erikson, Kohlberg, and Marcia were preoccupied with social and identity development in children, Jean Piaget was focused on their cognitive development. Piaget proposed four stages of cognitive development, emphasizing the importance of stimulation so that children could reach their full potential. During the *sensorimotor* stage (birth to age 2), children begin to develop motor skills, to differentiate

TABLE 8.2   Lawrence Kohlberg's Moral Development Theory

Level 1: Pre-Conventional Morality

Stage 1: Obedience and Punishment

> Rules are seen as fixed and absolute
>
> Obeying rules is important to gain a reward or avoid punishment
>
> Common in young children but also expressed by adults

Stage 2: Individualism and Exchange

> Children account for individual points of view
>
> Actions are judged on how they serve individual needs
>
> Reciprocity is possible, but only if it serves one's own interests

Level 2: Conventional Morality

Stage 3: Interpersonal Relationships (also referred to as the "good boy–good girl" orientation)

> Focus on living up to social expectations and roles
>
> Emphasis on conformity and being "nice"
>
> Consideration of how choices influence relationships

Stage 4: Respecting Authority and Maintaining Social Order

> Society as a whole considered when making judgments
>
> Focus on law-and-order morality

Level 3: Post-Conventional Morality

Stage 5: Social Contract and Individual Rights

> Differing values, opinions, and beliefs of other people begin to be accounted for
>
> Civic-mindedness; rules of law considered important for maintaining a society

Stage 6: Universal Ethical Principles

> Moral reasoning based upon universal ethical principles and abstract reasoning
>
> Internalized principles of justice are followed, even if they conflict with laws and rules

---

themselves from objects, to recognize themselves as agents of action, and to act intentionally (for example, shaking a rattle to make a noise). Nevertheless, sensorimotor-stage children show little or no ability for symbolic representation or object permanence—the ability to conceive of things existing outside their immediate vicinity. In the *preoperational* stage (ages 2–7), children begin to use language and to represent objects by images and words, and even discuss things or people who are not physically present. Nevertheless, preoperational-stage children show egocentric thought—that is, difficulty taking the viewpoint of others. In the *concrete operational* stage (ages 7–12), children overcome their egocentrism and begin to develop clearer methods of thinking and better understanding of time and spatial relationships, but they are largely bound by the concrete world and have trouble conceiving abstract thought. In the *formal operational* stage (age 12 to adulthood), individuals develop the ability to think logically, to understand abstractions, and to recognize the concepts of causality (that different actions can produce different outcomes) and choice (that people have freedom to choose between various actions, depending on the desired outcome).

Moral Development

While Piaget (1932) studied many aspects of moral judgment, Lawrence Kohlberg provided a more elaborate theory on how children formulate moral reasoning at various stages of cognitive development, and proposed moral development as a continuous lifespan process (Crain, 1985; Kohlberg & Lickona, 1976). Kohlberg's moral development theory identified six stages of moral reasoning grouped into three levels: pre-conventional, conventional, and post-conventional (Table 8.2). In the *pre-conventional* level, children's moral decisions focus on avoidance of punishment and gaining of awards. In the *conventional* level, they are preoccupied with the conventions of society (or of family, religion, or some other social order). In the *post-conventional* level, they focus on personal beliefs.

POINTS TO REMEMBER

Personality theories vary in the factors they consider essential for describing and explaining personality. The psychoanalytic, neopsychoanalytic, humanistic, and social–cognitive perspectives are explanatory—they attempt to explain how personality develops and functions. Trait theories are descriptive—they attempt to identify essential traits that account for similarities and differences among people's personalities and to predict human behaviour.

The psychoanalytic and neopsychoanalytic perspectives view people as being controlled by unconscious forces. The humanistic perspective views people as rational individuals striving to achieve their potential. The trait perspective views people as individuals with a set of stable internal dispositions. The social–cognitive perspective views people as shaped by and shaping their social environment. In non-Western cultures, personality is likely to be shaped as an interdependent self that strives for connectedness with family, kin, and in-groups.

Developmental and personality psychologists have focused on the interplay between genetic and environmental factors and theorized about identity formation, cognitive development, and moral development.

KEY TERMS

basic anxiety	personality
collective efficacy	pleasure principle
collective unconscious	positive regard
conditional positive regard	psychoanalysis
defence mechanism	psychoticism
extraversion	reality principle
five-factor theory	reciprocal determinism
fixation	self-concept
humanistic psychology	self-control
identity	self-efficacy
incongruence	social–cognitive approach
inferiority complex	sublimation
introversion	trait
neopsychoanalytic perspective	trait perspective
neuroticism	unconditional positive regard
Oedipus complex	

REFERENCES

Ansbacher, H., & R. Ansbacher. (1956). *The individual psychology of Alfred Adler: A systematic presentation in selections from his writings.* New York: Basic Books.

Bandura, A. (1977). *Social learning theory.* Englewood Cliffs, NJ: Prentice Hall.

Bandura, A. (1989). Human agency in social cognitive theory. *American Psychologist, 44,* 1175-84.

Costa, P.T., & R.R. McCrae. (1992). The five-factor model of personality and its relevance to personality disorders. *Journal of Personality Disorders, 6* (4), 343–59.

Crain, W.C. (1985). *Theories of Development.* Englewood Cliffs, NJ: Prentice Hall.

Erikson, E. (1963). *Childhood and society* (2nd ed.). New York: Norton.

Freud, S. (1940/1949). *An outline of psychoanalysis.* J. Strachey, Trans. New York: Norton.

Highroad Films. (1996). *Criminal profilers.* Television documentary, The Learning Channel.

Hjelle, L.A., & D.J. Ziegler. (1981). *Personality theories: Basic assumptions, research, and application* (2nd ed.). New York: McGraw-Hill.

Hofer, S.M. (1995). On the structure of personality and the relationship of personality to fluid and crystallized intelligence in adulthood. *Dissertation Abstracts International, 55* (8-B), 3625.

Horney, K. (1926/1967). *Feminine psychology.* New York: Norton.

Kazarian, S.S., & M.D. Boyadjian. (2008). Validation of the multigroup ethnic identity measure among ethnic Armenian adolescents in Lebanon. *Identity: An International Journal of Theory and Research, 8,* 335–47.

Kohlberg, L. (1966). A cognitive-development analysis of children's sex role concepts and attitudes. In E.E. Maccoby & R.G. D'Andrade (Eds.), *The development of sex differences.* Stanford, CA: Stanford University Press.

Kohlberg, L., & T. Lickona (Eds.). (1976). *Moral development and behavior: Theory, research and social issues.* New York: Holt, Rinehart and Winston.

Lorr, M., & S. Strack. (1994). Personality profiles of police candidates. *Journal of Criminal Psychology, 50,* 200–7.

MacDonald, J.M. (1999). The corruption process of a law enforcement officer. Comment. *Journal of American Academy of Psychiatry and the Law, 27,* 178–79.

Marcia, J.E. (1966). Development and validation of ego identity status. *Journal of Personality and Social Psychology, 3,* 551–58.

Markus, H.R., & S. Kitayama. (1991). Culture and self: Implications for cognition, emotion, and motivation. *Psychological Review, 98,* 224–53.

Maslow, A. (1970). *Motivation and personality* (2nd ed.). New York: Harper & Row.

Orgler, H. (1963). *Alfred Adler, the man and his work: Triumphs over the inferiority complex.* New York: New American Library.

Phinney, J.S., & A.D. Ong. (2007). Conceptualization and measurement of ethnic identity: Current status and future directions. *Journal of Counseling Psychology, 54,* 271–81.

Piaget, J. (1932). *The moral judgment of the child.* London: Kegan Paul, Trench, Trubner.

Stajkovic, A.D., D. Lee, & A.J. Nyberg. (2009). Collective efficacy, group potency, and group performance: Meta-analyses of their relationships and test of a mediation model. *Journal of Applied Psychology, 94,* 814–28.

Twersky-Glasner, A. (2005). Police personality: What is it and why are they like that? *Journal of Police and Criminal Psychology, 20,* 56–67.

Wood, D. (1996). Issues in policing: Lecture notes. University of Alaska, Anchorage. http://local.uaa.alaska.edu/~afdsw/police3.html.

EXERCISES AND REVIEW

Self-Test

Circle the correct answer.

1. Staff Sergeant Jessica and her husband are failing to recognize obvious signs of substance use in their teenage daughter. Which defence mechanism is operating in the parents?

    a. projection

    b. denial

    c. sublimation

    d. intellectualization

2. A woman is suspected of seducing men, then murdering them. According to Freud, which of the following applies in her case?

    a. Electra complex

    b. penis envy

    c. phallic personality

    d. all of the above

3. Officer Ben has difficulty working with female supervisors. Which of the following is a likely explanation for his problem?

    a. Electra complex

    b. penis envy

    c. Oedipus complex

    d. projection

4. Officer Narina is best described as a recluse. Which of the following is consistent with this personality style?

    a. moving away

    b. moving against

    c. moving toward

    d. standing still

5. In Cattell's terms, intelligence is a

    a. source trait

    b. surface trait

    c. deep trait

    d. convoluted trait

6. Which of the following types of personality theorists would be most interested in having Mother Teresa participate in a personality study?

   a. social–cognitive

   b. neopsychoanalytic

   c. humanistic

   d. trait

7. Officer Roger seems to have a natural ability to detect the fake, the phony, and the dishonest. Which of the following self-actualization characteristics does he possess?

   a. efficient perception of reality

   b. problem centring

   c. peak experience

   d. creativity

8. Officer Martina has the ingrained belief that the only way to earn her boss's acceptance and respect is to feel, act, and think as her boss wants her to. Officer Martina's view of her self exemplifies

   a. unconditional positive regard

   b. conditions of worth

   c. need for negative regard

   d. need for self-actualization

9. Constable Lise is strongly against physical violence yet must use force to subdue an angry, out-of-control suspect. According to Rogers, Officer Lise is in a state of

   a. congruence

   b. total recall

   c. sudden impact

   d. incongruence

10. Officer Hans is new to law enforcement and has doubts about the effectiveness of the group of officers he will be working with. Which of the following is relevant to his personality, according to Bandura?

   a. self-efficacy

   b. collective efficacy

   c. reciprocal determinism

   d. extraversion

Thinking About Psychology and Law Enforcement

1. Jenny is a 20-year-old white woman attending college to become a police officer. As a youngster, she was taught that premarital sex is a major sin, that heterosexual relations are the only acceptable relationships in God's eyes, and that interracial marriages are bad for the blood. Her parents preached these values and acted in a manner consistent with their beliefs. Jenny believed and respected her parents' values and internalized them over time. In high school and later in university, however, Jenny was exposed to attitudes and values that were different from those of her parents. For example, she heard her peers support premarital sex with someone one truly loves. She became more aware of stories of peers having sex. She also saw on television ample examples of unmarried couples doing their thing in the bedroom, on the kitchen table, or even in the closet. One of her friends even confided that she was in love with another woman, and that she had already gone to bed with her female lover more than once. Jenny continued to accept her parents' values about premarital sex, heterosexual relations, and same-race relations. However, after graduation and acceptance as a recruit in a local police department, she found herself gradually falling in love with a fellow recruit, Denzel. Denzel is a young, handsome, charming, and considerate black man. He is in love with Jenny as well and committed to her. He sees nothing wrong in making love to the woman he loves. After a year of courtship and commitment to getting married, Denzel and Jenny willingly had intercourse. Jenny found the experience "heavenly." Three weeks later, however, she started to worry about what she did.

   a. How might each of the personality perspectives described in this chapter help explain Jenny's personality development; current thoughts, feelings, and actions; and future behaviour?

   b. How might Jenny's personality background affect her duties as a law enforcement officer?

2. Monitor your use of defence mechanisms for a week. Which ones do you use, and how often? How might the defence mechanisms you use differ from those of others, such as troubled teenagers, offenders, and prisoners?

3. Which personality perspective should society generally, and the criminal justice system particularly, consider in dealing with social and criminal issues? Why?

4. What do you think is the typical personality of law enforcement officers? Explain.

CHAPTER 9

Stress, Coping, and Health

CHAPTER OBJECTIVES

After completing this chapter, you should be able to:

- Define the concept of health.
- Describe the stress response, the nature of stressors, and approaches to coping.
- Understand the impact of stress on law enforcement work.
- Identify major health issues.

PREVIEW SCENARIO

Law enforcement is a highly stressful occupation. In fact, it involves a significantly higher degree of job-related and personal stressors than other occupations. Law enforcement officers experience threats of physical harm, dangerous—sometimes fatal—situations such as being shot at, psychological abuse from irate citizens, pain and suffering among the people they serve and protect, a sense of uselessness and powerlessness, rapid changes in the nature of police work, and critical incidents or post-traumatic stress caused by a line-of-duty death, a police suicide, or use of deadly force. A significant proportion of police officers who use deadly force are likely to leave law enforcement within five years.

Compared with other occupations, the personal stressors that police experience as a result of job-related stress include a higher incidence of cancer (particularly of the colon and the liver), diabetes, and heart disease. The longer law enforcement officers remain in their job, the higher their risk for these diseases. The divorce rate is higher among law enforcement officers than among the general population, as are the rates of alcoholism and death from cancer (particularly of the colon and the esophagus), heart disease, and ulcers. The suicide rate for law enforcement officers is the highest in comparison with any other occupational group. Finally, the rate for premature death among law enforcement officers is higher than that in other occupations. (North Carolina Coalition of Police, 2000)

INTRODUCTION

health psychology
scientific and practice field that contributes to understanding health behaviour and the treatment, rehabilitation, and prevention approaches that evolve from such an understanding

Health psychology is the scientific and practice field that contributes to understanding health behaviour and the treatment, rehabilitation, and prevention approaches that evolve from such an understanding. Why people become ill, how they react to being ill, and what they do to ruin their health or to stay healthy are some of the important questions that health psychologists examine.

The field of health psychology is highly relevant to the personal and professional lives of those who are or intend to become law enforcement officers. This chapter discusses factors that have a negative influence on health, such as stress, as well as major health issues.

HEALTH AND STRESS

health
the absence of disease; a positive state of physical, mental, and social well-being; a resource that can be used to influence the quality of life

stress
physical or psychological reaction to threat

Health is not an easy concept to define: it may mean the absence of disease; a positive state of physical, mental, and social well-being; or a resource that can be used to influence the quality of life. While we may have different views on the definition of health, most of us seem to agree that health is more than just not being sick.

Of the many factors that affect health, stress is key. **Stress** can be the spice of life when it allows growth and development. Hans Selye (1907–1982), a Canadian scientist who contributed much to our understanding of stress, coined the term *eustress* to describe positive stress (Selye, 1975). On the other hand, negative stress (*distress*) can be the kiss of death when it takes its toll on health.

Stress and law enforcement work go hand in hand. Stress is described as the silent killer within the ranks of law enforcement. Its negative effects are seen in the high rates of alcoholism and drug dependency, divorce, heart problems, marital conflict, suicide, stomach problems, and premature death among police officers (Briant, 2000; Leach, 2000; North Carolina Coalition of Police, 2000; Picore, 2000).

Like health, stress is not an easy concept to define, and it is viewed differently by different stress experts (Martin, 1989; Martin, Kazarian, & Breiter, 1995). The following sections present three perspectives on stress: the stimulus view, the response view, and the stimulus–response view.

Stimulus View of Stress: Changes in Life

The *stimulus view*, or life-change model, considers stress an event that requires physiological, cognitive, or behavioural adjustment or adaptation, and that compromises an individual's physical or psychological well-being. Events that cause stress reactions are called **stressors**. **Acute stressors** are temporary or last a short time, such as awaiting surgery. **Chronic stressors** are continuous or longer-lasting and include poverty, unemployment, or ill health that lasts a long time. Four types of stressors are described below.

stressors
events that cause stress reactions or responses

acute stressors
stressors that are temporary or last a short time

chronic stressors
stressors that are continuous or last a long time

CATASTROPHIC EVENTS

Catastrophic events are extreme or out-of-the-ordinary human experiences that are either witnessed or experienced directly. Examples include violent personal assaults (sexual assault, physical attack, robbery, mugging, and so on), natural or human-made disasters (for example, plane crash, earthquake, fire, severe car accident), torture, ethnic cleansing, and genocide.

The shooting of a law enforcement officer, being taken hostage, and prison riots are examples of catastrophic events in law enforcement. Jack Ritchie, a Toronto Police Association executive, described "traumatic nightmare" situations as those in which the spouses of police officers hear a knock at their door in the middle of the night and are informed that their partners have been shot—and that is *all* the information they have (Gray, 2000). As described in Chapter 10, catastrophic events can cause post-traumatic stress disorder.

MAJOR LIFE EVENTS

Major life events are ordinary personal experiences that most people find stressful and that require adjustment and adaptation. A well-known measure of major life events is the *Social Readjustment Rating Scale* (Holmes & Rahe, 1967), which ranks various life events from those that require the least life changes and the least adaptation to those that require the greatest life changes and the greatest adaptation. Life events that require the greatest life changes and adaptation are considered the most stressful—some examples include the death of a spouse, a jail term, marriage, and the birth of a child. As you can see, major life events do not have to be negative to be stressful. Positive life events can create stress responses because they also require varying degrees of adaptation. Still, negative life events are likely to produce greater stress responses than those that are positive. In addition, some life events that are seen as negative (for example, separation or divorce) may in fact be welcome and have positive consequences for a person's well-being.

The *Social Readjustment Rating Scale* is used in research that attempts to show the relationship between stress and health. A high level of stressful events has been shown to be bad for a person's health, both physical (for example, by contributing to diabetes, heart disease, leukemia, and colds and influenza) and psychological (for example, by contributing to depression).

MINOR LIFE EVENTS

The little ongoing hassles in life also adversely affect a person's physical and psychological well-being. Negative minor life events are everyday irritants that create a stress response (Delongis, Folkman, & Lazarus, 1988): misplacing your eyeglasses or keys, the car not starting first thing in the morning, the irritating behaviour of co-workers, a colleague breaking a promise, criticism from a supervisor, waiting in a long line at the store, and spilling your coffee are some examples. Positive minor life events are **uplifts**, or events that make people feel good about themselves and life (Kanner et al., 1981). Examples of uplifts include receiving a compliment from your boss, being invited to a party, and doing something well. Their frequent occurrence enhances personal well-being.

uplift
positive minor life event

Daily hassles can accumulate and negatively affect a person's physical or psychological well-being to the same extent as major life events. Such health problems as backache, headache, sore throat, and flu are all linked to minor life events (Delongis et al., 1988).

DIVERSITY-RELATED LIFE EVENTS

Notably absent in mainstream stress theory and research is consideration of stressors that are specific to diversity. Diversity-related stress refers to negative life events that people experience because they differ from the mainstream culture around them. Diversity stressors include those related to age, sex, ethnicity, physical or mental disability, race, culture, or socio-economic level (Kazarian, 2001).

Racism-related stress refers to the multiple ways that racism is experienced in life (Harrell, 2000). An important aspect of racism-related stress is racism-related life events, stressful experiences that involve race and occur across a variety of life domains. Examples of such events include being harassed by law enforcement officers and being discriminated against in housing. People who are subjected to "alive and sick" racism-related stress tend to do poorly physically, psychologically, socially, functionally, and spiritually (Harrell, 2000).

A Heart and Stroke Foundation survey showed that workplace demands, family needs, and finances were the top three sources of stress (Turner, 2000). The burdens of major life events, daily hassles, and diversity-related life events seem disproportionately heavy for women, people who live in a host culture that views diversity negatively, and lower-income individuals (Federal, Provincial, and Territorial Advisory Committee on Population Health, 1999; World Health Organization, 2000a).

acculturation
process of adaptation or change that results from people of diverse cultures being in continuous contact with one another

Acculturation is the process of adaptation or change that results from people of diverse cultures being in continuous contact with one another. Psychological, socio-economic, and physical environmental (excessive noise and pollution) stressors produce stress responses that contribute to psychological and physical ill health. Psychological ill health may take the form of anxiety, depression, substance use, or suicide. Physical ill health may present in the form of cancer, chronic pain, common colds, heart attacks, hypertension, or ulcers. People facing acculturation in a new host culture may experience **acculturative stress**, the negative consequence of acculturation, which may also result in psychological or physical ill health (Berry, 1998).

acculturative stress
negative consequence of acculturation

Compared with men, women are likely to experience more illiteracy, less pay for comparable work, sex discrimination, and sexual harassment. Similarly, newcomers, immigrants, refugees, and people from diverse "minority" cultures (ethnic groups, gays and lesbians, people with mental and physical disabilities) in intolerant host cultures are more likely to experience acculturative stress and to encounter threatened, perceived, and actual discrimination than those from the "majority" groups. Finally, people from lower-income groups are at higher risk for exposure to unsafe work conditions and occupational stress than those from higher-income levels. Income seems to be the single most powerful predictor of health status. Wealth means health. People in the lowest income bracket are less likely to report their health as being very good or excellent, and are more likely to die earlier and suffer more illnesses than higher-income individuals (Federal, Provincial, and Territorial Advisory Committee on Population Health, 1999).

STRESSORS AND LAW ENFORCEMENT

Stressors that are common to law enforcement work include organizational demands, lack of involvement in organizational decisions, shift work, career development and advancement, killing someone, and losing a fellow officer in the line of duty. The last two are ranked most stressful to officers (North Carolina Coalition of

Police, 2000). Diversity factors (such as culture, sex, and sexual orientation) are related to the level of stress and types of stressors experienced.

Response View of Stress: Fight or Flight

Dr. Hans Selye was a proponent of the *response view* of stress, which considers the body's physical and psychological reactions to biological stressors. *Biological stressors* are events that challenge or offend the body, such as viral or bacterial infection, physical trauma, disease, and malnutrition. Selye offered the **General Adaptation Syndrome** as an approach to understanding the relationship between stress and physical health (Selye, 1976). He described the General Adaptation Syndrome as consisting of three phases:

General Adaptation Syndrome
sequence of reactions to stressors

1. Alarm/mobilization stage: This is the "call to arms" stage. Stressors alert the body to act, in much the same way that burglar alarms alert police to act (Selye, 1956). The sympathetic nervous system (see Chapter 2) reacts immediately to the assault: the individual may experience increased blood pressure and blood sugar, a rapid heartbeat, and more muscle tension. Stress hormones, such as cortisol, are released to help the body cope with the stressor.

2. Resistance stage: In this stage, the body continues to defend against the injury or disease, tries to destroy it, or decides to coexist and "sleep with the enemy." If adaptation to the disease is successful, the symptoms disappear. Needless to say, the battle against the enemy consumes the individual's body and mind. The continued release of stress hormones weakens the body's immune system and may also lead to cognitive impairments.

3. Exhaustion stage: In this stage, the individual's physical and psychological ammunition are so depleted that he or she is prepared to declare defeat and suffer the humiliation of surrender. Those who surrender or are allowed to surrender develop physical problems (for example, ulcers) or psychological problems (for example, depression), their immune system may be suppressed, or they may even die. It is important to note that exhaustion or surrender is not inevitable. The bodies and minds of people in the resistance stage may bounce back so that they never progress to the exhaustion stage. In addition, those who advance to this stage may retreat or may be forced to retreat to rest.

Originally, the General Adaptation Syndrome was a way of understanding the body's physical response to biological stressors. The model allowed the possibility that people experiencing the same set of stressors might develop different physical and psychological symptoms. Stressors may primarily affect the weakest organs in individuals, causing impairment and disease. This may explain why one person develops heart disease in the face of continual stressors while another person develops ulcers or hypertension.

Since its development, Selye's stress response (or "fight or flight") model has been found to be useful in explaining bodily wear and tear due to a wide variety of stressors: psychological (assault on self-esteem, physical bullying), socio-economic (crowding, poverty), cultural (acculturation and diversism, explained in Chapter 12), and physical environmental (excessive noise, pollution).

Stimulus–Response View of Stress: In the Eye of the Beholder

The major weakness of the stimulus view of stress is its limited focus on external events that trigger the stress reaction. The major weakness of the response view of stress is its exclusive concern with the body's reaction to troublesome events. The factors that both views miss are captured by the *stimulus–response view* of stress. A champion of this view of stress and coping, Richard Lazarus (1966), introduces *cognition* as a factor in the stress process. Lazarus suggests that the experience of stress is highly personal and subjective (Lazarus & Folkman, 1984). He and his colleagues claim that an event in and of itself does not cause the stress response, but a person's perception or appraisal of the event does. The perceptions of the same event reported by two people may be completely different. For example, taking psychological tests for entry into a city police service may be overwhelmingly stressful for Sandra but may be experienced as a positive challenge by Cassandra. In general, stressors that are *predictable* and *controllable* are perceived as less stressful than those that are unpredictable and uncontrollable.

Lazarus identifies four phases of the stress response process:

1. Causal agent: This is an objective internal or external event that has the potential to be perceived as stressful, conflictual, frustrating, or requiring change. Causal agents are the same as stressors—for example, responding to a crisis call, chasing a suspect, and trouble with the boss.

2. Primary appraisal: This is the process in which an individual evaluates the meaning or significance of an event according to its potential effect on personal well-being. Events are appraised as challenging (positive), irrelevant, or stressful (negative).

3. Secondary appraisal: This is the process in which individuals evaluate their coping approaches (options and potential decisions) and resources. Coping resources are physical (such as health and level of energy), social (such as availability of family and friends for support), psychological (such as self-esteem and skills), and material (such as money). People with adequate resources to cope with a stressful event experience lower levels of stress than those with limited resources.

4. Stress reaction: The stress reaction consists of physiological, emotional, and behavioural patterns of responding to the stressful event. Physiological reactions to stress include autonomic arousal (for example, sweating, increased heart rate) and hormonal fluctuations. Emotional reactions include anger, anxiety, depression, fear, and grief. Behavioural reactions include lashing out at others and problem solving.

STRESS AND COPING

Stress and coping are an integral part of the lives of law enforcement officers. Officers must always be physically and mentally alert to respond effectively and efficiently to crises and threats. Failure to respond quickly or to cope competently with threats can cost officers their lives or can cost the lives of others.

Everyone handles personal and work stress differently. Officer Raj is poor at coping with stress in life. He tends to throw in the towel and give up when the slightest thing goes wrong at work. Officer Tranh copes well with stress. He sees stressors at work as challenging opportunities for problem solving and creativity. Unfortunately, there are more Rajs than Tranhs. A Heart and Stroke Foundation survey showed that three-quarters of those surveyed reported harmful coping strategies—that is, eating fatty comfort foods, watching television, smoking, or drinking alcohol (Turner, 2000).

Coping is the process of dealing with stressors for the purpose of minimizing, reducing, or learning to tolerate physical and psychological wear and tear. People use a variety of conscious and unconscious coping strategies to deal successfully with stressful events. Effective coping makes stressors considerably less troublesome than does ineffective coping.

coping
process of dealing with stressors to minimize, reduce, or learn to tolerate physical and psychological wear and tear

Coping strategies at the unconscious level are the *defence mechanisms*. As discussed in Chapter 8, defence mechanisms are approaches to dealing with stressors that allow people to distort or deny threats associated with stressful events. Defence mechanisms are effective coping strategies in the short term but are ineffective in the long term because they fail to deal with reality. Like a coverup, they hide reality, but reality will resurface sooner or later.

Coping strategies at the conscious level are emotion-focused or problem-focused (Folkman & Lazarus, 1980, 1988).

Emotion-Focused Coping

Emotion-focused coping involves consciously regulating the feelings evoked by stressful events. Here are some emotion-focused coping strategies:

emotion-focused coping
approach to dealing with stress that involves consciously regulating the feelings evoked by stressful events

- perceiving the stressor as a challenge rather than a threat;
- looking at the bright side of a stressor;
- seeking emotional support and comfort from others;
- praying;
- looking at the situation with a sense of humour;
- overeating;
- using alcohol or drugs;
- engaging in promiscuous sex;
- fantasizing; and
- engaging in wishful thinking.

These coping strategies can be healthy or unhealthy. For example, a good laugh can ease tension and make a threatening situation less stressful. However, humour can be unhealthy when it is used excessively to put oneself or others down (Roelofsen, 2000).

Problem-Focused Coping

problem-focused coping
approach to dealing with stress that involves facing the stressor for the purpose of solution and resolution

Problem-focused coping involves facing the stressor squarely for the purpose of solution and resolution. Staff Sergeant Leslie realized that she and her family were suffering because of her seemingly irrational outbursts of anger at home. She decided to seek counselling to help her understand her issues with domestic anger and to learn anger management skills. In this case, Staff Sergeant Leslie used a problem-focused coping strategy to deal with a personal stressor that involved her husband and children. The following are some problem-focused coping strategies:

- acting to resolve the stressful situation;
- getting help from others to deal with the stressor;
- seeking professional advice;
- removing oneself from the stressful situation; and
- acting proactively to prevent similar situations from happening again.

Law Enforcement and Coping

 Both emotion-focused and problem-focused coping may be applied in stressful situations, though emotion-focused strategies may be used more for personal stressors than for work-related stressors. Stress management training, anger management training, critical incident debriefings, circuit weight training, and sleep management training are also being offered to law enforcement officers to promote department wellness, increase morale, improve job performance, and decrease burnout. Research suggests that managing leisure pursuits is associated with effective coping among police officers (Box 9.1).

Stress experts ("stressperts") point out that using multiple coping strategies is more likely to reduce job stress and burnout and buffer against stress-related illness than using a single coping strategy. Here are a number of useful stress management strategies:

- Identifying key personal symptoms and sources of stress: Stress symptoms may include tense muscles, headaches, and feelings of edginess or wanting to withdraw.

- Progressive muscular relaxation: This technique involves learning to induce relaxation by tensing and then releasing various muscle groups in the body. Alternative forms of relaxation include meditation and yoga.

- Stress-inoculation training: Stress inoculation can be used to deal with anxiety, anger, or pain. It involves using coping statements or appropriate self-talk to prepare for a stressor, in the face of the stressor, in the face of feeling overwhelmed by the stressor, and after facing the stressor. Examples of self-statements to deal with anxiety-provoking stressors include "Take a slow, deep breath and relax" and "It will be over soon." Examples of self-statements to deal with anger-provoking stressors include "I'll know what to do if I start getting upset" and "Don't take things personally, keep your cool." Examples of self-statements to deal with pain-provoking stressors include "I will focus on what I have to do" and "Don't think about the pain, just use your coping skills."

Ray Novaco (1977) has used the stress inoculation model to teach law enforcement officers anger management. There are three stages to his approach: (1) the *cognitive preparation* stage helps officers understand stressful situations that they encounter in policing and their reactions to these situations (typical situations include being called a pig, a drunk throwing up in the police cruiser, someone refusing to carry out a police order, and being assaulted); (2) the *skill acquisition and rehearsal* stage involves strategies to handle various policing situations; and (3) the *practice* stage comprises applying the learned coping techniques in a series of simulated policing incidents.

- Physical fitness: A person who is physically fit has more physical resources to deal with stress.

- Working off stress: Working off stress means using physical activity to blow off steam.

- Proper nutrition: Proper nutrition contributes to physical fitness and health.

BOX 9.1   The Benefits of Leisure

What do you do in your leisure time? People occupy their leisure with many different pursuits, including fitness activities, spending time with friends, relaxing in front of the TV, exploring nature, attending concerts or movies, pursuing hobbies, travelling, and so on. As in these examples, leisure is often taken to mean a specific activity (such as gardening), but it may also be described more broadly to include a psychological experience involving emotions, moods, and attitudes.

Researchers at the University of Manitoba and the University of Waterloo have found that for police officers and emergency response workers, leisure is related to coping effectiveness and mental and physical health. Among the findings of this research:

- Relaxing leisure activities (for example, listening to music, reading, meditation) were most strongly associated with effective coping with stress.

- The frequency of engaging in relaxing leisure was associated with mental health outcomes; more frequent relaxing leisure predicted better mental health.

- Physically active leisure activities were not associated with coping effectiveness or with health (perhaps because police work involves high levels of physical activity).

- More frequent engagement in social leisure was associated with better mental health outcomes.

- Engagement in cultural leisure pursuits and outdoor recreation were associated with better physical and mental health, respectively.

- Greater reported enjoyment of leisure was associated with coping effectiveness and better mental health outcomes.

Source: Iwasaki et al. (2005).

STRESS BUFFERS

stress buffers
factors that reduce the negative outcomes of high stress

Stress buffers are factors that protect people from the negative effects of stress. Stress experts identify hardiness and a supportive social environment as stress buffers.

Hardiness

hardiness
personal characteristics of commitment, willingness to face challenge, and sense of control that help to make a person more resistant to stress

Hardiness includes the personal characteristics of *commitment*, *willingness to face challenge*, and *sense of control*. Commitment is active participation in life and a sense that personal activities are important and meaningful. The opposite of commitment is alienation. A willingness to face challenge is a belief that change is a fact of life and a motivator for growth rather than a threat to security. The opposite of challenge is the perception of threat. A sense of control reflects the belief that events in life can be influenced by one's actions. The opposite of control is powerlessness. Hardy people are optimistic and use direct approaches to deal with stressors. This makes them less susceptible to the negative effects of stress.

Law enforcement work allows some control in the form of discretion. However, many aspects of this work prevent officers from having a sense of control (North Carolina Coalition of Police, 2000):

- Law enforcement officers must follow to the letter all policies and procedures associated with their respective police services.

- Law enforcement officers have to deal with situations that require change, but such change is often beyond their control—for example, they may be unable to meet the needs of the community owing to inadequate resources.

- Law enforcement officers encounter incidents in which their efforts and actions do not produce the desired outcomes—for example, they are unable to prevent fatalities or save innocent victims of crime.

Supportive Social Environment

A *supportive social environment* refers to the emotional, financial, and moral support, help, care, and respect a person receives in times of stress from family, friends, relatives, and neighbours (Kazarian & McCabe, 1991; Baker, Kazarian, & Marquez-Julio, 1994). Social support may cause a person to feel a stronger sense of identity and community. It may even stimulate the immune system (Baron et al., 1990). The absence of social support is loneliness. The overabundance of social support is overprotectiveness. A balanced support system for law enforcement officers is essential. Support may range from someone to talk to to an employee assistance program.

HEALTH AND DISEASE

The stress-related diseases that cause the majority of deaths in industrialized countries are coronary heart disease and cancer. Human immunodeficiency virus/acquired immunodeficiency syndrome (HIV/AIDS) is also affected by stress. These diseases are strongly influenced by behavioural factors. Another behavioural factor in compromising health is substance abuse.

Coronary Heart Disease

Coronary heart disease is the number one killer of men and women in North America, and costs Canadians $19 billion every year in medical services and loss of income and productivity (Hackam, 2000). Coronary heart disease is a result of coronary atherosclerosis. This condition occurs when cholesterol and fatty substances accumulate and form plaque on the inner walls of the coronary arteries, which feed blood to the heart. Atherosclerosis narrows the arteries to the point that the heart becomes starved for oxygen.

Angina, or chest pain, is the earliest recognizable symptom of coronary heart disease. The person having an angina attack may experience sensations of squeezing, fullness, or pain in the centre of the chest in episodes that last for several minutes and recur periodically. Pain may also spread to the shoulders, neck, or arms. Additional symptoms of coronary heart disease that women tend to experience more than men include swelling of the ankles or lower legs, chronic fatigue, dizziness, rapid heartbeat, shortness of breath, and stomach upset.

Atherosclerosis causes heart attacks, which are in turn the result of a blood clot or obstruction completely blocking an artery. The Heart and Stroke Foundation of Canada (2001) lists these warning signs of a heart attack:

- heaviness, pressure, squeezing, fullness, burning, or discomfort in the centre of the chest that may spread to the neck, jaw, shoulders, arm, or back;

- shortness of breath, paleness, sweating, and weakness;

- nausea, vomiting, or indigestion; and/or

- fear, anxiety, or denial.

The following are ten risk factors for coronary heart disease (National Heart Foundation, 1999):

- age—older people are at greater risk;

- gender—men are at greater risk at a younger age than women, but women who have passed menopause have a risk equal to men at the same age;

- genetic predisposition—a family history of heart disease;

- diabetes;

- high cholesterol level;

- high blood pressure;

- smoking;

- obesity;

- sedentary lifestyle—physical inactivity; and

- stress.

Type A personality
personality that is generally aggressive, competitive, hostile, in a rush all the time, doing several things at once, and constantly striving for achievement

Type B personality
personality that is generally easygoing, patient, and relaxed

The Type A personality is a group of behavioural patterns that place the individual at higher risk for heart attack than the Type B personality. The **Type A personality** is aggressive, competitive, hostile, in a rush all the time, doing several things at once, and constantly striving for achievement. The **Type B personality** has the opposite behavioural patterns—that is, easygoing, patient, and relaxed. The personality traits associated with the Type A personality are necessary ingredients for successful policing (North Carolina Coalition of Police, 2000). Time urgency is part of the daily routine of police work. Similarly, hostile and angry encounters with citizens are a usual part of policing.

It is likely that not all of the Type A characteristics impair health. Attempts to separate the less risky from the more risky behavioural patterns have identified anger and hostility as the main culprits in heart disease. It seems that anger kills (Williams & Williams, 1993; Iribarren et al., 2000), and that teaching people effective ways of dealing with their hostility is more helpful in lowering their risk of heart attack than asking them to slow down in life.

Cancer

cancer
disease in which cells become abnormal and keep dividing and forming more cells without order or control

Cancer is second only to cardiovascular disease as the leading cause of death in North America. **Cancer** is a biological disease process in which cells become abnormal and keep dividing and forming more cells without order or control (Canadian Cancer Society, 2001). All bodily organs are made of cells. Whenever the body requires more cells to stay healthy, cells divide in an orderly fashion and generate the needed cells. When cells keep dividing and exceed the requirement for the new needed cells, a mass of extra tissue forms that is called a growth or *tumour*.

A tumour can be benign or malignant. A benign tumour is not cancerous or life-threatening, and it does not spread to other parts of the body. It can usually be removed with the promise that, in most cases, it will not come back. A malignant tumour is cancerous. Cancerous cells can invade and damage nearby tissues and organs. They also have the potential to spread cancer from the original tumour and form new tumours in other parts of the body. Cancerous cells spread cancer by splitting up or breaking away from a malignant tumour and entering the bloodstream or the lymphatic system. The spread of cancer is known as metastasis.

There are more than 100 different types of cancer. Common ones include breast cancer, lung cancer, prostate cancer, and skin cancer. Note that early cancer usually does not cause pain, so a person should not wait to feel pain before consulting a doctor.

Cancer is believed to develop gradually as a result of a complex interplay among environmental, hereditary, and lifestyle factors. The following are risk factors for cancer (National Cancer Institute, 2001; Temoshok & Dreher, 1992):

- smoking and being exposed to other people's tobacco smoke;

- high-fat diet;

- being overweight;

- being exposed to ultraviolet radiation from the sun and from other sources (such as sun lamps and tanning booths);

- consuming large amounts of alcohol (more than one or two drinks a day);

- being repeatedly exposed to X-ray radiation;

- being exposed to chemicals and other substances in the workplace (for example, asbestos, dust, metals, pesticides, uranium);

- using hormone replacements during menopause, such as estrogen (increased risk for cancer of the uterus) and progesterone in combination with estrogen (increased risk of breast cancer);

- using or being exposed to diethylstilbestrol, a form of estrogen used from the early 1940s until 1971 to prevent miscarriage;

- suffering prolonged stress or depression;

- having a family history of cancer; and

- having a Type C personality (see below).

Some research suggests a link between stress and cancer, but the evidence is not conclusive. Stress may not have the capacity to make normal cells cancerous, but it may interfere with the ability of the immune system to kill cancerous cells (Evans, 1991). A link between cancer and depression is evident because the death rate from cancer among people with depression is twice the norm (Shekelle et al., 1981). Finally, Type C behaviour is a risk factor for cancer (Temoshok & Dreher, 1992). The **Type C personality** is inhibited about talking with others about problems, uptight, emotionally unexpressive, and constrained.

Coping strategies for cancer include an optimistic attitude, a realistic acceptance of the cancer, a sense of humour, the ability to be distracted from thinking about the cancer all the time, the ability to discuss personal matters with others, and social support (Temoshok & Dreher, 1992).

Type C personality personality that is generally inhibited about talking with others about problems, uptight, emotionally unexpressive, and constrained

Acquired Immunodeficiency Syndrome (AIDS)

AIDS is caused by the human immunodeficiency virus (HIV). AIDS is a worldwide epidemic but is particularly prevalant in sub-Saharan Africa (World Health Organization, 2000b). As of 2007, an estimated 33 million people worldwide (adults and children under 15 years old) were living with HIV/AIDS (CIA World Factbook, 2010). In Canada, an estimated 58,000 people were HIV-positive in 2005 (Public Health Agency of Canada, 2006). Among Canadians with HIV/AIDS in 2002, about 59 percent were white, 13 percent Aboriginal, 18 percent black, and 6 percent Asian (Public Health Agency of Canada, 2004).

The AIDS rate in US state and federal prisons is seven times higher than that in the general population. The exceptional risk of prisoners for HIV is primarily due to the link between imprisonment and injection drug use (Kantor, 1998). While there is no confirmed case of a Canadian or US corrections officer being infected from contact with inmates, an Australian report documents an incident in which an officer was "injected by an infected inmate with a syringe full of his own blood" (cited in Kantor, 1998).

HIV is carried in bodily fluids, including blood, breast milk, semen, and vaginal secretions. Contact with these fluids from an infected person—through unprotected sexual intercourse of any kind, from sharing contaminated needles, through broken skin, or during birth or breastfeeding—can result in infection. HIV cannot be contracted through social contact, coughs and sneezes, cutlery, crockery, food, mosquito bites, touching or hugging, or toilet seats. An HIV-positive person has a positive blood test for the virus; being HIV-positive does not mean that the person has AIDS.

HIV infects and kills or functionally impairs cells of the immune system, notably T-helper cells, and gradually destroys the body's ability to fight infections and certain cancers. **T-helper cells** are a type of white blood cell that is important in regulating the immune system and stimulating other cells in the immune system to attack invading germs. A decline in T-helper cells can result in the collapse of the immune system, leaving the person defenceless against infections and malignancies.

The following are early symptoms of HIV infection:

- enlarged lymph glands;

- enlarged tonsils;

- mild fever;

- shingles (a viral infection that causes extremely painful skin lesions around a person's torso, among other symptoms);

- night sweats; and

- weight loss.

As the disease advances with the progressive failure of the immune system, the individual fails to thrive and develops *opportunistic infections*—for example, certain forms of cancer or pneumonia. It takes an average of eight to ten years from infection with HIV to develop full-blown AIDS. After HIV has progressed to diagnosable AIDS, the average survival time with antiretroviral therapy has been estimated at over five years (Schneider et al., 2005). People who die from AIDS and related diseases often experience a slow, undignified death due to the gradual loss of control of bodily functions, loss of memory, and suffering due to rejection and social stigma. People with AIDS are at high risk for depression, feelings of hopelessness, and suicide.

People with AIDS need dignified medical, psychological, and social care. Trials on new anti-HIV drugs seem encouraging, but a cure for HIV/AIDS is not yet in sight. The following are useful strategies in helping people cope with HIV/AIDS:

- education and information about the disease;

- self-care to prevent infection;

- adequate nutrition;

- psychotherapy;

- self-help groups; and

- emotional support from friends and family.

T-helper cell
type of white blood cell that is important in regulating the immune system and stimulating other cells to attack invading germs

Substance Abuse

Tobacco and alcohol abuse are among the leading causes of preventable death in North America. One hundred million people died in the 20th century from tobacco-related causes (Canadian Institutes of Health Research, 2009). Ethyl alcohol is a small, water-soluble molecule. It can reach just about any tissue in the body, and its abuse is associated with increased risks of heart attack, liver damage, cognitive impairment, and a host of cancers.

One of the major goals of health psychologists is to change health-compromising behaviours such as substance abuse. Many techniques have been developed to help addicts into recovery. *Multi-modal* approaches combine various techniques including psychological strategies (for example, stress-management and coping skills, counselling) and biological strategies (for example, nicotine patches, conditioning aversive reactions to drugs). *Harm reduction* is an approach to treat not the addiction itself, but the harmful behaviours that co-occur with the addiction. Providing safe injection sites and clean needles for drug addicts is one example and may reduce the spread of HIV infection. Methadone is sometimes administered to heroin addicts in the hope that it may reduce criminal activities (such as prostitution and break-and-enters) that support addiction to heroin. The first safe injection facility in North America, InSite, opened in Vancouver in 2003. Since opening, InSite has been associated with fewer deaths from overdose and reduced crime rates (Hathaway & Tousaw, 2008). However, the federal government is currently contemplating closing the facility.

POINTS TO REMEMBER

Health is a personal resource that should be treasured. Health psychology is the scientific and practice field that contributes to understanding health behaviour and the treatment, rehabilitation, and prevention approaches that evolve from such an understanding.

Of the many factors in the social and economic environments that affect individual and collective well-being, stress is key. The three major views of stress are the response view, the stimulus view, and the stimulus–response view. Coping is the process of dealing with stressors for the purpose of minimizing or learning to tolerate physical and psychological wear and tear. People use unconscious and conscious coping strategies to deal successfully with stressful events. Hardiness and social support serve as buffers against the negative effects of stress. Three diseases related to stress are coronary heart disease, cancer, and HIV/AIDS. Behaviours that compromise good health include smoking, sedentary lifestyle, and substance abuse.

KEY TERMS

acculturation	health psychology
acculturative stress	problem-focused coping
acute stressors	stress
cancer	stress buffers
chronic stressors	stressors
coping	T-helper cell
emotion-focused coping	Type A personality
General Adaptation Syndrome	Type B personality
hardiness	Type C personality
health	uplift

REFERENCES

Baker, B., S.S. Kazarian, & A. Marquez-Julio. (1994). Perceived interpersonal attitudes and psychiatric complaints in patients with essential hypertension. *Journal of Clinical Psychology, 50,* 320–24.

Baron, R.S., C.E. Cutrona, D. Hicklin, D.W. Russell, & D.M. Lubaroff. (1990). Social support and immune responses among spouses of cancer patients. *Journal of Personality and Social Psychology, 59,* 344–52.

Berry, J.W. (1998). Acculturation and stress: Theory and research. In S.S. Kazarian & D.R. Evans (Eds.), *Cultural clinical psychology: Theory, research and practice* (pp. 39–60). New York: Oxford University Press.

Briant, J.H. (2000). *Stress and diverticulosis: A warning for law enforcement officers.* http://www.communitypolicing.org/publications/artbytop/w6/w6briant.htm.

Canadian Cancer Society. (2001). *What is cancer?* http://www.cancer.ca/indexe3.htm.

Canadian Institutes of Health Research. (2009). *The science behind combating the greatest threat to global health: Tobacco use.* http://www.cihr-irsc.gc.ca/e/40292.html.

CIA World Factbook. (2010). *Country comparison: HIV/AIDS: People living with HIV/AIDS.* https://www.cia.gov/library/publications/the-world-factbook/rankorder/2156rank.html?countryName=Bhutan&countryCode=bt&regionCode=sas&rank=162#bt.

Delongis, A., S. Folkman, & R.S. Lazarus. (1988). The impact of daily stress on health and mood: Psychological social resources as mediators. *Journal of Personality and Social Psychology, 54,* 486–95.

Evans, M.G. (1991). The problem of analyzing multiplicative composites: Interactions revisited. *American Psychologist, 46,* 6–15.

Federal, Provincial, and Territorial Advisory Committee on Population Health. (1999). *Toward a healthy future: Second report on the health of Canadians.* Ottawa: Minister of Public Works and Government Services Canada.

Folkman, S., & R.S. Lazarus. (1980, December). An analysis of coping in a middle-aged community sample. *Journal of Health and Social Behaviour, 21,* 219–39.

Folkman, S., & R.S. Lazarus. (1988). Coping as a mediator of emotion. *Journal of Personality and Social Psychology, 54* (3), 466–75.

Gray, B. (2000, May 23). On-duty shooting cop's nightmare. *The London Free Press,* p. A10.

Hackam, D. (2000). Progress in cardiovascular medicine. *University of Western Ontario Medical Journal, 70,* 6.

Harrell, S.P. (2000, January). A multidimensional conceptualization of racism-related stress: Implications for the well-being of people of color. *American Journal of Orthopsychiatry, 70* (1), 42–57.

Hathaway, A.D., & K.I. Tousaw. (2008). Harm reduction headway and continuing resistance: Insights from safe injection in the city of Vancouver. *International Journal of Drug Policy, 19,* 11–16.

Heart and Stroke Foundation of Canada. (2001). *Heart attack warning signs.* http://www.na.heartandstroke.ca/cgi-bin/English/Catalog/Public/bR.cgi.

Holmes, T.H., & R.H. Rahe. (1967). The Social Readjustment Rating Scale. *Journal of Psychosomatic Research, 11,* 213–18.

Iribarren, C., S. Sidney, D.E. Bild, K. Liu, J.H. Markowitz, J.M. Roseman, & K. Matthews. (2000, May 17). Association of hostility with coronary artery calcification in young adults: The CARDIA study. *Journal of the American Medical Association, 283* (19), 2546–51.

Iwasaki, Y., R.C. Mannell, B.J.A. Smale, & J. Butcher. (2005). Contributions of leisure participation in predicting stress coping and health among police and emergency response services workers. *Journal of Health Psychology, 10,* 79–99.

Kanner, A.D., J.C. Coyne, C. Schaeffer, & R.S. Lazarus. (1981). Comparison of two modes of stress measurement: Daily hassles and uplifts versus major life events. *Journal of Behavioral Medicine, 4* (1), 1–39.

Kantor, E. (1998, May). HIV transmission and prevention in prisons. *HIV InSite Knowledge Base.* http://HIVInSite.ucsf.edu/InSite.jsp?page=kb-07-04-13#SIX.

Kazarian, S.S. (2001). *Diversity issues in law enforcement* (2nd ed.). Toronto: Emond Montgomery.

Kazarian, S.S., & S.B. McCabe. (1991). Dimensions of social support in the MSPSS: Factorial structure, reliability and theoretical implications. *Journal of Community Psychology, 19,* 150–60.

Lazarus, R.S. (1966). *Psychological stress and the coping process.* New York: McGraw-Hill.

Lazarus, R.S., & S. Folkman. (1984). *Stress, appraisal and coping.* New York: Springer.

Leach, J. (2000). *A killer is within our ranks.* http://www.communitypolicing.org/publications/artbytop/w6/w6leach.htm.

Martin, R.A. (1989). Techniques for data acquisition and analysis in field investigations of stress. In R.W.J. Neufeld (Ed.), *Advances in the investigation of psychological stress* (pp. 195–234). New York: John Wiley.

Martin, R.A., S.S. Kazarian, & H.J. Breiter. (1995). Perceived stress, life events, dysfunctional attitudes, and depression in adolescent psychiatric inpatients. *Journal of Psychopathology and Behavioural Assessment, 17* (1), 81–95.

National Cancer Institute. (2001). *Dictionary of cancer terms.* http://cancernet.nci.nih.gov/dictionary.html.

National Heart Foundation. (1999). *About heart disease and stroke: Symptoms.* http://www.ahaf.org/hrtstrok/about/hssymp.htm.

North Carolina Coalition of Police. (2000). *Police stress, psychosomatic disorders and premature death: A proposal advocating early retirement for police officers.* http://www.nccops.org/reference/police_stress.htm.

Novaco, R. (1977). A stress-inoculation approach to anger management in the training of law enforcement officers. *American Journal of Community Psychology, 5,* 327–46.

Picore, D. (2000). *Behind the badge: The hidden stress.* http://www.communitypolicing.org/publications/artbytop/w2/w2-picor.htm.

Public Health Agency of Canada. (2004). *HIV/AIDS epi update—May 2004.* http://www.phac-aspc.gc.ca/publicat/epiu-aepi/epi_update_may_04/8-eng.php.

Public Health Agency of Canada. (2006, July 31). *Estimates of the number of people living with HIV in Canada, 2005.* http://www.phac-aspc.gc.ca/media/nr-rp/2006/20060731-hiv-vih-eng.php.

Roelofsen, M. (2000, February 6). Did you hear the one about the UWO prof? *The London Free Press,* p. C10.

Schneider, M.F., S.J. Gange, C.M. Williams, et al. (2005). Patterns of the hazard of death after AIDS through the evolution of antiretroviral therapy: 1984–2004. *AIDS, 19* (17), 2009–18.

Selye, H. (1956). *The stress of life.* New York: McGraw-Hill.

Selye, H. (1975). Confusion and controversy in the stress field. *Journal of Human Stress, 1* (2), 37–44.

Selye, H. (1976). *The stress of life* (2nd ed.). New York: McGraw-Hill.

Shekelle, R.B., W.J. Rayner, A.M. Ostfield, D.C. Garron, L.A. Bieliauskas, S.C. Liu, C. Maliza, & O. Paul. (1981). Psychological depression and 17-year risk and death from cancer. *Psychosomatic Medicine, 43* (2), 117–25.

Temoshok, L., & H. Dreher. (1992). *The Type C syndrome.* New York: Random House.

Turner, J. (2000, February 25). Feeling a bit stressed? *The Toronto Star*, p. G2.

Williams, R., & V. Williams. (1993). *Anger kills.* New York: Random House.

World Health Organization. (2000a, June). *Gender, health and poverty.* Fact sheet no. 251. http://www.who.int/inf-fs/en/fact251.html.

World Health Organization. (2000b, June 4). *WHO issues new healthy life expectancy rankings: Japan number one in new "health life" system.* Press release. http://www.who.int/inf-pr-2000/en/pr2000-life.html.

EXERCISES AND REVIEW

Self-Test

Circle the correct answer.

1. This chapter has presented the following view of stress and law enforcement work:

    a. stress is an everyday feature of law enforcement work

    b. law enforcement work not only causes work-related stress but also personal stress

    c. law enforcement officers must learn effective coping strategies for the sake of their own lives and the lives of others

    d. all of the above

2. Thelma welcomes the opportunity to speak to young people about safe sex. Louise, on the other hand, dreads the thought and views such an assignment as a threat. The reactions of Thelma and Louise support what view of stress?

    a. stimulus–response

    b. General Adaptation Syndrome

    c. stimulus

    d. all of the above

3. Which of the following represents the stimulus view of stress?

    a. losing a job

    b. dealing with a hostage situation

    c. confronting a prison riot

    d. all of the above

4. Officer Pierre's house burned down because of faulty wiring. Psychologists are likely to classify this event as

   a. a minor hassle

   b. a catastrophic experience

   c. an uplift

   d. something to ponder over

5. Which of the following characterizes emotion-focused coping with a marital problem?

   a. laughing and joking about it with other officers

   b. going to church more often

   c. denying that a problem exists

   d. all of the above

6. Which of the following is likely to buffer the effects of stress on illness?

   a. optimism

   b. the belief that one's actions have an effect on outcomes

   c. supportive friends and relatives

   d. all of the above

7. Which of the following would prevent the spread of HIV among prison inmates?

   a. donating blood or sperm

   b. sharing handmade syringes (from parts of pens and lightbulbs) with other inmates

   c. sharing toothbrushes with other inmates

   d. none of the above

8. Which of the following helps law enforcement officers handle day-to-day challenges in their work?

   a. exercise

   b. balanced diet

   c. relaxation

   d. all of the above

9. Which of the following occupations is the second-most stressful job in North America?

   a. law enforcement officer

   b. air traffic controller

   c. psychologist

   d. solicitor general

10. Illnesses such as heart disease and cancer are likely to

    a. shorten the life expectancy of law enforcement officers

    b. adversely affect the quality of life of law enforcement officers

    c. a and b

    d. none of the above

Thinking About Psychology and Law Enforcement

1. List minor life events (hassles and uplifts) associated with law enforcement work. Compare your list with those of others. Generate strategies to cope with hassles and to increase uplifts to make life less stressful.

2. Why should police services consider making stress-reduction programs and counselling services available for police officers and their families to help them deal with job stress and burnout?

3. Toronto Police Detective Greg Groves was accidentally shot in the abdomen by a fellow officer. Groves's wife, Lisa, was informed about the incident by another officer who knocked at her door. She was whisked to the hospital. The Toronto Police Service makes available to the Groveses, other officers, and dispatchers the Employment Family Assistance Plan to help them deal with the aftermath of catastrophic events. Should police services consider approaches other than "a knock at the door" to inform family members of job-related catastrophic events? If so, what approaches? Is the expense of an Employment Family Assistance Plan a wise investment by police services? Explain.

CHAPTER 10

Psychological Disorders

CHAPTER OBJECTIVES

After completing this chapter, you should be able to:

- Understand the definition and classification of psychological disorders.

- Identify the major psychological disorders.

- Describe the symptoms and causes of major psychological disorders.

- Recognize the personal and occupational importance of mental health in the context of law enforcement.

PREVIEW SCENARIO

Paul Bernardo, a smart and charmingly persuasive 23-year-old, met Karla Homolka, a pretty 17-year-old veterinary assistant, during a Toronto pet industry convention. Within hours, they had sex in a hotel room. Before meeting Homolka, Bernardo had committed at least 14 sexual assaults in the Scarborough, Ontario area, crimes to which he later confessed. Bernardo became engaged to Homolka on December 24, 1989. A year later, he lost his job and began smuggling cigarettes to make money. On December 23, 1990, Homolka "gave" Bernardo her 15-year-old virgin sister, Tammy, as a Christmas present after her fiancé complained that Karla was not a virgin when they met. The pair served Tammy spaghetti spiked with diazepam that Homolka had stolen from the clinic where she worked. Tammy was further sedated by a mixture of alcohol and triazolam, rendered unconscious with a cloth soaked in halothane, and then raped. During the assault, Tammy choked on her vomit and died. Her death was ruled an accident because the drugs in her system went undetected at the time.

Late one night in June 1991, Bernardo accosted and kidnapped 14-year-old Leslie Mahaffy while he was engaged in stealing licence plates for his cigarette smuggling operation. With Homolka, he repeatedly raped Mahaffy over the course of several days and videotaped these assaults. Mahaffy was eventually killed. Her body was dismembered, encased in cement, and thrown into a lake, later to be found by a couple out canoeing.

One year after their lavish wedding in Niagara-on-the-Lake, Bernardo and Homolka kidnapped 15-year-old Kristen French and subjected her to humiliation, torture, and sexual abuse while videotaping these acts. French's dead body was later found in a ditch in Burlington.

Homolka left her husband in January 1993, alleging constant physical abuse from him over a period of six months. Bernardo's increasingly ferocious attacks culminated in his beating her with a flashlight. Homolka was hospitalized after sustaining two black eyes, a hemorrhage in the left eye, a contused forehead, bruises on her neck, arms, and legs, and a puncture wound above her knee. The physician who saw her called it "the worst case of wife assault I have seen." Bernardo was arrested a month later.

Realizing that they were going to be caught, Homolka confessed that Bernardo was a serial rapist and murderer, and negotiated a plea bargain in exchange for testimony against her husband. She quickly agreed to the government's offer of eligibility for parole after serving three years in prison with good behaviour. Later, after all the evidence was in, the plea bargain became known in the press as the "deal with the Devil": although Homolka had portrayed herself as an abused wife forced into abetting Bernardo's criminal activity, later evidence revealed her as a willing participant. Homolka had managed to manipulate the system and escape retrial for her crimes. (Montaldo, various dates; Kari & Associates, 2006)

INTRODUCTION

abnormal psychology
scientific study of behaviours that are seemingly unhealthy, strange, or unusual

Psychological disorders are the subject matter of abnormal psychology. **Abnormal psychology** is the scientific study of behaviours that are seemingly unhealthy, strange, or unusual.

The topic of psychological disorders is highly relevant to law enforcement, which is a high-stress occupation. Officers are expected to maintain a healthy mental balance in the face of daily encounters with dangerous, emotionally charged, and horrific situations, and to endure intrusive public scrutiny and personal accountability. Law enforcement is also embedded in a hierarchical work environment and a "blue" culture that tends to consider discussion of the emotional impact of the job as "wussy crap" and views a police officer struggling with mental health issues as a "nutbar" (Canadian Mental Health Association, 2005).

This chapter discusses the definition and classification of psychological disorders, the consequences of psychiatric labelling, and major forms of psychological disorders, their likely causes, and their implications for law enforcement.

DEFINING AND CLASSIFYING PSYCHOLOGICAL DISORDERS

Distinguishing "normal" behaviour from "abnormal" behaviour is not an easy task. What may be construed as normal in one society or situation may be considered abnormal in another. Further, behaviour that was once considered abnormal may decades later be construed as normal. For example, homosexuality was considered a psychological disorder in the 1970 edition of the *Diagnostic and Statistical Manual of Mental Disorders* (DSM); a decade later, the American Psychiatric Association removed it from the psychiatric classification system.

abnormal behaviour
behaviour that is distressing, dysfunctional, and deviant

Despite the difficulty inherent in defining what is normal and what is pathological, **abnormal behaviour** may be described as behaviour that is distressing, dysfunctional, and deviant. The definition incorporates three criteria that tend to be used in judgments about abnormality. *Distress* refers to the experience of emotional or physical pain. Behaviours are more likely to be judged abnormal if they are intensely distressing to the individual. In many of the conditions described in this chapter, psychological pain such as intense anxiety and deep depression may overwhelm individuals and compromise their ability to function in society.

Similarly, behaviours are more likely to be labelled abnormal if they are *dysfunctional* either for the individual or for the community in which the individual lives. Dysfunctional behaviours are maladaptive and self-defeating conduct in that they interfere with a person's ability to function and hinder meaningful interpersonal relationships in life.

Finally, behaviours are more likely judged as abnormal if they *deviate* from societal or cultural norms. *Norms* are codified or implicit behavioural rules or scripts that dictate how individuals are expected to think, feel, and behave in social and cultural contexts. Laws represent codified norms, and their violation constitutes criminal behaviour. Implicit norms are unwritten cultural rules that govern individual behaviour, such that a person who deviates from the "script" is seen as psychologically disturbed. For example, a student in an introductory psychology for law enforcement class who persistently glares at the teacher in an attempt to intimidate her (don't try this unless you want to risk flunking or expulsion!) is likely to be viewed as psychologically disturbed. Staring at one's teacher in such a manner is inappropriate conduct in a classroom context.

Although any one of the three criteria for abnormal behaviour discussed above could serve as a basis for defining abnormality, two or more of the criteria may be used in describing psychological disorders. An important recognition is that individuals with psychological abnormalities are people with problems rather than "problem people." Another important distinction is that different terminology may be used and preferred in the mental health system than in the criminal justice system. For example, police prefer the term *emotionally disturbed person* (EDP) rather than *mentally ill person*. Similarly, the judicial branch of the criminal justice system emphasizes an individual's fitness to stand trial, whereas the correctional branch focuses on protection, prevention of reoffence, and release (Sinha, 2009).

Diagnosis of Psychological Disorders

In Canada, the *Diagnostic and Statistical Manual of Mental Disorders,* fourth edition (DSM-IV-TR) of the American Psychiatric Association (2000) is the most widely used classification system. It lists more than 350 diagnostic categories with inclusion and exclusion criteria, using five dimensions, or axes, for assessment. Axis I represents a person's current primary clinical diagnosis, such as schizophrenia or bipolar disorder. Axis II reflects mental retardation or long-standing personality disorders such as antisocial personality disorder. Axis III refers to relevant medical conditions, such as diabetes or hypertension. Axis IV identifies psychosocial and environmental problems, including those that relate to family, social relationships, schooling, and housing. Finally, Axis V reflects clinical judgment concerning overall level of functioning, with higher scores suggesting higher functioning.

Consequences of Diagnostic Labels

While classification systems are useful for the science and practice of abnormal psychology, there are important personal, social, and legal consequences to the diagnostic labels that people receive. Diagnostic labels that are construed as degrading and stigmatizing lead to diminishment of morale and self-esteem, and may be cause for social withdrawal. Diagnostic labels may also result in the "self-fulfilling prophecy": in accepting the diagnosis applied to them, people may act in ways that live up to the label. Alcoholics may continue to drink, justifying their actions on the basis that they are alcoholic.

stigma
a label that causes the labelled person to be perceived as different, and in negative light

Diagnostic labels also affect social perception and contribute to stigmatization of the person and the family. A **stigma** is a label that causes a person to be perceived as different, and in negative light. Stigmas are dehumanizing in that society may focus on the "tag" the individual is carrying more than on the person bearing the tag. Stigmatization of psychological disorders and discrimination against the people affected by them are common consequences, despite efforts at public education (Standing Committee on Social Affairs, Science and Technology, 2006). A third serious consequence of stigmatization is deterrence from help-seeking behaviour. Troubled people generally, and law enforcement officers in particular, may refrain from seeking help for fear of being stigmatized.

The legal consequences of psychiatric diagnoses relate to civil liberties. Many individuals with psychological disorders manage to cope with their mental health issues in the community, whereas others may require the protective environment of a general hospital or a mental health centre, and still others may come into conflict with the law (Sinha, 2009). Wilson-Bates (2008) has reported that 31 percent of 1,154 calls to the Vancouver Police Department over a 16-day period were identified as mental health contacts. Similarly, Crocker, Hartford, and Heslop (2009) have shown that 3 percent of interactions with the London (Ontario) Police Service involved men and women with a serious mental illness, even though they represented less than 1 percent of individuals who had contact with the police.

Many people with psychological disorders do not become involved with the criminal justice system. Others come into contact with the system through calls to the police, either as victims or as offenders. In such cases, the need for psychiatric and psychological assessment may arise for determination of safety to self and to the community. Those diagnosed as dangerous to self or to others and suffering from a mental disorder may be committed to a mental institution involuntarily and detained against their will until they are deemed safe to self and community.

Similarly, the competence and sanity of people accused of a crime may come into question. *Competence* is a legal term that refers to a defendant's state of mind at the time of a judicial hearing. A defendant may be subjected to psychiatric and psychological examinations, and if judged as "not competent to stand trial"—that is, too disturbed to understand the legal proceedings—the person may be institutionalized until judged competent. *Sanity* is also a legal term, and refers to the defendant's presumed state of mind at the time the crime was committed. Defendants judged "not criminally responsible"—that is, too severely impaired at the time of the crime to have the capacity to appreciate the wrongfulness of their act or to control their conduct—may be ordered to a mental hospital for treatment.

FORMS OF PSYCHOLOGICAL DISORDERS

Psychological disorders are estimated to affect over 450 million people worldwide (World Health Organization, 2001). In 2002, the Mental Health and Well-being Survey showed that 20 percent of Canadians (24.1 percent of women and 17.0 percent of men) met the criteria for a mood or anxiety disorder or substance dependence at some point during their lifetime (Government of Canada, 2006).

Anxiety Disorders

Anxiety disorder refers to the experience of excessive anxiety, fear, or worry that causes maladaptive behaviours, such as avoidance of situations, that lessen the anxiety. Anxiety symptoms can be physical (rapid heartbeat, sweating, dry mouth), cognitive (worrying, difficulty concentrating), emotional (depression, apprehension, panic), and behavioural (avoidance, escape, restlessness). Anxiety disorders are the most common of the psychological disorders, affecting 11.5 percent of the Canadian population (Government of Canada, 2006). Anxiety disorders affect twice as many women as men.

anxiety disorders
psychological disorders in which anxiety is the major disturbance

ANXIETY DISORDER TYPES

There are five types of anxiety disorders.

Panic Disorder

A person with **panic disorder** has repeated and unexpected panic attacks and worries about future panic attacks. During a panic attack, the person experiences intense fear and may have a rapid heart rate, shortness of breath or a feeling of suffocating, chest pain, nausea, fear of losing control or going crazy, and fear of dying. Panic attacks are often mistaken for heart attacks. Panic disorder occurs with or without agoraphobia (see below). About 3.7 percent of Canadians meet the criteria for panic disorder.

panic disorder
recurrent and unexpected panic attacks

Phobias

Phobias are a set of anxiety disorders in which people have persistent and unrealistic fears about specific objects or situations, become intensely fearful when exposed to those objects or situations, and avoid the sources of the fear at all costs. Even celebrities can suffer from phobias. TV's vampire-slayer Sarah Michelle Gellar ("Buffy") is reported to have a fear of graveyards, while Carmen Electra, of *Baywatch* fame, is scared of water.

phobia
persistent and unrealistic fear of an object or situation

- *Agoraphobia* is an intense fear of being in public places in which escape or help may not be readily available. About 1.5 percent of Canadians meet the criteria for agoraphobia.

- *Social phobia* is an intense fear of being examined and evaluated in social situations or performing in public—for example, attending a party, talking in meetings or classes, or working out in front of others. About 8.1 percent of Canadians meet the criteria for social phobia.

■ *Specific phobia* is an extreme fear of a specific object or situation—for example, animals, the natural environment, blood, injections, injury, airplanes, elevators, or heights.

Generalized Anxiety Disorder

Generalized anxiety disorder refers to experiencing excessive anxiety, apprehension, and worry in a number of situations, not just in response to specific objects or situations.

Obsessive–Compulsive Disorder

obsessive–compulsive disorder
disorder characterized by obsessions and compulsions

People with **obsessive–compulsive disorder** are trapped in repetitive thoughts, impulses, and behaviours. These are recognized as foreign by the person experiencing them, and he or she attempts to resist or suppress them. Common obsessions include fear of contamination (in the form of germs and dirt), images of harm to self or others, intrusive sexual thoughts or urges, excessive religious or moral doubt, unacceptable thoughts, and a need to confess or seek reassurance. Common compulsions include checking, washing, touching, counting, ordering and arranging, and hoarding. In the television series *Monk*, detective Adrian Monk (played by Tony Shalhoub) suffers from obsessive–compulsive disorder.

Post-Traumatic Stress Disorder

post-traumatic stress disorder
severe anxiety disorder that occurs after exposure to a traumatic event

traumatic event
disastrous or extremely painful stressor with severe psychological and physiological consequences

Post-traumatic stress disorder (PTSD) is a severe anxiety disorder seen in many people who have been exposed to traumatic events. A **traumatic event** is a disastrous or an extremely painful stressor with severe psychological and physiological consequences. Traumatic events that are associated with PTSD include encountered or witnessed natural disasters (such as earthquakes), mass-fatality terrorist attacks (such as the attacks on the World Trade Center on 9/11), serious accidents, intentional life-threatening violence by another person (such as rape), or betrayal by someone depended upon for survival. The person experiences repeated and intense memories and dreams of the traumatic event; shows increased arousal in the form of sleep disturbance, irritability and temper outbursts, cynicism, concentration difficulties, and being easily startled; and attempts to ward off thoughts of the event and remain avoidant or detached from it. PTSD affects 9.2 percent of the Canadian population (Hamilton Health Sciences, 2008). The most common reported traumas associated with PTSD are the sudden death of a loved one, sexual assault, and witnessing someone being badly injured or killed.

CAUSES OF ANXIETY DISORDERS

A variety of explanations are offered for the genesis of anxiety disorders (Antony, Federic, & Stein, 2009). The biological explanation of anxiety disorders stresses heredity, structural brain dysfunction, and chemical deficiencies in the brain. In the case of panic disorders, for example, high levels of the neurotransmitter norepinephrine in the brain are implicated. Another theory suggests underactivity or low levels of the neurotransmitter gamma-aminobutyric acid (GABA). In the case of specific phobias, the biological preparedness theory proposes that humans are essentially programmed to fear certain stimuli and situations such as death, disaster, or injury that are likely to threaten human survival. In relation to obsessive–compulsive disorder, the biological perspective suggests dysfunction in the brain circuitry connecting the subcortical and cortical regions that are involved in the inhibition of behaviour. Finally, genetic predisposition, structural change in the brain (for example, in the hippocampus) following the experience of a traumatic event, and neurotransmitter alterations (for example, levels of norepinephrine or dopamine) are suggested in the case of PTSD.

The psychoanalytic approach views anxiety disorders as expressions of unconscious conflicts displaced to external objects or situations. For example, phobia of horses may symbolically represent unconscious hostility toward an authoritarian figure, such as a castrating father.

The behavioural approach explains anxiety disorders as learned responses. The classical conditioning perspective (see Chapter 5) views anxiety disorders as conditioned emotional responses to objects or situations. For example, a police officer who is shot and wounded in a high-crime neighbourhood may develop a fear or phobia about the neighbourhood. Similarly, people with post-traumatic stress disorder may react negatively toward objects or events associated with the original traumatic event. The operant conditioning perspective views anxiety disorders as behaviours that are learned through direct reinforcement, reduction of anxiety, or both.

The cognitive approach emphasizes learning by observation or faulty thinking as a cause of anxiety disorders. People who are exposed to anxiety in others learn its characteristics and may copy them in their own lives. The cognitive approach blames faulty cognitions for causing anxiety disorders—that is, negative ideas, catastrophic thoughts, overappraisal of the world as dangerous, and overattentiveness to internal bodily sensations. For example, people with panic disorder may believe that they will lose control or die on an airplane. While on the airplane, they are likely to interpret minor physical symptoms as signs that they are passing out or are out of control. Similarly, people with a specific phobia, such as claustrophobia (fear of enclosed spaces), may find themselves thinking that they will be trapped or will suffocate and die. Finally, people with a checking compulsion may spend endless hours making absolutely sure that the gas oven is off for fear that if it is left on the house will blow up or burn down.

LAW ENFORCEMENT AND ANXIETY DISORDERS

Law enforcement professionals may be vulnerable to anxiety disorders, particularly post-traumatic stress disorder, because they are at risk for significant exposure to traumatic events. (See Box 10.1.)

Somatoform Disorders

Somatoform disorders are a group of disorders in which people experience physical symptoms that have no apparent physical cause.

somatoform disorders
psychological disorders in which people experience physical symptoms that have no apparent physical cause

SOMATOFORM DISORDER TYPES

There are five types of somatoform disorders.

Conversion Disorder

Conversion disorder is a condition in which an individual has a physical or neurological complaint that has no organic basis—for example, paralysis, blindness, or loss of hearing. This disorder may come on suddenly and may occur after extreme psychological stress.

Somatization Disorder

Somatization disorder is a condition in which an individual has pain and bodily symptoms that have no organic basis. People with this disorder are likely to be "doctor shoppers" and may undergo unnecessary operations.

Pain Disorder

Pain disorder is a condition in which pain is predominant and psychological factors play an important role in when the pain begins, how severe it is, what aggravates it, and so on. This is a relatively common disorder that often involves back pain from a work-related injury.

BOX 10.1   Post-Traumatic Stress Disorder and Law Enforcement

Law enforcement officers confront particular traumatic experiences, such as gruesome accidents, homicides, school or workplace shootings, vicious crimes and grisly crime scenes, personal brushes with death, familial violence, the death or serious injury of partners, and shootings of suspects or innocent civilians. Such intense stressors and other traumatic critical incidents, coupled with the cumulative weight of mundane job-related stressors, can challenge law enforcement officers to the breaking point, induce full-scale post-traumatic stress disorder, and precipitate other quality-of-life issues such as leaving the job, substance abuse, spousal abuse, divorce, and suicide.

Law enforcement professionals tend to view themselves as indestructible, preferring to "swim through boiling oil" rather than admit they need assistance to cope with intense work-related stressors or those on the home front. There is increasing recognition that the prevailing police "macho" culture is a barrier to helping law enforcement officers deal with the stressors and traumas they experience on the job. This barrier has consequences for officers' psychological, physical, and family well-being.

There is also increasing recognition that police are better served with evidence-based supports and services. Critical incident stress debriefing (CISD) following traumatic events and other crisis management alternatives allow emotional processing of the traumatic experiences through ventilation and normalization of feelings. Such interventions have the advantage of better preparing law enforcement officers for similar intense traumas in the future. Ongoing supportive and psychotherapeutic measures can help law enforcement officers and their families deal with psychological distress, such as depression, trauma, aftermath of suicide, and grief.

Sources: Becker et al. (2009); Miller (2006a, 2006b, 2007).

Hypochondriasis

Hypochondriasis is a disorder in which an individual shows persistent preoccupation with his or her state of health and physical well-being.

Body Dysmorphic Disorder

With body dysmorphic disorder, individuals are overly concerned about an imagined fault in their appearance even though they have a normal appearance. These people look in the mirror a lot and target their hair (too much or too little), or size or shape of nose, face, eyes, breasts, or penis for "investigative reporting" (Phillips et al., 1993).

CAUSES OF SOMATOFORM DISORDERS

A variety of factors are implicated in the development of somatoform disorders (Trimble, 2004). The biological perspective suggests the possibilities that somatoform disorders may run in families or that people with these disorders may be more sensitive to internal sensations or pain because of genetically based abnormal arousal levels.

The psychoanalytic and more contemporary psychodynamic approaches view somatoform disorders as unconscious expressions of hostile and sexual conflicts. These conflicts take the form of physical symptoms to defend against anxiety. For example, a "sandwich generation" parent who is overwhelmed with responsibilities to her own children and must also look after her overly critical father may suddenly develop paralysis in her arm. The "psychogenic" paralysis is an unconscious "solution" to the woman's aggressive impulses to strike her father with the "paralyzed" arm.

LAW ENFORCEMENT AND SOMATOFORM DISORDERS

Somatoform disorders are not the same as deliberately faking a symptom to gain something, such as an insurance settlement after a car accident. They are also not the same as factitious disorders, which may come to the attention of law enforcement professionals. **Factitious disorders** are psychological conditions in which physical or mental symptoms are induced or simulated for no apparent reason. For example, Adler and Gosnell (1979) reported the case of a nurse who underwent four exploratory surgeries before it was found that she was injecting herself with fecal matter. Factitious disorder by proxy occurs when a person deliberately feigns or induces illness in another person. Adler and Gosnell (1979) also reported the case of a mother who was caught on a hidden camera suffocating her baby, whom she had brought to hospital for treatment.

factitious disorders
psychological conditions in which physical or mental symptoms are induced or simulated for no apparent reason

Dissociative Disorders: Splitters of Personality

Dissociative disorders are psychological disturbances in which people's identity, memory, and consciousness are changed or disrupted. These disorders are rare. In her autobiography, actress Anne Heche reported dissociative symptoms, attributing them to abuse by her father from the time she was a toddler.

dissociative disorders
psychological disorders in which people's identity, memory, and consciousness are changed or disrupted

DISSOCIATIVE DISORDER TYPES

There are four types of dissociative disorders.

Dissociative Amnesia

Dissociative amnesia is partial or total loss of important facts about one's personal life and identity (for example, name, address, and friends). The disorder tends to occur suddenly and following a stressful or traumatic experience. People with dissociative disorders may be involved with the criminal justice system. In a well-known US case, Lorena Bobbitt, who was in an abusive marriage for years, cut off her husband's penis and later claimed she had no memory of what she had done.

Dissociative Fugue

Dissociative fugue includes the partial or total loss of important facts about one's personal life, a movement away from home, and an assumption of a new identity.

Depersonalization Disorder

People who have depersonalization disorder experience episodes in which they feel detached from their own body or mind—for example, they may describe feeling robot-like.

Dissociative Identity Disorder

dissociative identity disorder
disorder in which two or more separate personalities exist in the same individual

Also called multiple personality disorder, **dissociative identity disorder** (DID) is said to occur when two or more separate personalities exist in the *same* individual. This disorder is a favourite of horror-story writers. The condition is highly controversial in that there are critics who question the very existence of DID.

CAUSES OF DISSOCIATIVE DISORDERS

Various theories have been advanced to explain the genesis of dissociative disorders (Dell & O'Neil, 2009). Repression is at the core of the psychoanalytic explanation of dissociative disorders. People with these disorders are believed to block from their conscious awareness traumatic or unpleasant experiences (for example, physical or sexual abuse). However, when the blocking-out process is incomplete, dissociation may result. In extreme cases, two or more personalities emerge that are sealed off from each other. The trauma-dissociation theory also proposes that new personalities may develop in response to severe stress, typically beginning in early childhood (Putnam, 1989). Children exposed to the trauma of physical or sexual abuse may create an alternate identity to detach themselves from the trauma. The creation of the alternate personality blunts the psychological pain as it transfers what is happening to someone else who is able to handle it.

Recovered-memory therapy is used to treat multiple personality disorder to uncover forgotten sexual abuse. It is now known that some therapists have "uncovered" memories of sexual abuse that they have inadvertently planted in the minds of their patients. An Iowa woman was awarded $13.5 million for being subjected to recovered-memory therapy in which she recalled incidents of Satanism, torture, cannibalism, rape, and child abuse that never happened (Laurence, 1997).

Cognitive–behavioural psychologists believe that reinforcement of illness and parental modelling play a role in causing dissociative disorders. The "sick role" that people with these disorders assume is reinforced because it allows them to escape from unpleasant circumstances or stressors, avoid responsibilities, and gain attention and sympathy from others.

LAW ENFORCEMENT AND DISSOCIATIVE DISORDERS

Law enforcement officers may be called to assist in the search for a person with dissociative fugue. Dissociative disorders also present special challenges to the criminal justice system. For example, the court has to judge the guilt or innocence of the individual when the facts show that one of the multiple personalities committed the crime without the awareness of the other personalities.

Mood Disorders: The Ups and Downs of Mood

Mood disorders are psychological conditions in which depression and mania are the primary mood disturbances. Mood disorders affect 13.4 percent of adult Canadians (10.5 percent of men and 16.1 percent of women), and they may frequently co-occur with anxiety disorders.

mood disorders
psychological disorders in which the primary symptom is mood disturbance

MOOD DISORDER TYPES

People with mood disorders feel extreme lows (depression) or extreme highs (mania), or both. There are two major categories of mood disorders: depression and bipolar disorder.

Depression

Depression refers to a state of mood and behaviour that suggests sadness and loss of interest. Depression is a common psychological disorder, occurring in 12.2 percent of adult Canadians (9.2 percent of men and 15.1 percent of women). Symptoms of depression may be physical (for example, change in eating habits, sleep disturbance), cognitive (for example, loss of self-esteem, feelings of worthlessness, pessimism), emotional (for example, feelings of sadness, loss of pleasure or interest, guilt), behavioural (for example, lethargy, social withdrawal, suicidal acts), and motivational (for example, inability to "get started" or to perform behaviours that result in pleasure or accomplishment). Depressed people do not shed phony tears, nor do they respond to commands to "snap out of it."

depression
mood disturbance characterized by persistent feelings of sadness and loss of interest

Four types of depressive disorders are major depression, dysthymic disorder, seasonal affective disorder, and postpartum depression.

Major depression is an intense depressed state that interferes with the person's ability to function effectively in life. At least five letters of the acronym SAD FACES are present in a major depressive disorder (Wyeth-Ayerst Canada, 1996):

- Sleep—increased or decreased;
- Appetite—increased or decreased, or weight change;
- Depressed mood or loss of interest or pleasure;
- Fatigue—loss of energy;
- Agitation/retardation—anxious or slowed down;
- Concentration—decreased ability to concentrate;
- Esteem—feelings of worthlessness or guilt; and
- Suicidal thoughts.

Dysthymic disorder is a psychological condition in which an individual suffers a less intense form of depression that has less dramatic effects on personal and occupational functioning. "Double depression" refers to a person who suffers from major depressive disorder and dysthymic disorder.

Seasonal affective disorder (SAD) is another form of depression. People with SAD find that their moods change with the seasons, either during the winter or during the summer. Many people feel "blue" in winter, particularly when there are long periods of overcast days. People who suffer from winter SAD can benefit from light therapy.

Postpartum depression is a disturbance in mood in women that occurs within weeks or months of having a baby.

Bipolar Disorder

mania
mood disturbance characterized by persistent feelings of emotional high, agitation, pressured speech, and impulsivity

In *bipolar disorder*, depression alternates with periods of mania. **Mania** refers to a state of highly excited mood and behaviour that suggests euphoria. Manic symptoms may be physical (for example, decreased need for sleep, increased sexual activity), cognitive (for example, distractibility, grandiosity or inflated self-esteem, increased talkativeness and pressure to keep talking, racing thoughts), affective (for example, elated or euphoric mood, extreme irritability), and behavioural (for example, overspending, sexual indiscretion, agitation). Bipolar disorder occurs in 2.4 percent of adults in Canada (2.4 percent of men and 2.3 percent of women).

Three forms of bipolar disorder are bipolar I disorder, cyclothymia, and bipolar II disorder.

Individuals with *bipolar I disorder* experience manic behaviours (extreme highs) and major depression (extreme lows), usually with relatively normal periods in between. People who have four or more cycles of depression and mania within a year are likely suffering from rapid cycling bipolar disorder. People with a bipolar I disorder in a manic state may pose danger to themselves and others. For example, someone may believe that his blood has exceptional qualities and can cure all sickness, and may insist that blood be drawn from him and distributed around the world. If such demands are not immediately met, the person may turn violent.

With *cyclothymia*, an individual suffers chronic hypomania (low-level mania) and depression that are not severe enough to be classified as manic episodes or major depressive episodes.

People with *bipolar II disorder* have experienced one or more major depressive episodes and at least one hypomanic episode.

CAUSES OF MOOD DISORDERS

Biological, psychological, and social factors are likely to contribute to the development of mood disorders (Craighead, Miklowitz, & Craighead, 2008). Mood disorders tend to run in families, hereditary factors being stronger in the bipolar disorders than in the other mood disorders. Genetic factors influence the amount of certain chemicals—norepinephrine, dopamine, and serotonin—in the brain. These neurotransmitters seem to be involved in brain circuits that produce reward and pleasure. It is believed that depression is caused by an undersupply of neurotransmitters and that mania is caused by an oversupply of neurotransmitters.

Loss is a core concept in the psychoanalytic approach to depression. Depressed people are believed to be fixated at the oral stage (see Chapter 8) and develop a dependent "hungry for love" personality. A real or symbolic loss and rejection can shatter their fragile self-esteem and produce anger against the lost object. The anger is then turned against the self, resulting in depression.

Cognitive theorists view depression as a disturbance in thought rather than a disturbance in mood. A major cognitive theory of depression is the cognitive distortion model (Beck, 1967, 1976), which asserts that people with depression have thoughts that distort reality. Some kinds of distorted thoughts include making sweeping generalizations about oneself based on one piece of information, exaggerating negative events, and devaluing positive events. The cognitive distortion model also asserts that beliefs and knowledge about the self are organized into *schema*, or belief systems that help people make sense of their experiences in life and process and organize information. People tend to focus selectively on information that fits their schema and to ignore or distort information that does not. Depressed people are believed to have a depressive cognitive triad of negative schema: negative thoughts about the self, the world, and the future.

Learned helplessness is another major cognitive model of depression. Seligman (1975) defined depression as belief in one's own helplessness. Learned helplessness is the process in which people acquire the belief that they are helpless and cannot control outcomes in their lives. The learned helplessness model was reformulated to explain how cognitive factors might explain different reactions to negative events (Abramson, Seligman, & Teasdale, 1978). This model suggests that people with learned helplessness explain experiences and events in life in terms of three contexts: internal to the individual versus external, stable in time versus unstable, and global versus specific to a particular life domain. Depressed people are believed to explain events in terms of internal, stable, and global contexts. For example, Natasha blames her less-than-desirable performance in her introductory psychology for law enforcement course to being stupid (internal) rather than to having a lousy instructor (external), to a lack of smarts (stable) rather than not having enough study time (unstable), and to being a born loser (global) rather than not doing well just in this course (specific).

Social relationship is at the core of the interpersonal approach to depression, which asserts that poor social support, lack of social skills, or a rocky marriage are bad for people's mental health generally and depression in particular. For example, people are more likely to develop depression if they do not have enough social contacts or others they can confide in, and if they have negative interactions with those who are part of their social support system. The social support available to people may provide a buffer against the negative effects of the stressful events they experience (Brown & Harris, 1978).

Stressors and culture are at the core of the socio-cultural approach to explaining mood disorders (Brown & Harris, 1989; Johnson & Roberts, 1995). For example, the prevalence of mood disorders is likely to be lower in cultures with strong familial and social support systems than in cultures low in familial and social support. Similarly, depression may be less prevalent in peaceful countries than in war-torn countries.

LAW ENFORCEMENT AND MOOD DISORDERS

Law enforcement is a high-stress profession, and law enforcement officers are considered a highly stressed community owing to the nature of their work. One study has shown that exposure to multiple negative life events is associated with depression in police officers, suggesting the need for psychological services to help affected officers cope with major life events and deal with depression (Hartley et al., 2007).

Suicidal Behaviour

suicide
the action of wilfully
taking one's own life

Suicide is the action of wilfully taking one's own life. It is a serious issue nationally and worldwide. The 2002 Mental Health and Well-Being Survey showed that 13.4 percent of Canadians (14.4 percent of women and 12.3 percent of men) over the age of 15 years reported that they had seriously thought about suicide during their lifetime, and 3.1 percent (2.0 percent of men and 4.2 percent of women) had attempted suicide (Government of Canada, 2006). Similarly, Statistics Canada (2009) reported that 3,743 Canadians, representing a rate of 11.6 per 100,000 population, committed suicide in 2005. Hanging, poisoning, and firearms were the most prevalent methods of suicide.

TYPES OF SUICIDAL BEHAVIOUR

Suicidal behaviour takes the form of ideation (thinking about suicide), suicide threat (expression of self-destructive intentions), suicide attempt (self-destructive act with clear death intent), suicide gesture (self-destructive act with little or no death intent), and completed suicide (death by suicide). It is estimated that the suicide of one Canadian costs society $849,877.80 in direct or indirect costs ("Study Puts Suicide Cost," 1999).

Risk factors that increase the likelihood of suicidal behaviour include a suicide plan; history of suicide attempts; lack of community support; recent loss (actual, threatened, or imagined); physical illness, including AIDS or another terminal illness; change in lifestyle, behaviour, or personality; giving away possessions or valuables; putting one's affairs in order (for example, making a will); depression, including feelings of hopelessness and helplessness; substance use; recent discharge from hospital; and anniversaries (for example, death of a loved one).

Protective factors that reduce the risk of suicide include personal resilience, frustration tolerance, adaptive coping skills, optimism, sense of humour, and social support, including the availability of a confidant (Morgan, 2008).

CAUSES OF SUICIDAL BEHAVIOUR

A variety of theories have been advanced as explanations for suicide (Palmer, 2007). Suicide is blamed on a range of factors, from video lottery terminals (Canadian Press, 1997) to the media (copycat suicides) (McCabe, 1997). The biological approach views suicide as a disease or symptom of a disease such as depression, possible defects in genes, and abnormalities in neurotransmitters such as serotonin. Studies of families, twins, and adoptions support the theory of genetic susceptibility to suicide. Actress Margaux Hemingway committed suicide in 1996 at the age of 41 by overdosing on sedative pills. She was the fifth person in her family to commit suicide; her grandfather, Ernest Hemingway, had killed himself 35 years earlier.

According to Durkheim's (1897/1951) sociological approach, suicide is a consequence of individual failure to integrate in religious, communal, or family groups. Vulnerability is even higher for individuals whose previous pattern of social integration is challenged or disrupted (for example, by immigrating to a new country).

Psychological explanations of suicide implicate genetic family history, personality traits (such as impulsivity), substance abuse, and lack of social supports (Kazarian & Persad, 2001). Protective factors against suicide include cognitive flexibility, positive social supports, hopeful outlook, and treatment for psychiatric or personality disorder. Precipitating factors that drive a person "over the edge" include the availability of methods for committing suicide and recent life events, including those seen as humiliating.

SUICIDE AND LAW ENFORCEMENT

Suicide in law enforcement needs to be considered at both the occupational and personal levels. A unique form of suicide in the context of policing is **suicide by cop**, seen when a troubled individual provokes police into shooting him or her (Mohandie, Meloy, & Collins, 2009). In one incident, a 43-year-old woman entered a police station and pointed a realistic-looking pellet gun through bulletproof glass at a police officer. Fortunately, the officer was able to talk to her, persuade her to drop the gun, and arrange her admission to a crisis intervention unit (Associated Press, 2000). Suicide in jails and lock-ups is a second, highly stressful occupational hazard in the context of the criminal justice system (Blasko, Jeglio, & Malkin, 2008). The most critical time is from midnight to 8 a.m., especially on weekends. High-risk periods during an inmate's incarceration include time of entry, times when legal decisions are made (for example, indictment), times of significant loss (for example, breakup of marriage), significant dates (for example, birthdays), and after visits (Ulster County Community Mental Health Services, 1990). Over 95 percent of inmate suicides are accomplished by hanging.

Suicide is a hush-hush topic in law enforcement circles, even though reports in both Canada and the United States suggest that the suicide rate among police is higher than in the general population, and that more law enforcement officers die by suicide than in the line of duty (International Association of Chiefs of Police, 2009; Ritter, 2007; Schaer, 2006). There are many facets to suicide in the context of law enforcement. Belinda Rose, an Ontario Provincial Police constable, was recommended for a bravery citation for dramatically saving the life of a suicidal man ("Officer Saves Suicidal Man," 2001). Sergeant J.W.P. was a married father of two, a 27-year veteran of the highway patrol in Barstow, California, and 1995 Officer of the Year. At age 49 he was found dead on a dirt road by a couple out jogging. He had apparently committed suicide one month after he was arrested on charges of raping a woman in his patrol car. It seems that he left his car, sat down on an old couch near the road, and shot himself in the head with a rifle (Associated Press, 1996).

There is global leadership in law enforcement to jolt the "blue" macho culture in an effort to eliminate the stigma of mental illness generally and suicide in particular. In relation to reducing suicides, law enforcement services are introducing suicide awareness and prevention initiatives specifically designed for law enforcement personnel (Baker, 1996; International Association of Chiefs of Police, 2009; Morgan, 2008). Police suicide awareness training program modules tend to include

suicide by cop
suicide committed by a person by provoking police into shooting him or her

breaking the "blue wall of silence," understanding stress in law enforcement, identifying warning signs and handling a suicidal officer, delineating issues and responsibilities of officer and agency when a suicide occurs, and describing issues of survivors, including guilt and anger.

Schizophrenia: Cancer of the Mind

schizophrenia
psychological disorder characterized by psychotic thoughts, perceptions, feelings, and actions

Schizophrenia refers to severe disturbances in thinking, speech, perception, emotion, and behaviour. The disorder has been described as cancer of the mind. Schizophrenia is considered a psychotic disorder because it involves some loss of contact with reality, together with bizarre behaviours and perceptions. Schizophrenia does not imply laziness, malicious activity, multiple personalities, or a life sentence in a mental hospital (Fernando & Kazarian, 1995). It is a merciless psychological disorder, and people with schizophrenia are often treated as social outcasts. As a result of changes in mental health therapeutics and public policy in the 1960s and 1970s, many individuals with schizophrenia were "deinstitutionalized" (see Chapter 11), and now a shameful number of people with the disorder are homeless and living on the street, in jails and prisons, or in substandard housing. Their quality of life is as cruel as the disorder they suffer from. Schizophrenia affects about 1 percent of the population. Approximately 10 percent of people with schizophrenia are likely to kill themselves (Government of Canada, 2006).

There are positive and negative symptoms of schizophrenia. A positive symptom is an add-on feeling or behaviour; a negative symptom is a loss or deficit in feeling or behaviour.

Positive symptoms

hallucination
sensory experience that is disturbed or disturbing and is real only to the person experiencing it

- **Hallucinations** are sensory experiences without external sensory stimulation. An auditory hallucination is the experience of hearing one or more voices that don't exist. The voices are often frightening and even terrifying, may be accusatory or threatening, or may tell the person to harm herself or others. It is not unusual to see people with schizophrenia on city streets talking back to voices.

    Visual hallucination is the experience of seeing things others do not see. This type of hallucination may accompany auditory hallucinations.

- Disorganized thought and speech are disturbances in thinking and language. These can include loosening of association—the tendency to jump from one topic to another, unrelated one; tangentiality—answering a question in a way that is irrelevant or unrelated to the question; having a severe disturbance in speech that makes it incomprehensible; or linking words on the basis of sound rather than meaning (for example, using only rhyming words).

delusion
fixed belief that is real only to the person holding it

- **Delusions** are false beliefs or unusual misperceptions of reality. They include believing that others are plotting against the schizophrenic person or intend to harm or kill him or her (delusions of persecution); that the schizophrenic person is someone famous or has special abilities (delusions of grandeur); that the schizophrenic person's thoughts and actions are controlled by external powers, people, or objects (delusions of control); that the schizophrenic person's thoughts can be heard by others (delusions of thought broadcasting);

that the schizophrenic person's thoughts are being sucked out of his or her mind like a vacuum cleaner (delusions of thought withdrawal); and that thoughts are being inserted into the schizophrenic person's mind (delusions of thought insertion).

- Disorganized behaviour involves unpredictable or socially disapproved of acts, including agitation, shouting, swearing, pacing, masturbating in public, and wearing clothes that are inappropriate for the weather (few clothes on cold days and heavy clothes on warm days).

- Catatonic behaviour is extreme unresponsiveness to the external world. In catatonic stupor, the schizophrenic person sits motionless for hours and is completely unaware of the outside world. In catatonic posture, the person stays in a bizarre position for a long period of time. Finally, in catatonic excitement the person is extremely agitated and difficult to manage.

Negative symptoms

- Alogia is a deficit in the quality and quantity of speech. The person with schizophrenia does not initiate meaningful speech with others or gives only brief replies to questions.

- Mood disturbances may take the form of anhedonia, inability to feel pleasure; little or no emotion in situations where strong reactions are expected; expressionless face and voice; lack of eye contact with others; and inappropriate emotions (such as laughing while describing the death of a loved one).

- The person with schizophrenia may withdraw from social relationships, become socially isolated, lack close friends, or be unable to sustain friendships.

- The schizophrenic person may lack drive or motivation, be unable to make a decision or complete a task, be disorganized and careless, or spend her day just sitting around and watching television.

SCHIZOPHRENIA TYPES

There are four types of schizophrenia.

- Paranoid schizophrenia: The individual experiences delusions of grandeur and persecution.

- Catatonic schizophrenia: The individual is in a stupor—oblivious to reality, stays in one posture for a long time, or is excessively agitated and excited.

- Disorganized schizophrenia: The individual shows confusion and incoherence, in addition to inappropriate emotional reactions, silliness, laughter, bizarre mannerisms, and deterioration in such adaptive behaviours as personal hygiene.

- Undifferentiated schizophrenia: The individual shows a symptom pattern that does not conform to the other types of schizophrenia or that conforms to more than one type.

CAUSES OF SCHIZOPHRENIA

There is increasing consensus that biological, psychological, and social-environmental vulnerabilities may be implicated in schizophrenia (Hersen & Rosqvist, 2008). In relation to biological considerations, the belief that heredity or genetic predisposition is an important determinant of schizophrenia is supported by research involving blood relatives, twins, adoptions, and children who are at high risk for schizophrenia. Brain abnormalities in the form of enlargement of the ventricles and loss or deterioration of neurons in the cerebral cortex and limbic system are also hypothesized. Finally, the role of neurotransmitters, particularly dopamine, is postulated. The dopamine hypothesis suggests that the dopamine system in areas of the brain that regulate emotional expression, cognition, and motivation may be overactive in people with schizophrenia.

Psychological explanations of schizophrenia are either psychoanalytic and psychodynamic or cognitive in focus. Psychoanalytic and psychodynamic theorists suggest that schizophrenia essentially represents retreat from unbearable stress and conflict or a painful social climate. Cognitive theorists, on the other hand, consider an information processing approach, proposing a defect in the attentional processes of people with schizophrenia. More specifically, they suggest that people with schizophrenia feel overwhelmed by the external and internal stimulus overload that they experience because they are unable to sort the relevant from the irrelevant. The stimulus overload seen in people with schizophrenia may be due to structural malfunction in the brain, particularly the thalamus.

The diathesis–stress explanation focuses on biological, psychological, and environmental vulnerabilities. It proposes that schizophrenia is both a biological disease and a stress-related condition, and suggests that the course of the illness is influenced by environmental stressors. This model implies that people with genetic vulnerability for schizophrenia may be able to prevent the disorder if their social and familial environments contribute to psychological well-being.

LAW ENFORCEMENT AND SCHIZOPHRENIA

Law enforcement professionals may respond to mental health calls that involve people with psychological disorders, including schizophrenia (Hoffman & Putnam, 2004). Law enforcement encounters with people with schizophrenia may occur in response to infractions such as loitering or disorderly conduct, or because the schizophrenic individual is a victim of crime, abuse, or injury, or because a family is in immediate crisis and needs police help to hospitalize the schizophrenic member (Kazarian, Crichlow, & Bradford, 2007). In such cases, the person with schizophrenia may be confused or disoriented, may demonstrate bizarre behaviour, or become aggressive, destructive, assaultive, or violent. Such encounters may escalate into confrontation and the tragic shooting of the person with schizophrenia (Tucker, Van Hasselt, & Russell, 2008).

Personality Disorders

personality disorders
psychological disorders in which people show enduring, pervasive, and inflexible patterns of inner experiences and behaviours that deviate from cultural expectations and cause distress or impairment

Personality disorders are a set of psychological conditions in which people show enduring, pervasive, and inflexible patterns of inner experiences and behaviours that differ from cultural expectations and cause distress or impairment. Canadian studies

TABLE 10.1   Types of Personality Disorders

Disorder	Characteristics
Antisocial personality disorder	Irresponsibility, antisocial attitudes and behaviour, impulsivity, lack of empathy, manipulative behaviour, absence of remorse or guilt
Avoidant personality disorder	Fear of rejection and humiliation, reluctance to enter into meaningful social relationships
Borderline personality disorder	Instability of emotion, self-image, and interpersonal relations; categorical approach to emotions and thoughts; manipulative suicidal behaviour
Dependent personality disorder	Submissiveness, dependency, inability to assume responsibility for self
Histrionic personality disorder	Attention-seeking, overly dramatic behaviour; sexual provocation; suggestibility
Narcissistic personality disorder	Exaggerated sense of self-importance and entitlement; oversensitive to evaluation, craves admiration and attention; lack of empathy
Obsessive–compulsive personality disorder	Perfectionism, excessive orderliness, rigidity, need to control interpersonal relationships
Paranoid personality disorder	Suspiciousness, lack of trust, hypersensitivity, defensiveness; takes offence easily, holds grudges
Schizoid personality disorder	Indifference to social relationships, emotional frigidity
Schizotypal personality disorder	Eccentric thoughts, appearance, and behaviour; poor social relations

on the prevalence of personality disorders are lacking, but US estimates suggest they occur in 6 percent to 9 percent of the population (Government of Canada, 2006).

TYPES OF PERSONALITY DISORDERS

The ten major personality disorders are briefly described in Table 10.1. The two personality disorders that are most likely to be encountered in the context of law enforcement are antisocial personality disorder and borderline personality disorder.

Antisocial Personality Disorder

People with antisocial personality disorder (ASPD) are sometimes referred to as psychopaths or sociopaths, even though psychopathy is a more severe form of antisocial personality disorder. People with ASPD show little anxiety or guilt and callous disregard for the rights and feelings of others; are manipulative, impulsive, selfish, aggressive, and reckless; exhibit difficulty in dealing with authority figures; break the law willingly, lie, cheat, or exploit others for personal gain without feeling remorse; and lack responsibility as indicated by failing to hold jobs or to honour financial obligations. The acronym ANTISOCIAL captures diagnostic features associated with antisocial personality disorder: **A**bsence of anxiety or guilt; **N**o remorse; **T**heft; **I**rresponsibility; **S**ocial norms violated; **O**thers' rights violated; **C**unning; **I**mpulsive; **A**ggressive; **L**ying. You may wish to reread the Preview Scenario of this chapter with a view to extracting possible diagnostic features of ASPD represented in the ANTISOCIAL acronym. This disorder is diagnosed more frequently in men than in women.

People with ASPD present a danger to society because they lack the capacity to care about others, and their callous disregard can lead to a pattern of unrestrained and vicious victimization. It is easy to fall victim to people with antisocial personality disorder, particularly women, as they often appear very intelligent and charming, verbalize feelings and commitments with convincing sincerity, and can easily talk their way out of trouble. Hannibal Lecter, as played by Anthony Hopkins in *Silence of the Lambs*, vividly exemplifies the person with antisocial personality disorder.

Borderline Personality Disorder

People with borderline personality disorder (BPD) are unstable in mood, behaviour, self-image, and social relations; have an intense fear of being abandoned; exhibit impulsive and reckless behaviour; and perform self-mutilating acts (such as slashing their wrists and watching in fascination as the blood pours out). This disorder is diagnosed more frequently in women than in men. Alex, as portrayed by Glenn Close in the movie *Fatal Attraction*, exemplifies the emotions and behaviours of a person with borderline personality disorder.

BPD makes others "walk on eggshells" because people with the disorder can be a Dr. Jekyll at one moment and a Mr. or Ms. Hyde the next. People living or dealing with a person with BPD can never anticipate whether he or she is going to see the world as black or as white, or is going to hug them or attack them.

CAUSES OF PERSONALITY DISORDERS

A variety of factors are thought to contribute to the predisposition or development of personality disorders (Dobbert, 2007). On the genetic side, criminal behaviour is higher in identical twins (50 percent) than in fraternal twins (20 percent or lower). Similarly, the criminal records of adopted males are more similar to the criminal record of the biological father than of the adoptive father. People with antisocial personality disorder also show low levels of arousal, which may explain their need for stimulation and sensation and their impulsive and dangerous acts.

The psychological and social factors that contribute to antisocial personality disorder are home environments that are harsh, unstable and chaotic, and social climates that foster antisocial and aggressive patterns of behaviour. In the case of borderline personality disorder, experiences of physical and sexual abuse in early childhood are noted. Impaired regulation of the brain circuits that control emotion, and dysfunctional attitudes and beliefs are also likely possibilities.

LAW ENFORCEMENT AND PERSONALITY DISORDERS

People with antisocial personality disorder come to the attention of the criminal justice system as they wreak havoc in society. People with ASPD are habitual and repeat offenders and commit the most serious crimes, including serial or mass murder. It is estimated that up to one-half of prisoners have antisocial personality disorder (Government of Canada, 2006).

People with borderline personality disorder also come to the attention of the criminal justice system because of legal disputes or as defendants in violent incidents. Law enforcement officers are also likely to be called when a person with BPD "acts out," is a "terror in the household," is "totally out of control," or is "combative," verbally or physically. The erratic nature of people with BPD makes their management a challenge for law enforcement officers.

Cognitive Disorders: Memory, Language, and Executive Functions Lost

Cognitive disorders are significant disturbances in memory, language, and activities of daily living.

cognitive disorders psychological disorders characterized by significant disturbances and deterioration in cognition and memory

TYPES OF COGNITIVE DISORDERS

There are three types of cognitive disorders.

Delirium

Delirium is a disturbance in consciousness and sudden change in cognition that develops in a short period of time, usually hours to days. Delirium may be due to a general medical condition, such as brain injury, infection that causes high fever, or reduction of oxygen supply to the brain. It may also be substance-induced, as in alcohol or drug intoxication, alcohol or drug withdrawal, medication side effects, or toxin exposure. People with delirium may have no sense of time or place. They may be unable to sustain attention for long periods of time or on more than one thing at a time. They may also show an inability to relate past events to present behaviour and may display disjointed thinking. Finally, they may have hallucinatory and dreamlike experiences, act restless and agitated, and move constantly and aimlessly. In its severe form, delirium produces major problems in thinking, reasoning, and problem solving.

Dementia

A person with dementia shows a gradual and usually permanent decline in general intellectual functioning as well as changes in personality and mood. For example, these people may be overcome by paranoia and suspicious thinking in the advanced stages of dementia.

The two most common types of dementia are Alzheimer's and vascular dementia. A person with Alzheimer's suffers many cognitive impairments, including memory impairment—a decreased ability to learn new information or to recall previously learned information—and one or more of the following:

- short-term and long-term memory loss;

- aphasia, or deterioration in the ability to speak and to understand speech;

- apraxia, or deterioration in the ability to carry out common actions;

- agnosia, or impairment in the ability to recognize people or objects; and

- loss of executive functioning, or impairment in the ability to initiate, plan, monitor, and stop complex activities of everyday living. A person who can no longer prepare a meal may be showing a loss of executive functioning.

Alzheimer's is estimated to be the most prevalent type of dementia, affecting 2 percent to 4 percent of the population over age 65. The prevalence of dementia is known to increase with age, particularly after age 75. Alzheimer's is slightly more common in women than in men.

People with vascular dementia experience several of the above symptoms, typically following a stroke (prolonged oxygen deprivation of the brain). It usually affects people between the ages of 60 and 75. Vascular dementia is slightly more common in men than in women.

Amnestic Disorder

With amnestic disorder, a person experiences impairment in memory and perception. People with amnestic disorder show difficulty learning new information and an inability to recall previously learned information.

CAUSES OF COGNITIVE DISORDERS

Many different factors can cause cognitive disorders: head injuries, alcohol abuse, malnutrition, toxic substances, brain surgery, oxygen deprivation, stroke, or brain infection, among others.

LAW ENFORCEMENT AND COGNITIVE DISORDERS

Law enforcement officers may be involved with people with cognitive disorders who have gotten lost because of confusion, or who are showing disturbing behaviour such as aggression.

Paraphilias

paraphilias
group of sexual and gender identity disorders in which people have recurrent and intense sexual urges, fantasies, and behaviours

Also referred to as sexual deviations, **paraphilias** are a set of disorders in which people have recurrent and intense sexual urges, fantasies, and behaviours involving unusual objects, activities, or situations.

TYPES OF PARAPHILIAS

Table 10.2 briefly describes the most common paraphilias. Generally, paraphilias are diagnosed more often in men than in women.

TABLE 10.2 Types of Paraphilias

Disorder	Characteristics
Exhibitionism	Flashing; intense sexual fantasies, urges, and behaviours that involve exposing the genitals to unsuspecting strangers
Fetishism	Intense sexual fantasies, urges, and behaviours that involve inanimate objects, such as women's shoes or undergarments; some individuals shoplift fetishistic items from stores
Frotteurism	Intense sexual fantasies, urges, and behaviours that involve touching or rubbing against an unsuspecting, non-consenting person, usually in crowded places such as a bus or subway
Pedophilia	Child molestation; intense sexual fantasies, urges, and behaviours that involve a prepubescent non-familial child; incest with children or stepchildren
Sexual masochism	Intense sexual fantasies, urges, and behaviours that involve being humiliated, beaten, bound, or otherwise made to suffer
Sexual sadism	Intense sexual fantasies, urges, and behaviours that involve acts in which the psychological or physical suffering of the consenting victim is sexually exciting to the person inflicting the suffering
Transvestic fetishism	Intense sexual fantasies, urges, and behaviours involving cross-dressing in heterosexual males
Voyeurism	Intense sexual fantasies, urges, and behaviours that involve watching an unsuspecting person naked, undressing, or engaging in sexual activity. A voyeur is also called a peeping Tom.

CAUSES OF PARAPHILIAS

A variety of explanations have been offered for the development of sexual deviance (Laws & O'Donohue, 2008). Paraphilias are linked to hormonal or endocrine abnormalities, deep psychological disturbances, faulty learning processes (for example, a boy who accidentally touches a woman's shoe while aroused may develop a shoe fetish), and alcohol and drug abuse.

LAW ENFORCEMENT AND PARAPHILIAS

People with paraphilias, such as pedophiles and exhibitionists, often come to the attention of the criminal justice system.

Psychological Disorders: Cultural Considerations

While psychological problems are universal, psychological disorders may be defined differently in different cultures. Further, psychological symptoms may manifest differently in people from different cultures. For example, in North Americans and Europeans, depression may manifest as either psychological or somatic symptoms, whereas a person born in the Middle East may exhibit mixed psychological and somatic expressions of negative mood (see, for example, Kazarian, 2009; Kazarian & Taher, 2010). Finally, the genesis of psychological disorders may be attributed to different causes in different cultures, ranging from biological disorders to the "evil eye."

POINTS TO REMEMBER

Law enforcement officers are likely to encounter many different kinds of mental health issues in their work and in their personal lives. Each disorder manifests in different symptoms. While the exact causes of most disorders are not known, a variety of biological, psychological, and social factors are involved. It is important to recognize that people with psychological disorders who come in contact with the criminal justice system are people with problems rather than "problem people." It is also important to recognize that law enforcement by its very nature is a challenge to the mental health of the dedicated law enforcement professional.

KEY TERMS

abnormal behaviour

abnormal psychology

anxiety disorders

cognitive disorders

delusion

depression

dissociative disorders

dissociative identity disorder

factitious disorders

hallucination

mania

mood disorders

obsessive–compulsive disorder

panic disorder

paraphilias

personality disorders

phobia

post-traumatic stress disorder

schizophrenia

somatoform disorders

stigma

suicide

suicide by cop

traumatic event

REFERENCES

Abramson, L.Y., M.E.P. Seligman, & J. Teasdale. (1978). Learned helplessness in humans: Critique and reformulation. *Journal of Abnormal Psychology, 87* (1), 49–74.

Adler, J., & M. Gosnell. (1979, December 31). A question of fraudulent fever. *Newsweek*, p. C5.

American Psychiatric Association (APA). (2000). *Diagnostic and statistical manual of mental disorders* (4th ed. text rev.) (DSM-IV-TR). Washington, DC: Author.

Antony, M.M., A. Federic, & M.B. Stein (Eds.). (2009). *Oxford handbook of anxiety and related disorders.* New York: Oxford University Press.

Associated Press. (1996, January 11). Officer of the Year raped woman in patrol car. http://www.NETural.com/lip/polabuse/0383.html.

Associated Press. (2000, June 8). Woman tries to commit suicide by cop. http://www.worknews.pwpl.com/content/letn/letn0600/1060800s1.htm.

Baker, J.P. (October 1, 1996). Preventing police suicide. *The FBI Law Enforcement Bulletin.* http://www.the freelibrary.com.

Beck, A.T. (1967). *Depression: Clinical, experimental, and theoretical aspects.* New York: Harper & Row.

Beck, A.T. (1976). *Cognitive therapy and the emotional disorders.* New York: International University Press.

Becker, C.B., G. Meyer, J.S. Price, M.M. Graham, A. Arsena, D.A. Armstrong, et al. (2009). Law enforcement preferences for PTSD treatment and crisis management. *Behavior Research and Therapy, 47,* 245–53.

Blasko, B.L., E.L. Jeglio, & S. Malkin. (2008). Suicide risk assessment in jails. *Journal of Forensic Psychology Practice, 8,* 67–76.

Brown, G.W., & T.O. Harris. (1978). *Social origins of depression.* London, UK: Tavistock.

Brown, G.W., & T.O. Harris. (1989). Depression. In G.W. Brown and T.O. Harris (Eds.), *Life events and illness* (pp. 49–93). New York: Guilford Press.

Canadian Mental Health Association. (2005, Winter). Busting the stigma. *Network.* http://www.ontario.cmha.ca/network_story.asp.

Canadian Press. (1997, December 5). VLT-blamed suicides spark call for help in Manitoba. *The London Free Press,* p. A11.

Craighead, W.E., D.J. Miklowitz, & L.W. Craighead (Eds.). (2008). *Psychopathology: History, diagnosis, and empirical foundations.* New York: John Wiley & Sons.

Crocker, A.G., K. Hartford, & L. Heslop. (2009). Gender difference in police encounters among persons with and without serious mental illness. *Psychiatric Services, 60,* 86–93.

Dell, P.F., & J.A. O'Neil. (2009). *Dissociation and the dissociative disorders: DSM-V and beyond.* London, UK: Routledge.

Dobbert, D.L. (2007). *Understanding personality disorders: An introduction.* Westport, CT: Praeger Publications.

Durkheim, E. (1897/1951). *Suicide: A study in sociology.* J.A. Spaulding and G. Simpson (trans). Glencoe, IL: Free Press.

Fernando, M.L.D., & S.S. Kazarian. (1995, April). Patient education in the drug treatment of psychiatric disorders: Effect on compliance and outcome. *CNS Drugs, 3,* 291–304.

Government of Canada. (2006). *The human face of mental health and mental illness in Canada.* Catalogue no. HP5-19/2006E. Ottawa: Author.

Hamilton Health Sciences. (2008, September 15). High rates of posttraumatic stress disorder in Canada. News release. http://www.macanxiety.com/PTSD%20press%20release(Sep18-08).pdf.

Hartley, T.A., J.M. Violanti, D. Fekedulegn, M.E. Andrew, & C.M. Burchfiel. (2007). Association between major life events, traumatic incidents, and depression among Buffalo police officers. *International Journal of Emergency Mental Health, 9,* 25–35.

Hersen, M., & J. Rosqvist (Eds.). (2008). *Handbook of psychological assessment, case conceptualization, and treatment: Vol. 1. Adults.* New York: John Wiley & Sons.

Hoffman, R., & L. Putnam. (2004). *Not just another call… police response to people with mental illnesses in Ontario: A practical guide for the frontline officer.* London, ON: Centre for Addiction and Mental Health & St. Joseph's Healthcare.

International Association of Chiefs of Police. (2009, March 18). Preventing law enforcement officer suicide—CD. http://theiacp.org/PublicationsGuides/ ResearchCenter/ Publications/tabid/299/Def.

Johnson, S.L., & J.E. Roberts. (1995). Life events and bipolar disorder: Implications from biological theories. *Psychological Bulletin, 117*, 434–49.

Kari & Associates. (2006, May 23). *Paul Bernardo and Karla Homolka—The Ken and Barbie murderers.* http://karisable.com/skazpaulkarla.htm.

Kazarian, S.S. (2009). Validation of the Armenian Center for Epidemiological Studies Depression Scale (CES-D) among ethnic Armenians in Lebanon. *International Journal of Social Psychiatry, 55*, 442–48.

Kazarian, S.S., W. Crichlow, & S. Bradford. (2007). *Diversity issues in law enforcement* (3rd ed.). Toronto: Emond Montgomery.

Kazarian, S.S., & E. Persad. (2001). Cultural aspects of suicidal behaviour. In S.S. Kazarian & D.R. Evans (Eds.), *Handbook of cultural health psychology.* San Diego: Academic Press.

Kazarian, S.S., & D. Taher. (2010). Validation of the Armenian Center for Epidemiological Studies Depression Scale (CES-D) in a Lebanese community sample. *European Journal of Psychological Assessment, 26*, 68–73.

Laurence, C. (1997, November 7). The devil didn't make her do it. *The Gazette* (Montreal), pp. A1–A2.

Laws, D.R., & W.T. O'Donohue. (2008). *Sexual deviations: Theory, assessment, and treatment.* New York: Guilford Press.

McCabe, A. (1997). Media don't cause "copy-cat" suicides: Expert. *The Gazette* (Montreal), p. B8.

Miller, L. (2006a). *Practical police psychology: Stress management and crisis intervention for law enforcement.* Springfield, IL: Charles C. Thomas.

Miller, L. (2006b). Officer-involved shooting: Reaction patterns, response protocols, and psychological intervention strategies. *International Journal of Emergency Mental Health, 8*, 239–54.

Miller, L. (2007). Line-of-duty death: Psychological treatment of traumatic bereavement in law enforcement. *International Journal of Emergency Mental Health, 9*, 13–23.

Mohandie, K., J.R. Meloy, & P.I. Collins. (2009). Suicide by cop among officer-involved shooting cases. *Journal of Forensic Science, 54*, 456–64.

Montaldo, C. (Various dates). Karla Homolka—Child rapist, torturer and killer. http://crime.about.com/od/murder/p/homolka.htm.

Morgan, T. (2008). Chaplain's column: The dark epidemic of law enforcement suicide. A confidant is available. http://www.officer.com/web/online/Police-Life/Chaplains-Column—The-Dark-Epidemic-of-Law-Enforcement-Suicide/17$35065.

Officer saves suicidal man. (2001, April 23). *The National Post*, p. A5.

Palmer, S. (2007). *Suicide: Strategies and interventions for reduction and prevention*. London, UK: Routledge.

Phillips, K.A., S.L. McElroy, P.E. Keck, H.L. Pope, & J.I. Hudson. (1993). Body dysmorphic disorder: 30 cases of imagined ugliness. *American Journal of Psychiatry, 150* (2): 302–8.

Putnam, F.W. (1989). *Diagnosis and treatment of multiple personality disorder*. New York: Guilford Press.

Ritter, R. (2007, February 8). Suicide rates jolt police culture. *USA Today*. http://usatoday.com/news/nation/2007-02-08-police-suicides_x.htm.

Schaer, J. (2006). Suicide prevention in law enforcement: The Toronto Police Service experience. http://efap.torontopolice.on.ca/sucide.html.

Seligman, M.E.P. (1975). *Helplessness: On depression, development, and death*. San Francisco: Freeman, Cooper.

Sinha, M. (2009, March). *An investigation into the feasibility of collecting data on the involvement of adults and youth with mental health issues in the criminal justice system*. Ottawa: Statistics Canada, Catalogue no. 85-561-M-016.

Standing Committee on Social Affairs, Science and Technology. (2006). *Out of the shadows at last: Transforming mental health, mental illness and addiction services in Canada*. http://www.parl.gc.ca/common/Committee_SenRep.asp?Language=E&Parl=39&Ses=1&comm_id=47.

Statistics Canada. (2009, April 30). Suicides and suicide rate, by sex and by age group. http://www40.statcan.gc.ca/l01/cst01/perhlth66a-eng.htm.

Study puts suicide cost at $849,877 per person. (1999, September 7). *The London Free Press*, p. A7.

Trimble, M. (2004). *Somatoform disorders: A medicolegal guide*. Cambridge, UK: Cambridge University Press.

Tucker, A.S., V.B. Van Hasselt, & S.A. Russell. (2008). Law enforcement response to the mentally ill: An evaluative interview. *Brief Treatment and Crisis Intervention, 8*, 236–50.

Ulster County Community Mental Health Services. (1990). *Suicide prevention and crisis intervention in county jails and police lock-ups: Officer's handbook*. New York: Author.

Wilson-Bates, F. (2008). *Lost in transition: How lack of capacity in the mental health system is failing Vancouver's mentally ill and draining police resources*. Vancouver: Vancouver Police Department.

World Health Organization. (2001). A public health approach to mental health. http://www.who.int/whr/2001/chapter1/en/index.html.

Wyeth-Ayerst Canada. (1996). *The symptoms of clinical depression* (adapted from Dr. Mark J. Berber and DSM-IV). Montreal: Author.

EXERCISES AND REVIEW

Self-Test

Circle the correct answer.

1. People who experience severe mood swings from the highest of highs (manias) to the lowest of lows (depression) suffer from

    a. schizophrenia

    b. bipolar disorder

    c. mood disorder

    d. somatoform disorder

2. A disease in which the person experiences hallucinations and delusions is

    a. schizophrenia

    b. bipolar disorder

    c. multiple personality disorder

    d. dissociative disorder

3. Marta has a habit of checking the stove, windows, and front door of her house over and over to make sure that the house is safe before she leaves. Marta is likely suffering from

    a. obsessive–compulsive disorder

    b. schizophrenia

    c. sexual dysfunction

    d. paraphilia

4. Ted is brutal and sadistic. He served time in prison for chopping off the arms of a teenaged hitchhiker he raped, and after his release from prison he viciously stabbed to death a woman who tried to befriend him. Ted's most likely diagnosis is

    a. antisocial personality disorder

    b. schizophrenia

    c. pedophilia

    d. sexual sadism

5. Which of the following is a cognitive disorder?

    a. dementia

    b. delirium

    c. amnestic disorder

    d. all of the above

6. Which of the following is a syndrome experienced by many people who have survived such events as genocide, natural disaster, sexual assault, or major car accident?

   a. post-traumatic stress disorder

   b. anxiety disorder

   c. social phobia

   d. panic disorder

7. Garo gets excited from rubbing against unsuspecting women on the subway. Which of the following best describes Garo's condition?

   a. transvestic fetishism

   b. exhibitionism

   c. frotteurism

   d. voyeurism

8. Stephanie was reported missing for over a month. She was found living in a different province and holding a secretarial job under a different name. She told her neighbours and co-workers that she was raised by an uncle beginning at age 3 following the death of her parents in a car accident. When questioned by the police, Stephanie admitted that she had no memories of herself from before that month. Stephanie was most likely suffering from

   a. dissociative identity

   b. dissociative amnesia

   c. dissociative fugue

   d. police-induced memory loss

9. Police have been called many times to take away Antonella for cutting her wrists after minor arguments with her boyfriend or mother. Evidently, she is very afraid of being abandoned by these people after an argument. Antonella is most likely suffering from

   a. post-traumatic stress disorder

   b. antisocial personality disorder

   c. borderline personality disorder

   d. depression

10. Don dresses in women's clothing to become sexually aroused. He finds that his urge to cross-dress is stronger during times of stress. He loves his wife but is distressed about her increased objections to his cross-dressing. Don is likely suffering from

    a. exhibitionism

    b. pedophilia

    c. fetishism

    d. transvestic fetishism

Thinking About Psychology and Law Enforcement

1. Should seriously mentally ill people have the "right to be crazy," including the right to refuse treatment (medication) and live homeless? Debate the issue in class.

2. As a class, discuss and debate the "mad versus bad" issue in the mental health system and criminal justice system. The mental health system cites evidence that people with psychological disorders are criminalized—that is, society imprisons people and treats them as "bad" when in fact they are "mad." On the other hand, the criminal justice system is against the practice of psychologizing criminals—that is, society treating criminals as "mad" when in fact they are "bad."

3. What legal challenges do people with dissociative identity disorder present to law enforcement officers—for example, when an officer apprehends them and reads them their rights?

4. Law enforcement officers who need professional help may be reluctant to seek treatment for two main reasons. The first is denial. Everyone, beginning with the affected officer and including friends, co-workers, and the department's hierarchy, may fail to acknowledge that a problem exists. The second reason is the stigma associated with seeking help. Troubled law enforcement officers may feel shame for failing to live up to the macho image promoted in law enforcement culture. The officers may also feel that their problem will be exposed to public ridicule or that they will lose their job or be demoted. As a group, discuss approaches to de-stigmatize, in law enforcement, psychological disorders generally and suicide in particular.

CHAPTER 11

Treatment of Psychological Disorders

CHAPTER OBJECTIVES

After completing this chapter, you should be able to:

- Describe the major psychological treatments for psychological disorders.

- Describe the major biological treatments for psychological disorders.

- Identify major issues associated with psychological and biological treatments of psychological disorders.

- Describe evolving views regarding the treatment of psychological disorders and their impact on society.

PREVIEW SCENARIO

Officer Emond was a proud and dedicated law enforcement service employee. He was well prepared for police work, and related well to his superiors and peers. After a while, however, shift work, demands for overtime, and exposure to physical danger and risk (being assaulted, witnessing the murder of his partner, and having to kill a suspect out of duty) started taking their toll. Officer Emond found himself increasingly distressed and emotionally exhausted during and after work. He began to experience a range of unsettling emotions such as anxiety, anger, and frustration. Two additional factors deepened his depression. The first factor was his contact with disrespectful and often hostile members of the public. The second factor was the effect of circumstances beyond his control (such as his hours) on his family life. Officer Emond felt torn between his job and his life with his wife and kids. He began calling in sick more frequently and spending days at home wallowing in self-pity. An unfavourable personnel evaluation made things even worse. Officer Emond succumbed to a self-destructive path of cynicism, binge drinking, and withdrawal because of his self-perceived weakness.

Fortunately, the law enforcement service to which Officer Emond belonged recognized his need for psychological help before it was too late, and supported his involvement in therapy with a qualified psychologist. His organization's experience with Officer Emond and many other male and female law enforcement officers inspired the implementation of service-wide psychosocial interventions for early detection of police officers at high risk for job-related psychological problems and the prevention of psychological disorders in law enforcement personnel. Psychosocial interventions included evidence-based psychological therapies (cognitive, behavioural, and psychodynamic) in conjunction with biological interventions (medication). (Peñalba, McGuire, & Leite, 2009)

INTRODUCTION

People with psychological disorders need help to diminish their distress, dysfunction, and deviation, and to improve their quality of life. There is no shame in asking for help, nor does wanting help indicate personal weakness. A number of professional groups provide treatments for psychological disorders in private clinics, general hospitals, community mental health centres, and mental hospitals. These include psychologists, psychiatrists, psychiatric social workers, marriage and family counsellors, pastoral counsellors, and substance-use counsellors. Clinical and counselling psychologists typically hold a doctorate in philosophy (PhD) or doctorate in psychology (PsyD) from university psychology or educaiton departments. The PhD is a more science-oriented academic degree, while the PsyD is a more clinically oriented degree. Clinical and counselling psychologists spend five or more years in intensive training and supervision in psychological treatments. Psychiatrists, on the other hand, specialize in psychological disorders after receiving their medical degree, and their training tends to focus more on biological treatments of psychological disorders.

This chapter explores a variety of psychological and biological treatments for psychological disorders, as well as their implications for law enforcement and society.

PSYCHOLOGICAL TREATMENTS

psychological treatment
a psychotherapeutic approach to help people change maladaptive thoughts, feelings, and behaviours and to improve their psychological, biological, social, cultural, and spiritual functioning

psychotherapy
process in which a client and a trained professional interact for the purpose of improving the client's quality of life

insight-oriented psychotherapy
psychological treatment to increase psychological well-being through self-understanding

Psychological treatment is a psychotherapeutic approach to help people change maladaptive (inappropriate) thoughts, feelings, and behaviours and to improve their functioning in the psychological, biological, social, cultural, and spiritual domains. In **psychotherapy**, a person with a psychological disorder and a trained professional engage in a therapeutic relationship for the purpose of addressing the client's psychological problems and improving the client's quality of life.

Psychotherapists practise with individuals, groups, couples, and families. This section discusses seven kinds of psychotherapy.

Insight-Oriented Psychotherapies

Insight-oriented psychotherapy is grounded in psychoanalytic theory and consists of traditional and contemporary psychoanalytic practice. Psychoanalytic and psychodynamic theories view behaviour as a product of the unconscious. Both classical psychoanalysis and contemporary psychoanalytic practices are used mainly in cases of clients who have general feelings of unhappiness or unresolved issues from childhood.

Traditional psychoanalytic practice relies on orthodox psychoanalytic theory (see Chapter 8) and five major therapeutic techniques that are used to uncover underlying unconscious conflicts, work through difficulties, and gain insight—that is, an understanding of the past in relation to the present:

- *Free association* is a technique in which a client is instructed to say anything that comes to mind, regardless of whether it seems relevant. Freud (see Chapter 8) believed that this would minimize distraction and maximize the free flow of the person's thoughts and feelings.

- *Dream interpretation* involves analyzing a client's dreams. Dreams consist of manifest content (what the dreamer tells) and latent content (the underlying meaning of the dream).

- *Analysis of resistance* is a technique in which the therapist identifies instances of client unwillingness to discuss or reveal particular thoughts, feelings, memories, or motivations and attempts to interpret their meaning and help the client work through the unconscious resistance. Examples of resistance include not showing up for a session, being late or early for the appointment, getting drunk before the session, and forgetting to pay the therapist's bill.

- *Transference* is a technique in which the therapist helps the client work through re-enactments of past relationships. Re-enactments may take the form of intense positive feelings directed toward the therapist (for example, falling in love with him or her) or intense negative feelings (hostility toward him or her). In *countertransference*, the therapist develops feelings, either positive or negative, toward the client.

- *Interpretation* is a technique in which the therapist suggests connections between the client's past experiences and present thoughts, feelings, and behaviours. The client gains insight into his or her condition through the interpretive process.

Traditional psychoanalysis has the limitation of requiring intensive training and self-analysis, in addition to being expensive and time-consuming. Classical psychoanalysis typically requires five sessions per week for five or more years, and its effectiveness may not be related to the level of intensity. Contemporary psychoanalysis is based on adaptations of orthodox psychoanalysis that place more emphasis on the ego, or the self, and interpersonal relationships. In contrast to traditional psychoanalysts, contemporary, insight-oriented psychotherapists are active in therapy sessions, limit the number of visits, and focus on current rather than past relationships. Interpersonal therapy is a short-term, insight-oriented psychological treatment that focuses primarily on important current relationships in a client's life (Weissman, Markowitz, & Klerman, 2007). This highly structured therapy helps clients examine reenactments of past relationships and identify current barriers to satisfying interpersonal relationships. Clients are helped to find solutions to interpersonal conflict and to strengthen social skills that initiate and maintain satisfying relationships.

Humanistic Psychotherapies

Humanistic psychotherapies are based on humanistic psychology. Humanistic theorists view individuals as responsible for their actions rather than victims at the mercy of unconscious forces, focused on the here and now rather than on the past, knowledgeable about themselves, and motivated by the impetus toward personal growth. Humanistic theorists suggest that distressed, dysfunctional, or deviant people are a product of childhood experiences that made them live according to the expectations of others rather than according to their own desires and feelings. Humanistic psychotherapy provides a helping relationship in which clients engage in self-exploration of distorted perceptions, denial of feelings, and negative views of themselves with a view to unblocking their capacity for self-healing and personal growth. In contrast to insight-oriented psychotherapies, in which the helping relationship is hierarchical and the focus is on the past, the human encounter in humanistic psychotherapies arises between equals and is focused on the here and now.

Humanistic psychotherapies are used primarily with clients who have general feelings of unhappiness or interpersonal issues. Practitioners consider themselves facilitators of change in their clients. The following are three types of humanistic psychotherapy:

- *Person-centred therapy:* Formerly called client-centred therapy, this approach was developed by Carl Rogers (see Chapter 8). The therapist provides a therapeutic climate of unconditional positive regard, empathy, and genuineness. *Unconditional positive regard* means accepting and valuing clients as they are without judging them. Such therapists allow clients to feel free to express and accept all their own thoughts and feelings without fear of rejection, and thus come to grips with previously distorted or denied experiences. *Empathy* refers to the therapist's ability to view the world from the client's eyes. Empathic therapists help clients understand themselves better through reflecting, a process in which therapists restate or rephrase vague feelings expressed by the client in a way that captures their meaning more clearly. Finally, *genuineness* refers to the consistency of the therapist's behaviours with his or her feelings in the context of the helping relationship. Therapists are genuine when they express both positive and negative feelings openly and honestly. Of course, expressing negative feelings to clients is trickier than expressing positive feelings. Nevertheless, "genuine" therapists can express disapproval of a client's behaviour yet at the same time convey acceptance of the client as a person. Therapists are "phony" when their behaviours are incongruent with their feelings. Incongruence damages the helping relationship. Person-centred therapy considers unconditional positive regard, empathy, and genuineness the active ingredients of effective therapy; that is, therapy that fosters client self-exploration, self-understanding, and personal growth.

- *Existential therapy:* In this approach, the therapist assists clients in finding meaning in life and identifying values that are worth living or even dying for. The therapist probes and challenges clients' worldviews to help them deal more effectively with alienation and increase their connectedness with the world around them. Existential therapists tend to be more directive than person-centred therapists—that is, they are more willing to offer their views and give advice to clients.

- *Gestalt therapy:* Gestalt therapy was developed by Fritz Perls. The therapist takes a directive approach to allow clients to express their feelings, thoughts, and actions freely so that they can get in touch with their feelings, finish "unfinished business" from the past, and assume responsibility for their conduct. Unfinished business may consist of unresolved issues with significant people that continue to affect the client's life. Gestalt therapists use verbal and non-verbal techniques to help clients identify and complete unfinished business and promote greater self-understanding and personal growth. In the "empty chair" technique, for example, clients express their thoughts and feelings about significant others (parents, siblings, and so on) as they imagine those people sitting in the chair. Clients can also switch places and role-play the responses of those people.

Behaviour Therapies

Behaviour therapies are based on three main assumptions. The first is that distressed, dysfunctional, and deviant behaviours are not merely symptoms of underlying problems such as disease or unconscious conflicts—rather, they *are* the problem. Thus, behavioural therapies focus on the maladaptive behaviours themselves rather than on their presumed underlying causes. A second assumption is that maladaptive behaviours are learned in much the same way as more suitable (adaptive) behaviours are learned, through behavioural and social learning principles—that is, classical conditioning, operant conditioning, and modelling (see Chapter 5). A third assumption is that maladaptive behaviours can be unlearned through the same principles that were operative in their learning.

Behaviour therapies are implemented in a variety of settings, such as clinics, mental hospitals, correctional services, and schools. They are used to treat many of the psychological disorders discussed in Chapter 10, including anxiety disorders, mood disorders, schizophrenia, substance-use disorders, and paraphilias. As therapeutic teachers, behaviour therapists choose empirically supported effective treatments and take a directive approach in helping clients unlearn maladaptive behaviours and learn new and more adaptive behaviours.

Behaviour therapies represent a range of techniques that are based on either classical conditioning procedures or operant conditioning procedures. Classical conditioning procedures are fear-reducing or aversion-inducing. *Fear-reducing* therapeutic techniques attempt to eliminate or minimize anxiety responses to irrationally feared objects, such as the sight of a dead body. *Aversion-inducing* therapeutic modalities condition aversive emotional responses to problematic objects such as alcohol or inappropriate sexual objects. The three most commonly used classical conditioning procedures are exposure therapies, systematic desensitization, and aversion therapies.

EXPOSURE THERAPIES

As fear-reducing treatments, exposure therapies assume that fears and phobias are classically conditioned emotional responses and that fear and phobias are maintained by avoidance responses. Avoidance responses to the feared objects are reinforced by anxiety reduction, and therefore maintain fears and phobias. According to the formulation of exposure therapies, fears can be overcome only through exposure and response prevention. *Exposure* refers to experience of the feared object, either in real life (in vivo) or in the imagination; *response prevention* refers to experiencing the feared object without the benefit of the avoidance behaviour. While exposure to the feared object is likely to evoke considerable anxiety, remaining in the presence of the feared object will eventually diminish if not eliminate (extinguish) the felt anxiety.

Exposure therapies are highly effective in the treatment of phobias and obsessive–compulsive behaviours, and are considered the treatment of choice for post-traumatic stress disorder (Choy, Fyer, & Lipsitz, 2007; Massad & Hulsey, 2006). Exposure therapies have also benefited from the application of computer technology in that virtual reality therapy is used for the treatment of anxiety disorders, particularly the treatment of height and flying phobias (Choy et al., 2007). Computer technology allows the integration of real-time computer graphics, visual displays, body tracking, and other sensory tracking devices. Virtual reality therapy involves computer program generation of a virtual environment that simulates the phobic situation, repeatedly exposing clients to their stressors in order to evoke the responses they experience in the real world.

SYSTEMATIC DESENSITIZATION

Systematic desensitization is another fear-reducing exposure therapy. This approach assumes that anxiety is a classically conditioned emotional response that requires a counterconditioning procedure for elimination. *Counterconditioning* refers to use of a new response that is incompatible with anxiety to counter the anxiety response. Whereas exposure therapies typically rely on the principle of extinction to overcome anxiety, systematic desensitization requires a substitute response to counter the anxiety response.

Three steps are associated with systematic desensitization. The first is learning how to relax, usually by tensing and releasing various muscles in the body. The second step is identifying a hierarchy of situations that the client fears, from those that are very mild to those that are very frightening. The third step is the desensitization process, in which the feared situations (starting with the least feared) are paired with the relaxation response in order to reduce anxiety and replace it with the relaxed state. While systematic desensitization relies on imagery, desensitization can also be implemented in vivo by systematic exposure to a hierarchy of real-life situations.

AVERSION THERAPIES

Aversion therapies are aversion-inducing therapeutic procedures. They involve the pairing of a stimulus that is attractive to a client and that triggers deviant behaviour with a noxious stimulus for the purpose of conditioning anxiety or discomfort to the stimulus and eliminating the undesirable behaviour. Clients are subjected to real or imagined discomfort or aversive stimuli to help them overcome a range of disorders, such as substance use and paraphilias (discussed in Chapter 10). Discomfort is created in one of three ways: chemically, through drugs that cause nausea and vomiting; electrically, through mild electric shocks; or cognitively, through the use of imagery that involves descriptions of physical distress (for example, nausea) or psychological distress (for example, feeling shame). The attractive stimuli eventually lose their appeal and cease triggering deviant behaviours. For example, pedophiles may undergo aversion therapy in which electric shocks are paired with images of children they have rated as sexually attractive with a view to building aversion to the images and reducing pedophile offences. Similarly, clients with alcoholism may undergo aversion therapy in which images of their favourite drinks are paired with electric shocks. More recently, self-applied aversion therapy has been used in an adult survivor of childhood sexual abuse to extinguish unwanted sexual fantasies arising from sexual abuse cues (Wilson & Wilson, 2008).

Aversion therapies have their limitations. Clients may refuse such treatments because of the treatment's aversive nature. Also, the responses acquired through aversion therapy may not generalize to the real world. Finally, aversion therapies may better succeed when they are part of more comprehensive treatment programs in which clients are taught coping skills and relapse-prevention strategies.

Operant Conditioning Therapies

Behaviour therapies that are based on operant conditioning procedures focus on increasing or decreasing specific behaviours. *Positive reinforcement techniques* are used to build new adaptive skills and increase or maintain existing adaptive behaviours, while *punishment techniques* are used to stop or decrease maladaptive behaviours. For example, children may be rewarded with verbal praise or the occasional tangible reward of ice cream so that they keep their rooms clean and tidy on all occasions. Similarly, children may be deprived of TV for a short period of time for hitting their younger siblings.

Behaviour therapies that are based on operant conditioning have been applied to many different behaviour disorders and in many settings. Operant conditioning procedures have been particularly successful with difficult-to-treat populations or those who have failed to respond to conventional treatments, such as institutionalized schizophrenics, profoundly disturbed children, and individuals with mental retardation. The psychosocial rehabilitation of people with chronic mental illness has benefited from positive reinforcement techniques, token economy programs in particular. *Token economy programs* use positive reinforcement to strengthen adaptive behaviours such as personal grooming, activities of daily living, social interaction, and participation in vocational rehabilitation. As a reward for engaging in a list of adaptive behaviours, patients receive plastic tokens that they later redeem for tangible rewards. Token economy has been shown to be more effective than conventional treatment in the case of chronic mental patients (Paul & Lentz, 1977). Token economy programs have also been successfully applied in such settings as businesses, schools, prisons, home environments, and hospitals.

Punishment techniques use aversive or noxious consequences to diminish or stop maladaptive behaviours. While punishment techniques tend to provide quick results, psychologists are generally inclined to use and evaluate the least aversive and intrusive treatments before implementing more painful approaches for behavioural change. In the case of severely disturbed autistic children engaged in self-destructive behaviours such as head-banging or self-mutilation, psychologists may have no option but to use punishment techniques, such as administering contingent electric shock. In such cases, parental consent is obtained and institutional ethics approval is secured.

Observational Learning and Social Skills Training

Observational learning procedures are used for the treatment of a variety of behavioural problems. Learning through observation can be an effective approach to learning new skills. Observational learning is particularly useful in teaching clients social skills. In social skills training, clients are taught interpersonal and problem-solving rules and responses. Therapists use observational learning principles and techniques, including role-play, in which clients act out new behaviours and receive constructive feedback from therapists for behavioural improvement. Interpersonal skills include effective verbal and non-verbal communication and assertiveness. Verbal communication entails basic and advanced conversational skills and rules, self-disclosure, and listening. The SMILE model (Kazarian, unpublished) identifies five skills and rules associated with effective interpersonal communication:

- **S**tarting a verbal interaction by introducing yourself, making a relevant comment or small talk, or offering assistance.

- **M**aintaining a verbal interaction by asking open-ended questions, volunteering information, and paying attention to the thoughts and feelings of the other person.

- **I**mparting information. Too much or too little self-disclosure does not make for a satisfactory verbal interaction. Two self-disclosure rules are "Start low and build up" and "Match personal self-disclosure with the self-disclosure level of the other person."

- **L**istening, which is a multidimensional skill. It involves using body orientation (avoiding falling all over the other person), eye contact (avoiding staring), facial expressions (avoiding a blank face), gestures (avoiding excessive use of hands), voice volume and tone (avoiding whispering), and non-verbal signals (such as nodding).

- **E**nding the verbal interaction at the appropriate time by, for example, telling the other person that you have enjoyed talking or that you would like the opportunity to talk again.

Non-verbal communication skills involve rules for using eye contact, body language, gestures, and personal space. For example, staring at people or standing too close to them makes them uncomfortable and makes the communication ineffective.

Assertiveness involves using positive responses (for example, compliments, receiving positive feedback from the other person), negative responses (for example, expressing anger and receiving negative feedback from others), and standing up for one's legitimate rights without violating the rights of others.

Problem solving is a five-step process for dealing effectively with life's problems (D'Zurilla & Goldfried, 1971): (1) defining the problem; (2) generating solutions to the identified problem using brainstorming—generating as many solutions as possible, using the generated solutions to generate more solutions, but not evaluating the solutions; (3) carefully evaluating each of the generated solutions and choosing the best option; (4) implementing the chosen solution; and (5) revisiting the entire process, or part of it, if the problem is not resolved in step 4.

2 # Cognitive Therapies

Cognitive psychotherapy assumes that distorted or dysfunctional thinking is at the heart of all psychological disturbances and that realistically evaluating and modifying thinking results in lasting improvement in psychological functioning (Beck, 1995). This therapy is used in cases in which clients have anxiety, panic disorder, general feelings of depression, and general feelings of unhappiness. There are various forms of cognitive therapy, including Albert Ellis's rational emotive therapy, Donald Meichenbaum's cognitive behavioural modification, Arnold Lazarus's multimodal therapy, and Aaron Beck's cognitive therapy. Cognitive therapy focuses on the present, is time-limited, and is oriented toward problem solving. It teaches clients to identify distorted thoughts they have about themselves, the world, and the future; to modify distressing beliefs; to relate to others in healthier ways; and to change behaviours (Beck, 1996).

Five steps are associated with Beck's cognitive therapy (Sacco & Beck, 1995). The first involves teaching clients to identify and monitor dysfunctional automatic thoughts about themselves, the world, and the future. For example, depressed people may have negative automatic thoughts that reflect their expectations of failure, rejection, and dissatisfaction. Clients may not recognize the automatic overthinking of their negative thoughts and the adverse effects of these thoughts on their mind and body. Clients are encouraged to identify dysfunctional thoughts and are given homework assignments for this purpose. The second step involves teaching clients to recognize thought–mood–behaviour connections so they can see the relationship between negative automatic thoughts and psychological ill health (negative mood and dysfunctional behaviour). The third step is teaching clients to assess the reasonableness of their negative automatic thoughts. Clients are instructed to ask themselves questions to evaluate the accuracy of their automatic thoughts and the logic behind them. Typical questions include "What is the evidence to support this thought?" and "Are there alternative interpretations of this event?" The fourth step is teaching clients to substitute more reasonable interpretations for their automatic responses. The final step is teaching clients to identify and change dysfunctional silent assumptions, the basic underlying beliefs that lead to psychological ill health such as depression. Examples of dysfunctional silent assumptions include "To be happy, everyone must accept me at all times," "If I make a mistake, it means I am hopeless," and "My value as a person depends on what others think of me."

cognitive psychotherapy
psychological treatment to change maladaptive behaviours and feelings by changing irrational thoughts, beliefs, and ideas

Family, Couple, and Group Therapies

In contrast to therapies that focus on the individual's personal issues, family, couple, and group therapies specialize in treating troubled interpersonal relationships.

In **family therapy**, members of the troubled family enter treatment as a group. Family therapy is conducted with either one or two therapists. Family therapy assumes that an individual's personal issues are caused, maintained, or worsened by problems within the family. It aims to heal wounds, foster open communication, and resolve family conflicts.

In marital or **couple therapy**, the therapist works with married couples. Couple therapy assumes that the individual's personal issues are caused, maintained, or worsened by problems in the marriage. Couple therapy aims to improve communication,

family therapy
psychological treatment in which the entire family is involved in therapy

couple therapy
psychological treatment in which the two partners in a relationship are involved in therapy

resolve conflicts, and improve the quality of the marriage. In some cases, the therapist supports the couple's decision to divorce and then helps the clients readjust.

In **group therapy**, the therapist works with a group of clients who have similar personal issues to help resolve these and foster a sense of belonging and support. *Psychodrama* is a form of group therapy in which group members act out their own issues or those of significant people in their lives to gain insight into their troubled interpersonal relationships. *Self-help groups* are non-professionally based support groups for people with a variety of physical or psychological problems and their families. Examples of self-help groups include Alcoholics Anonymous and Gamblers Anonymous.

PSYCHOLOGICAL TREATMENTS AND LAW ENFORCEMENT

Law enforcement officers can benefit from a range of psychological treatments that alleviate psychological and physical symptoms such as anxiety, depression, sleep disturbance, cynicism, anger, post-traumatic stress disorder, marital problems, and distress (Peñalba et al., 2009). Psychological treatments reportedly used to help law enforcement officers include cognitive and behavioural interventions, supportive therapies such as counselling and social support, and psychodynamic therapies (Peñalba et al., 2009).

BIOLOGICAL TREATMENTS

The **biological approach** (or biomedical approach) views psychological disorders as diseases that require biological treatments. Biological treatments are used with children, adults, and elderly people suffering from psychological disorders as an alternative to or in combination with psychological treatments. Descriptions of the three main intervention categories—drug therapies, electroconvulsive therapy, and psychosurgery—of the biological approach follow.

Drug Therapies

Of the three main biological interventions, drug therapies are the most common. **Psychopharmacology**, the study of the effects of drugs on thinking, feeling, and behaviour, contributes to the discovery of effective drugs for a range of psychological disorders. Four main groups of "wonder" drugs for psychological disorders are anti-anxiety drugs, antidepressant drugs, antimanic drugs, and antipsychotic drugs.

ANTI-ANXIETY DRUGS

Anti-anxiety drugs are also known as anxiolytics or minor tranquillizers. Introduced in the mid-1950s, these medications are used primarily to treat anxiety. Therapeutic doses of anti-anxiety drugs reduce anxiety without affecting concentration or alertness. Patients taking anti-anxiety drugs are able to enter and cope with feared situations. The most common drugs are from the class known as benzodiazepines. These drugs inhibit the activity of the neurotransmitter gamma-aminobutric acid (GABA) in the brain. Commonly used anti-anxiety drugs include Ativan, Miltown, Librium, Serax, Tranxene, Valium, Xanax, and BuSpar. These drugs are effective in treating generalized anxiety disorders and social phobias but may not

group therapy
psychological treatment in which several clients meet regularly to resolve personal issues

biological approach
approach to psychological disorders that assumes they are the result of underlying diseases that require biological treatments

psychopharmacology
study of the use of drugs for psychological disorders

be as effective for patients with phobic or obsessive–compulsive disorders. Xanax is the drug of choice for treating panic disorders.

A limitation of anti-anxiety drugs is side effects. Common side effects of these drugs include sleepiness, mild psychomotor impairment that may increase the risk of car accidents, and problems with attention and memory. A second limitation is psychological and physical dependence. The potential for addiction to benzodiazepines is high, particularly for people with a history of substance abuse. People who have developed physiological dependence on anti-anxiety drugs and who decide to stop taking them are likely to experience withdrawal symptoms such as intense anxiety and restlessness. As a result, many resume taking them. A third limitation of anti-anxiety medications is that anxiety symptoms often return when people are no longer taking them.

ANTIDEPRESSANT DRUGS

Antidepressant drugs are helpful in treating depression and certain anxiety disorders. Three major categories of antidepressant drugs are tricyclics, monoamine oxidase inhibitors, and selective serotonin reuptake inhibitors.

antidepressants
drugs that are used in treating depression and select anxiety disorders

Tricyclic Antidepressants

These are the traditional medications for reducing symptoms of depression. They affect brain functions by blocking the uptake of such neurotransmitters as norepinephrine or dopamine from the synapses (see Chapter 2). Common drugs in this group include Anafranil, Elavil, Norpramin, Pamelor, Sinequan, Surmontil, Tofranil, and Vivactil. Anafranil is also used as an anti-obsessional medication and Tofranil as an antipanic drug. Tricyclic antidepressants may take a number of weeks to show an effect. Their potential side effects are sleepiness, dizziness, nervousness, fatigue, dry mouth, forgetfulness, and weight gain. Weight gain is a major factor in people's discontinuing the use of these drugs, thereby prolonging their depression.

Monoamine Oxidase Inhibitors

People who are depressed and are unresponsive to other antidepressants may be given monoamine oxidase inhibitors (MAOIs) such as Eutonl, Marplan, Nardil, or Parnate. MAOIs reduce the activity of monoamine oxidase, an enzyme that breaks down neurotransmitters in the synapses. These drugs are also effective in treating certain anxiety disorders, including agoraphobia, panic attacks, and social phobias. MAOIs may be associated with severe side effects, in addition to causing serious hypertension when taken with certain foods such as chocolate or cheese, and some types of wine.

Selective Serotonin Reuptake Inhibitors

Selective serotonin reuptake inhibitors (SSRIs) are the newest breed of antidepressants. They were developed in the early 1980s and include Celexa, Effexor, Luvox, Paxil, Prozac, and Zoloft. Prozac is also used as an anti-obsessional medication. SSRIs increase the amount of serotonin in the synaptic cleft by inhibiting the uptake of serotonin into the presynaptic nerve ending. SSRIs are popular and have gradually replaced the tricyclics because they reduce depression faster, produce less severe side effects, and diminish anxiety symptoms that may accompany depression.

Nevertheless, SSRIs are not miracle cures for depression. Their side effects include anxiety, drowsiness, dry mouth, hypomania (low-level mania), nausea, and sexual dysfunction. Concern has been expressed over the use of Prozac and Zoloft with children, because neither drug has been approved for use with children in North America (Lewickyi, 1997). Concern has also been raised over the use of Prozac with the "worried well" for complaints of the stress of daily living, and the associated claim that the drug alters the fundamental constitution of personality (Woods, 1993).

ANTIMANIC DRUGS

These drugs are used primarily with people with a history of mania or hypomania. They include valproic acid (Depakote, Depakene, Epival), lithium (Eskalith, Lithane, Lithobid, Lithonate, Lithotabs), and carbamazapine (Tegretol).

Lithium is considered the drug of choice for manic–depressive or bipolar disorders. Lithium treatment requires careful and continuous monitoring for therapeutic effectiveness and to prevent lithium poisoning and permanent damage to the nervous system. Potential side effects associated with lithium treatment include stomach pain, diarrhea, nausea, tremors, twitches, and vomiting. Symptoms of lithium poisoning include loss of balance, shaking, dizziness, thirst, blurred vision, confusion, and convulsions. Because it is teratogenic (causes birth defects), it should not be taken during pregnancy. Getting people to adhere to lithium therapy can be an issue (Goodwin & Jamison, 1990). Some stop taking the drug because it can cause weight gain and memory problems; others complain of flat mood ("I don't miss my lows, but I do miss my highs").

Depakene and Tegretol are anticonvulsants. They are used with bipolar patients who do not respond to lithium therapy. Common side effects of Depakene include diarrhea, nausea, vomiting, and sexual dysfunction. Common side effects of Tegretol include slower thinking, confusion, dizziness, and nausea.

ANTIPSYCHOTIC DRUGS

antipsychotic drugs
drugs that are used to control severe mental disturbances such as delusions and hallucinations

Antipsychotic drugs are also known as neuroleptics or major tranquillizers. They are used mainly to treat severe psychological disorders such as schizophrenia. Antipsychotic drugs are also very helpful in controlling restlessness, agitation, and excitement. The discovery of antipsychotic drugs in the 1950s was revolutionary in that it allowed many severely disturbed patients leave mental hospitals to live in the community.

The conventional antipsychotic drugs inhibit the activity of dopamine, a neurotransmitter whose overactivity is implicated in schizophrenia, and control positive (add-on) symptoms of schizophrenia such as hallucinations and delusions but not negative (deficit) symptoms of schizophrenia such as apathy and social withdrawal. They include Haldol, Loxitane, Mellaril, Moban, Navane, Sandril, Stelazine, Taractan, and Thorazine. Antipsychotic drugs may have to be taken indefinitely.

These drugs produce unpleasant side effects such as restless pacing and fidgeting, muscle spasms and cramps, and a shuffling gait. Long-term use of these drugs can cause a severe movement disorder, tardive dyskinesia, a condition in which a person experiences involuntary twitching and jerking movements of the face and tongue, and squirming movements of the hands and torso. Another adverse reaction is neuroleptic malignant syndrome, which results in high fever, rigid muscles, fluctuating level of consciousness, rapid heart rate, increased sweating, elevated white blood count, and urine retention.

The newer atypical antipsychotic medications are effective in controlling both positive and negative symptoms of schizophrenia and have the added advantage of producing fewer undesirable side effects. These drugs include Clozaril (clozapine), Risperdal (resperidone), Serlect (sertindole), Zyprexa (olanzapine), and Seroquel (quetiapine). A limitation of Clozaril is that weekly blood tests are required to check for agranulocytosis, a fatal blood disease.

Electroconvulsive Therapy

Electroconvulsive therapy (ECT), also known as shock therapy, is another biological approach to treating psychological disorders. It was developed in 1938 by two Italian physicians, Ugo Cerletti and Lucio Bini, who were looking for a treatment for schizophrenia. Two faulty assumptions existed at this time: first, that schizophrenia was rare among people with epilepsy, and second, that epileptic seizures prevented schizophrenia. Cerletti and Bini reasoned that schizophrenia could be treated by inducing seizures. They discovered a method for doing so in a slaughterhouse they were visiting, where they saw animals convulsing and becoming unconscious after electric currents were passed through their brains. Cerletti and Bini introduced a modified electroconvulsive technique as an experimental intervention for schizophrenia.

Modern ECT is used mainly for conditions of severe depression and for psychological disorders that do not respond to other, less intrusive treatments. Modern ECT involves administering an electric current to the brain of a patient. The resulting seizure is believed to be necessary for treatment. All patients are given muscle relaxants before receiving ECT to minimize the likelihood of bone fractures and dislocations.

Modern ECT bears little resemblance to the treatment Murphy (played by Jack Nicholson) received in the movie *One Flew Over the Cuckoo's Nest*. Physical complications following the procedure are rare, as is experiencing pain. Nevertheless, ECT may cut depression short but is no permanent cure. This technique also continues to be controversial and to suggest horrific images of overuse and even abuse. Diehard opponents claim that ECT is an abusive instrument in the hands of oppressors and that it causes permanent brain damage and memory loss. Supporters of ECT point to the prevailing safeguards in using the procedure, dismiss the claims of its damaging effects, and highlight its value as a safe and highly effective treatment and intervention of last resort.

A non-intrusive experimental treatment that is claimed to have a similar antidepressant effect to that of ECT is repetitive transcranial magnetic stimulation (rTMS). In rTMS, a magnetic coil is placed over a person's skull, and an electric current is run through the coil repeatedly to create a series of brief but very powerful magnetic pulses. Electricity does not pass from the coil to the patient. Stimulation is delivered in trains of up to 10 seconds, with trains 30 seconds apart. The daily treatments produce only minimal discomfort, and the use of a general anesthetic is not required. RTMS is used to treat depression and bipolar disorder (Figiel et al., 1998). It is not recommended for patients who have a metal implant in the skull or brain.

electroconvulsive therapy
biological treatment in which an electrical current is passed through the brain to induce seizure and abort depression

Psychosurgery

psychosurgery
biological treatment in which brain surgery is performed to treat severe, unremitting, and debilitating psychological disorders such as obsessive–compulsive disorder

Psychosurgery, also known as lobotomy, involves surgically removing or destroying brain tissue to reduce the symptoms of serious and intractable psychological disorders and provide relief from unbearable chronic pain. Psychosurgery was developed by the Portuguese neurologist Elas Moniz in 1935 to treat psychological disorders. Moniz introduced the surgical procedure of lobotomy and received a Nobel prize in 1949 for his discovery of prefrontal lobotomy. Lobotomy involved severing the frontal lobes of the brain and deeper brain centres believed to control emotions. Ironically, one of Moniz's lobotomized patients shot him in the spine and left him paralyzed on one side.

Attitudes toward psychosurgery have shifted in three waves. In the first wave, tens of thousands of prefrontal lobotomies were performed around the world from 1935 to 1955. In the second wave, lobotomies were virtually stopped in the mid-1950s. The dramatic decline of the procedure was mainly due to its limited effectiveness and the introduction of antipsychotic drugs. The third wave began with the introduction of antipsychotic drugs and continues today. Psychosurgery today is rare and is used as a treatment of absolute last resort. The procedures are far less drastic than the earlier lobotomies and result in fewer cognitive impairments. However, there is still no guarantee of predictable results, and any negative surgical consequences are not reversible.

LAW ENFORCEMENT AND BIOLOGICAL TREATMENTS

Drug therapies revolutionized the treatment of psychological disorders and contributed to improved quality of life for many people. These drugs are effective and safe approaches to treating particular psychiatric disorders. However, critics of the biological approach condemn the use of these drugs on the ground that they are chemical lobotomies and brain-disabling agents, and not a cure for underlying pathology or psychological conflicts. Critics also charge the psychiatric profession with using chemistry on people with psychological issues—that is, overusing drugs and underusing psychological treatments and patient and family education (Fernando & Kazarian, 1995; Kazarian & Vanderheyden, 1992). Negative attitudes toward biological treatments play a significant role in refusal and non-adherence. Patient and family education has the advantage of exploration of anxieties and misconceptions associated with drug therapies with a view to correction.

It is important for law enforcement officers to know about drug therapies and to understand the issues associated with them. Law enforcement officers who encounter emotionally disturbed people need to find out if they have been refusing to take medication and as a result are causing disturbance in the community, or what kind of medication, if any, they are taking and the extent to which they have adhered to it. Emotionally disturbed people who have not been taking their medications regularly are in a state of relapse, reflected in the reappearance of their disturbing behaviours. Officers also need to be able to distinguish the side effects of drugs from the symptoms of substance abuse. Tremors, nausea, extreme lethargy, confusion, dry mouth, constipation, or diarrhea may all be due to medication side effects. People with mental illness who are detained need access to toilet facilities, food, and water, as well as their prescribed medication. Steps should be taken to obtain any necessary medications for people in custody.

EVALUATION OF BIOLOGICAL AND PSYCHOLOGICAL TREATMENTS

Alone Versus Together

Individuals with psychological issues who receive psychotherapy are better off than those who do not receive treatment. The different **psychological approaches** to treatment seem to be more or less equally effective, suggesting that the essential ingredient is the positive client–therapist relationship rather than the specific technique used.

The biological approach generally, and psychopharmacology particularly, dominates the treatment of psychological disorders. The value of psychological interventions, either alone or in combination with drug treatment for mental health issues, needs to be recognized. There is increasing evidence that psychological treatments may be as effective as drug therapy. For example, cognitive behavioural therapy, interpersonal therapy, and drug therapy all seem to lead to substantial relief from depression (Jacobson & Hollon, 1996). There is also growing evidence that psychological treatment increases the effectiveness of drug therapies (Barlow et al., 2000; Miklowitz, 1996; Miklowitz, Frank, & George, 1996). Increasingly, treatment research is revealing that drug therapies can often be used more effectively in conjunction with psychotherapy. In the case of schizophrenia, for example, patients who receive antipsychotic drugs, social skills training, and family therapy show a lower relapse rate than those on drugs only (Hogarty, 2002). Similarly, depression research shows superior recovery rate for patients receiving drugs and psychotherapy rather than drug therapy alone (Furokawa, Watanabe, & Churchill, 2006).

It appears that successful psychological interventions enhance people's personal competence and resilience to negative life events, sustain or improve the protective effects of their social and family environments, and increase their adherence to drug treatment. Unfortunately, Canada's health-care system does not provide universal access to psychological treatment. People in need of psychotherapy from psychologists are required to pay for such services, and not all Canadians can afford this treatment. Clearly, new non-discriminatory legislation with regard to psychological health-care services is warranted.

psychological approach
approach to psychological disorders that relies on psychotherapy or talk therapy to improve biological, psychological, social, cultural, and spiritual functioning

Treatment of Psychological Disorders: Cultural Issues

Biological and psychological treatments are embedded in mainstream Western thought and culture. Mainstream Western medicine and psychology construe the self as an independent agent and view distress, dysfunction, and deviance as originating within the person in the form of underlying disease, unconscious conflict, irrational and self-defeating cognition, or faulty learning (Kazarian, 2007). In addition, Western medicine and psychology assume that Western-grounded psychological and biological treatments that focus on changing internal factors through self-expression and medication are the best means of helping people with psychological disorders achieve improvement and autonomy.

These broad assumptions are not universally shared, even within pluralist societies such as the United States and Canada. For example, a depressed young woman of Middle Eastern heritage engaged in psychotherapy is highly unlikely to disclose family secrets to a "paid foreigner therapist" because in her culture such behaviour is construed as betrayal of family. The psychiatrist or clinical psychologist may not even be able to see the patient without a family member present. Similarly, discussing the therapeutic goal of living alone and away from family may baffle a patient of Southeast Asian heritage, because self-reliance and autonomy are foreign ideals. Youths in many non-Western cultures do not leave home at 18; they live with family indefinitely, until they marry, or even after they marry and have children. As a final example, people from non-Western cultures may be inclined in the direction of spiritual healing or alternative medicine, and thus Western-style interventions may be incompatible with their worldview.

Pluralist cultures with diverse and potentially conflicted cultural assumptions and values underline the importance of cultural knowledge, sensitivity, and competence in the delivery of psychological and biological treatments (Kazarian & Evans, 1998; Kazarian, 2007; Tseng, 2003).

Treatment of Psychological Disorders: Gender Issues

Gender competence refers to a good working knowledge of gender issues in biological and psychological treatments. Women present unique experiences that require consideration in their treatment. The stressors that women experience in life may differ from those experienced by men. First, women are more likely to experience sexism and its negative economic, psychological, social, and spiritual consequences. Second, women are more likely to feel the stress associated with taking care of their own families and members of their families-of-origin. Finally, women are more likely to have been sexually abused as children and to experience violence in adulthood.

Gender competence requires consideration of gender issues in the choice, implementation, and evaluation of psychological and biological interventions (Kazarian, 2007; Tseng, 2003).

Ethics and Boundaries

It is important that professionals maintain appropriate client–therapist boundaries so as not to compromise treatment effectiveness (Evans, 2004). The physical and sexual abuse by professionals of people with emotional disturbances is a serious issue. Abuse of trust is criminal and unethical. It harms the patient, and is grounds for litigation and loss of the therapist's licence. The College of Psychologists of Ontario revoked the licence of one therapist for making sexual advances to a client, thus "failing to maintain appropriate therapist/client boundaries" ("College Reveals Details," 1997). The woman and her husband also launched a civil suit against the psychologist (Hum, 1997a, 1997b). They alleged that the psychologist pursued a sexual relationship with the woman under the guise of therapy and sexually abused her for more than two years. A psychiatrist who became the head of the psychiatry department at a reputable North American university was charged, convicted, and sentenced to four years in prison for sexually assaulting his female patients, raping one of them, and forcing another to have oral sex (Reznek, 1992).

TREATMENT OF PSYCHOLOGICAL DISORDERS AND SOCIETY

Societal views of people with psychological disorders and their treatment have evolved over the years. The medieval belief that disturbed people were sinners possessed by the devil justified their persecution, excommunication, and even execution. The 16th century witnessed the beginnings of segregation of the mentally ill from society in insane asylums or "bedlams." These and later public mental hospitals warehoused the mentally ill in dark and cold cells, often chained to straw beds surrounded by their excrement, and offered them such "treatments" as bleeding and purging. Although sweeping reforms were initiated as early as the 18th century, mental hospitals offered only custodial care and a haven from the dangerous world outside. In the 1960s, institutionalization of the mentally ill was openly challenged in favour of deinstitutionalization.

Deinstitutionalization

Deinstitutionalization refers to transfer of the primary focus of treatment from inpatient care to community care. Advocates of the deinstitutionalization movement in North America and the United Kingdom described their efforts as "caring for people" and "putting people first" (Kazarian, McCabe, & Joseph, 1997). Human rights, cost containment, and accountability were important inspirational factors in the movement. Human rights considerations included rights of patients to live in the least restrictive environment, their right to a treatment setting free of maltreatment and abuse, and their right to receive treatment rather than be warehoused.

Deinstitutionalization resulted in the rapid release of thousands of emotionally disturbed people from psychiatric institutions. Over time, major weaknesses of the community-based movement became apparent:

- Communities were not prepared to care for the mentally ill people released.

- Mental health workers were inadequately trained in delivering community-based service.

- Mental health services were insufficiently coordinated and integrated.

- Resources for treatment and rehabilitation were inadequate in terms of available housing, case management, peer support, support for the family, and crisis intervention (Kazarian & Joseph, 1994; Kazarian, Joseph, & McCabe, 1996). As a result, deinstitutionalization contributed to homelessness, the "revolving door" phenomenon, and criminalization of the mentally ill.

Deinstitutionalization and community-based mental health care were intended to provide good-quality mental health care without relying on hospitals unless absolutely necessary (Police Executive Research Forum, 1997, p. 4). Instead, deinstitutionalization stripped psychiatric hospitals of their beds, dumped mentally ill people in the community, and forced those who were dumped to fend for themselves or end up in prisons. A comprehensive remedy to this situation would require significant improvements in institutional care, treatment and rehabilitation, and community supports and services (Kazarian et al., 1997). To facilitate the shift from institutional to community-based mental health care, a 2006 federal committee recommended a "targeted investment by the federal government ... in the form of a Mental Health Transition Fund" (Standing Committee on Social Affairs, Science and Technology, 2006).

LAW ENFORCEMENT AND DEINSTITUTIONALIZATION

A significant number of calls to urban police departments involve people with psychological disorders, or emotionally disturbed people (EDPs). Law enforcement officers who respond to such calls have very little theoretical and practical training in mental health issues. Critics suggest that deinstitutionalization, the prevailing ideology of community-based mental health care, and the traditional training of police in containing situations are the root causes of increased police encounters with mentally ill people and the housing of these people in jails. For example, a homeless mentally ill person who steals a sandwich from a convenience store because she is hungry may be arrested by officers whose training is based on containment rather than on referral to social services. As a result, many homeless people with mental illness wind up in jail. The need to recognize behaviour that is psychologically rather than criminally generated continues to be a pressing issue (APA, 1997).

On the positive side, deinstitutionalization, legislation (for example, the *Americans With Disabilities Act* in the United States), and community policing are causing police services and the mental health care system to address proactively the plight of mentally ill people and police mental health training. Growing communication and collaboration between the criminal justice system and the mental health care system for dealing with mentally ill people in the community in a humane and culturally appropriate manner is important, particularly for preventing violent behaviour. A strong partnership between the two is likely to correct known weaknesses in the mental health care system. It is also likely to enhance the effectiveness of the law enforcement response to people with mental illness, and their diversion into the mental health care system. Competently interacting and communicating with emotionally disturbed people and de-escalating confrontations before they turn violent may help to decrease killings of innocent people and law enforcement officers.

PREVENTION OF PSYCHOLOGICAL DISORDERS

Today, psychological interventions are being directed at preventing psychological disorders as well as treating them. Prevention can be targeted from the perspectives of tertiary prevention (after the disorder has occurred), secondary prevention (in a population with known risk factors), and primary prevention (before psychological disorders have occurred). As described in Table 11.1, primary prevention of psychological disorders can take the form of situation-focused prevention and competency-focused prevention (Cowen, 1985; Levonson, 2008; Paton et al., 2008). Ideally, prevention programs should consider a developmental perspective beginning as early in childhood as possible (Abela & Hankin, 2008) and should be culturally relevant (Knight, Roosa, & Umana-Taylor 2009) (see Box 11.1).

TABLE 11.1   Two Perspectives on the Prevention of Psychological Disorders

Situation-Focused Prevention	Competency-Focused Prevention
Aim: Reduce or eliminate environmental causes of psychological disorders or enhance situational factors that help prevent the development of disorders	Aim: Increase resilience and coping skills
Examples of Programs	**Examples of Programs**
Enhancing family functioning	Strengthening resistance to stress
Providing better educational opportunities for children	Improving social and vocational skills
Developing strong sense of connectedness to others and the community at large	Enhancing self-esteem
	Helping to develop skills needed to build stronger social support systems

---

BOX 11.1   Prevention of Psychological Disorders in Police Officers

People working in law enforcement are subject to on-the-job stressors and other stressors that are linked to organizational factors. These officers are not immune to developing psychological disorders that require professional attention. Yet, there is no definitive approach to dealing with the psychological problems they may develop.

Law enforcement agencies are increasingly using strategies to prevent psychological disorders in their personnel before such problems arise. While there are many psychosocial preventive approaches, it is important to identify those strategies that are most effective in preventing psychological problems in this select population.

A recent review of the literature has suggested the need for well-designed studies of psychosocial interventions with police and organization-based interventions to enhance the psychological health of police officers. The authors of this review add that available evidence suggests that the use of psychosocial interventions to prevent psychological problems in law enforcement personnel has no adverse effects, and that police officers may benefit from them both psychologically and physically.

Source: Peñalba, McGuire, and Leite (2009).

POINTS TO REMEMBER

Psychological and biological approaches are used to treat psychological disorders. The psychological approach includes insight-oriented psychotherapy, humanistic psychotherapy, behaviour therapies, operant conditioning therapies, observational learning and social skills training, cognitive therapies, and family, couple, and group therapies. The biological approach includes drug therapy, electroconvulsive therapy, and psychosurgery. Psychological and biological approaches combined are often more effective than either approach used alone. A positive client–therapist relationship seems to be a common component in the success of various forms of treatment.

Societal attitudes toward psychological disorders and their treatment have evolved over time. The deinstutionalization movement of the 1960s and 1970s had significant consequences for communities and the criminal justice system. Positive recent trends include improved police mental health training, and prevention of psychological disorders both in the general population and among law enforcement officers.

KEY TERMS

antidepressants

antipsychotic drugs

biological approach

cognitive psychotherapy

couple therapy

electroconvulsive therapy

family therapy

group therapy

insight-oriented psychotherapy

psychological approach

psychological treatment

psychopharmacology

psychosurgery

psychotherapy

REFERENCES

Abela, J.R.Z., & B.L. Hankin (Eds.). (2008). *Handbook of depression in children and adolescents.* New York: Guilford Press.

American Psychological Association (APA). (1997, November). More police opt for psychological training. *Monitor on Psychology, 28* (11). http://www.apa.org/monitor/nov97/police.html.

Americans With Disabilities Act of 1990, 42 USC 12101 et seq.

Barlow, D.H., J.M. Gorman, K.M. Shear, & S.W. Woods. (2000, May 17). Cognitive–behavioural therapy, imipramine, or their combination for panic disorder: A randomized control trial. *Journal of the American Medical Association, 283* (19), 2529–36.

Beck, J.S. (1995). *Cognitive therapy: Basics and beyond.* New York: Guilford Press.

Beck, J.S. (1996). *Questions and answers about cognitive therapy.* Bala Cynwyd, PA: Beck Institute for Cognitive Therapy and Research.

Choy, Y., A.J. Fyer, & J.D. Lipsitz. (2007). Treatment of specific phobias in adults. *Clinical Psychology Review, 27,* 266–86.

College reveals details of decision to revoke the therapist's licence. (1997, December 13). *The Ottawa Citizen,* p. C3.

Cowen, E.L. (1985). Person-centered approaches to primary prevention in mental health: Situation-focused and competence enhancement. *American Journal of Community Psychology, 13,* 31–48.

D'Zurilla, T., & M. Goldfried. (1971). Problem solving and behavior modification. *Journal of Abnormal Psychology, 78* (1), 107–26.

Evans, D.R. (2004). *The law, standards, and ethics in the practice of psychology.* Toronto: Emond Montgomery Publications.

Fernando, M.L.D., & S.S. Kazarian. (1995, April). Patient education in the drug treatment of psychiatric disorders. *CNS Drugs, 3,* 1–14.

Figiel, G.S., C. Epstein, W.M. McDonald, J. Amazon-Leece, L. Figiel, A. Saldivia, & S. Glover. (1998, February). The use of Rapid-Rate Transcranial Magnetic Stimulation (RTMS) in refractory depressed patients. *Journal of Neuropsychiatry, 10* (1), 20–25.

Furokawa, T.A., N. Watanabe, & R. Churchill. (2006). Psychotherapy plus antidepressant for panic disorder with or without agoraphobia: Systematic review. *British Journal of Psychiatry, 188,* 305–12.

Goodwin, F.K., & K.R. Jamison. (1990). *Manic–depressive illness.* New York: Oxford University Press.

Hogarty, G.E. (2002). *Personal therapy for schizophrenia and related disorders: A guide to individualized treatment.* New York: Guilford Press.

Hum, P. (1997a, December 10). Psychologist "had my heart": Woman alleges therapist had sex under guise of treatment. *The Ottawa Citizen,* pp. C1–C2.

Hum, P. (1997b, December 13). Psychologist "harmed" patient: Treatment "negligent," expert tells court. *The Ottawa Citizen*, p. C3.

Jacobson, N.S., & S.D. Hollon. (1996). Cognitive–behaviour therapy versus pharmacotherapy: Now that the jury's returned its verdict, it's time to present the rest of the evidence. *Journal of Consulting and Clinical Psychology, 64* (1), 74–80.

Kazarian, S.S. (Unpublished). The SMILE model of communication. London, ON: Author.

Kazarian, S.S. (2007). Psychological interventions and assessment. In D. Bhugra & K. Bhui (Eds.), *Textbook of cultural psychiatry* (pp. 424–33). Cambridge, UK: Cambridge University Press.

Kazarian, S.S., & D.R. Evans. (1998). *Cultural clinical psychology: Theory, research and practice.* New York: Oxford University Press.

Kazarian, S.S., & L.W. Joseph. (1994). A brief scale to help identify outpatients' level of need for community support services. *Hospital and Community Psychiatry, 45* (9), 935–37.

Kazarian, S.S., L.W. Joseph, & S.B. McCabe. (1996, June). A brief method of assessing adult inpatients' level of need for community support services. *Psychiatric Services, 47* (6), 654–56.

Kazarian, S.S., S.B. McCabe, & L.W. Joseph. (1997). Assessment and service needs of adult psychiatric inpatients: A systematic approach. *Psychiatric Quarterly, 68* (1), 5–23.

Kazarian, S.S., & E. Persad. (1995). *Training of police in community oriented psychiatric support: Recognizing mental illness module.* London, ON: Authors.

Kazarian, S.S., & D.A. Vanderheyden. (1992). Family education of relatives of people with psychiatric disability: A review. *Psychosocial Rehabilitation Journal, 15*, 67–84.

Knight, G.P., M.W. Roosa, & A.J. Umana-Taylor. (2009). *Studying ethnic minority and economically disadvantaged populations: Methodological challenges and best practices.* Washington, DC: American Psychological Association.

Levonson, R.L. (2008). Introduction to special issue focusing on resiliency and invulnerability in law enforcement. *International Journal of Emergency Mental Health, 10,* 85.

Lewickyi, M.A. (1997, July 28). Doctors wary as more children take Prozac. *The London Free Press*, p. C6.

Massad, P.M., & T.L. Hulsey. (2006). Exposure therapy renewed. *Journal of Psychotherapy Integration, 16,* 417–28.

Miklowitz, D.J. (1996). Psychotherapy in combination with drug treatment for bipolar disorders. *Journal of Clinical Psychopharmacology, 16* (2, Supplement 1), 56–66.

Miklowitz, D.J., E. Frank, & E.L. George. (1996). New psychosocial treatments for the outpatient management of bipolar disorder. *Psychopharmacology Bulletin, 32,* 613–21.

Paton, D., J.M. Violanti, P. Johnston, K.J. Burke, J. Clarke, & D. Keenan. (2008). Stress shield: A model of police resiliency. *International Journal of Emergency Mental Health, 10,* 95–108.

Paul, G.L., & R.J. Lentz. (1977). *Psychosocial treatment of chronic mental patients: Milieu vs. social learning programs.* Cambridge, MA: Harvard University Press.

Peñalba, V., H. McGuire, & J.R. Leite. (2009). Psychological interventions for prevention of psychological disorders in law enforcement officers (Review). New York: The Cochrane Collaboration, Wiley. http://www.library.nhs.uk/MENTAL HEALTH/ViewResource.aspx?rseID=29367.

Police Executive Research Forum. (1997). *The police response to people with mental illnesses: Trainer's guide and model policy.* Washington, DC: Author.

Reznek, L. (1992, March 7). Some psychiatrists need to have their heads examined: Review of C. Hyde's *Abuse of trust: The career of Dr. James Tyhurst. The Toronto Star,* p. J19.

Sacco, W.P., & A.T. Beck. (1995). Cognitive theory and therapy. In E.E. Becham & W.R. Leber (Eds.), *Handbook of depression* (2nd ed.) (pp. 329–51). New York: Guilford Press.

Standing Committee on Social Affairs, Science and Technology (2006). *Out of the shadows at last: Transforming mental health, mental illness and addiction services in Canada.* http://www.parl.gc.ca/common/Committee_SenRep.asp?Language=E&Parl=39&Ses=1&comm_id=47.

Tseng, W.S. (2003). *Clinician's guide to cultural psychiatry.* New York: Academic Press.

Weissman, M.M., J.C. Markowitz, & G.L. Klerman. (2007). *Clinician's guide to interpersonal psychotherapy.* New York: Oxford University Press.

Wilson, J.E., & K.M. Wilson. (2008). Amelioration of sexual fantasies to sexual abuse cues in an adult survivor of childhood sexual abuse: A case study. *Journal of Behavior Therapy and Experimental Psychiatry, 39,* 417–23.

Woods, R. (1993, November 28). Disturbing trend in use of Prozac. *The Toronto Star,* p. E2.

EXERCISES AND REVIEW

Self-Test

Circle the correct answer.

1. Chocolate lovers and cheese lovers who are depressed are best treated with

    a. MAOIs

    b. antipsychotic drugs

    c. electroconvulsive therapy

    d. none of the above

2. The saying "Actions speak louder than words" best represents which of the following psychological treatment approaches?

    a. behavioural therapy

    b cognitive therapy

    c. psychoanalysis

    d. none of the above

3. In the Bible, the Book of Proverbs (Chapter 23, Verse 7) states that a person is what he (she) thinks. Which of the following therapy principles does this statement, written over 2,000 years ago, represent?

    a. cognitive

    b. gestalt therapy

    c. humanistic

    d. insight-oriented

4. Which of the following is likely a dysfunctional silent assumption?

    a. I have to be successful in everything I do to be happy

    b. I can't live without you, baby

    c. if people disagree with me, it means they hate me

    d. all of the above

5. Cocaine Anonymous is an example of

    a. group therapy

    b. a self-help group

    c. psychodrama

    d. all of the above

6. Cognitive therapies are best suited to a person who

    a. has a gambling problem

    b. experiences general feelings of unhappiness

    c. has unresolved problems from childhood

    d. enjoys a martini once in a while

7. Which of the following antidepressants has fewer side effects than others and is therefore better tolerated?

    a. Prozac

    b. Zoloft

    c. Paxil

    d. all of the above

8. Which of the following statements is true?

    a. law enforcement officers and the mental health sector are responding most effectively to mentally ill people in the community

    b. relying only on the biological approach to treat mental health issues would be negligent

    c. in most cases, psychotherapy used alone is more effective than drug therapy

    d. all of the above

9. Which of the following is a negative outcome of deinstitutionalization?

    a. homelessness

    b. housing of emotionally disturbed people in jails

    c. a and b

    d. there is nothing negative about deinstitutionalization

10. Emotionally disturbed people on medication should be

    a. discouraged from taking their medication

    b. educated on the benefits of the medication

    c. encouraged to discuss the side effects of the medication with their physician

    d. b and c

Thinking About Psychology and Law Enforcement

1. Mr. Farris was a 40-year-old man with schizophrenia. Three police officers went to his home at the urging of relatives. The officers found him asleep and managed to wake him up after several minutes of trying. When Farris saw the officers, he picked up a fillet knife and a 41-cm steel rod and threatened to kill them. The officers started backing out of the apartment as they pleaded with Farris to calm down and drop the weapon. Suddenly, Farris raised both weapons over his head and lunged at one of the officers. The officer fired a shot from his service pistol, wounding Farris in the abdomen. He was pronounced dead on the operating table.

    Farris had been discharged from the military because of mental illness. He had been in and out of several mental health treatment centres and had not taken his medication for a month prior to the incident. The police officer who shot Farris was placed on administrative duties pending the outcome of an investigation. He had received numerous police awards and complimentary letters from citizens in his community for outstanding police work.

    a. What did the police officers do well in handling Farris?

    b. What could the police have done differently?

    c. Could the mental health sector and the criminal justice system prevent such a tragic incident from happening again? How could police services use mental health/law enforcement response teams specifically designed to deal with people with severe and persistent mental disorders? What sort of training should officers be given to deal with mentally ill people? Should police even deal with mental health calls? Explain.

2. In responding to an emotionally disturbed person, which of the following should law enforcement officers do and which should they avoid doing?

    a. Treat the person with respect and dignity.

        Do   Don't do

    b. Remain calm.

        Do   Don't do

    c. Be empathic and reassuring but firm.

        Do   Don't do

d. Touch the person without permission.

   Do   Don't do

e. Minimize distractions and overstimulation.

   Do   Don't do

f. Intimidate the person by using direct and continuous eye contact, invading his or her personal space, using inflammatory language and demeaning names, shouting, or criticizing.

   Do   Don't do

g. Recognize and acknowledge that the person's hallucinations and delusions are real to him or her.

   Do   Don't do

h. Challenge the person's hallucinations or delusions.

   Do   Don't do

i. Mislead the person into believing that the officer thinks and feels the way the person thinks and feels.

   Do   Don't do

j. Lie to the person so he or she allows the officer to help.

   Do   Don't do

k. Inform the person of the actions the officer intends to take before initiating them.

   Do   Don't do

l. Speak simply, slowly, and briefly to allow the person to process the information.

   Do   Don't do

m. Instruct the person hallucinating to listen to the officer's voice and not to other voices.

   Do   Don't do

n. Cheer up the person.

   Do   Don't do

o. Be alert to sudden changes in behaviour.

   Do   Don't do

p. Tell the person to shape up and stop acting crazy.

   Do   Don't do

q. Make sure the officer contains the situation—it's not the officer's job to make sure the person gets the service he or she needs.

   Do   Don't do

3. A mall security guard notices a dishevelled man who is apparently unaware of everything and everyone around him. The man is standing outside the mall on the corner of a busy intersection and singing out loud. A passerby approaches the security guard and says: "Why don't you take that man and put him in a nuthouse? He's going to hurt someone."

   Which of the following should the security guard consider in dealing with the situation? Why?

   a. Tell the passerby to mind her own business.

   b. Acknowledge the concern of the passerby and approach the singing man to assess his state of mind.

   c. Acknowledge the concern of the passerby and take the singing man into immediate custody.

   d. Ignore the passerby and the singing man.

   e. Acknowledge the concern of the passerby and observe the behaviour of the singing man from a distance to assess him and decide what to do.

4. While some law enforcement personnel may be amenable to seeking mental health services, others may be reluctant to do so—for example, because of fears of perception of weakness, or anxiety about confidentiality and job security. Consider these two factors and others that may limit officers' seeking help when they need it. Suggest possible strategies to make law enforcement officers more amenable to psychosocial intervention.

CHAPTER 12
Social Behaviour

CHAPTER OBJECTIVES

After completing this chapter, you should be able to:

- Define attitudes and attitude change strategies.
- Describe how people form impressions of others and explain their behaviours.
- Discuss social and group influences on behaviour.
- Discuss helping behaviour and aggression.

PREVIEW SCENARIO

Amadou Diallo was the good son who always smiled and never hurt anyone. On February 4, 1999, just after midnight, four white police officers who were looking for a black rape suspect spotted 22-year-old Diallo at the front door of his apartment building. According to police testimony, the African immigrant from Guinea fit the description of the suspect, and he acted in a way that made the police suspicious. Evidently, Diallo peered up and down the block and stepped back into the vestibule as the officers approached him, as if he did not want to be seen. He looked at the officers, his hands still on the doorknob, and started removing a black object from his right pocket. As Diallo pulled out the object, one of the officers thought he saw the slide of a black gun. The officer believed that Diallo was about to fire at his partner. He shouted "Gun!" and fired his weapon. In 8 seconds, the four officers fired 41 shots. Diallo's body slumped down, his head propped up against the wall. When one of the officers removed the object from Diallo's hand, he saw that it was a wallet. The officer held Diallo's hand, rubbed his face, and pleaded for him not to die. But Amadou Diallo was already dead.

The four police officers were tried on two counts each of second-degree murder and one count each of first-degree reckless endangerment. The trial took place in Albany, a less explosive location than the Bronx, where the shooting occurred. All four officers were fully cleared of the charges. All four were remorseful during the trial, and their ordeal was not yet over. Outside the courthouse, demonstrators were heard chanting "No justice, no peace." Diallo's father called the verdict the second murder of his son. For the Diallo family and supporters, there was a verdict but no closure.

In the weeks that followed, New York City witnessed protests and public outrage. Law-and-order advocates claimed that the police had made an honest mistake. They also believed that the conduct of the police had not been excessive because it involved perceived confrontation with deadly physical force. The advocates were outraged at the prevailing vicious anti-police bias.

Civil rights activists charged that the shooting was a case of racial profiling, concluding that Diallo's skin colour and race had a lot to do with it. They argued that if he had been white, his wallet would have been seen as a wallet. Civil rights activists charged that police created their own scenario of events surrounding the shooting of Diallo to justify their actions. Activists also felt insulted that the trial took place in Albany on the premise that 12 impartial people could not be found in the Bronx. (CNN, 2000; Chua-Eoan, 2000; Associated Press, 2000a, 2000b).

INTRODUCTION

social psychology
study of social situations that affect the thoughts, feelings, and actions of individuals

Amadou Diallo's tragic death touches on many aspects of **social psychology**, the study of social situations that affect the thoughts, feelings, and actions of individuals. Social psychologists attempt to explain:

- Attitudes and attitude change: How attitudes are developed and how they can be changed.

- Social perception or cognition: How people form impressions of others, how people try to understand why others behave the way they do, how people present themselves to other people, why people like other people, and why people dislike or even hate other people.

- Social influence: Factors that influence conformity, compliance, and obedience.

- Group influence: How groups influence performance, decision making, and social roles.

- Prosocial behaviour: Conditions under which people are likely to help other people.

- Aggressive behaviour: Conditions under which people are likely to hurt other people.

This chapter discusses these topics and highlights their relevance to law enforcement work.

ATTITUDES AND ATTITUDE CHANGE

attitude
predisposition to respond favourably or unfavourably toward objects, individuals, events, places, ideas, and situations

Attitudes are related to beliefs, behaviours, and feelings in complex ways (Albarracin, Johnson, & Zanna, 2005). Social psychologists define an **attitude** as a predisposition to respond favourably or unfavourably toward objects, individuals, events, places, ideas, and situations. The A-B-C model identifies three components of an attitude:

- **A**ffective component: How people *feel* about something—for example, inmates dislike corrections officers.

- Behavioural component: How people *act* toward something—for example, civil rights activists protest against police brutality toward non-whites.

- Cognitive component: What people *think* or *believe* about something—for example, police are fair and competent.

Cognitive Dissonance

There may be inconsistency in the three components of an attitude in the form of contradictions between beliefs and thoughts, between beliefs and feelings and behaviour, or between beliefs and feelings. This inconsistency or conflict can create **cognitive dissonance** (Festinger, 1957), the mental discomfort or pain a person experiences that is associated with being aware of attitude inconsistency.

People who are in a state of cognitive dissonance are motivated to reduce it. For example, Officer Nadia acknowledges that she is a smoker and holds the view that smoking causes cancer, and thus is in a state of cognitive dissonance. She may resolve her inner conflict in a number of ways:

- modifying one or more of her cognitions or thoughts—"I'm not really a smoker since I don't smoke that much";

- introducing additional cognitions—"I'm in excellent physical shape";

- introducing change in behaviour—"I think I'll quit smoking";

- advancing an argument that explains away the inconsistency—"Dad smoked till he was 93 and didn't die from cancer";

- diminishing the importance of the inconsistency—"They don't know for sure that smoking is linked to cancer"; or

- denying the link between the inconsistent cognitions—"There is no link between smoking and cancer."

cognitive dissonance
mental discomfort or pain a person experiences that is associated with being aware of attitude inconsistency

Prediction of Behaviour

The cognitive and affective components of an attitude may not always govern behaviour. A teenager may dislike security officers (affective component) and may think they are overpaid "pigs in disguise," but may obey their order to vacate a building. In this case, knowing what the teenager thinks and feels about security officers does not accurately predict the behaviour of the teenager toward the officers. An important reason for cognitive and affective components of an attitude being poor governors of behaviour is that beliefs and feelings may be weak or vague.

Behaviour may not be well governed or accurately predicted from the cognitive and affective components of an attitude for another reason. Factors that are more powerful than thoughts and feelings may override the governing power that thoughts and feelings have on behaviour. More influential factors may include cultural and social norms and values, and special circumstances. For example, some inmates may give in to group pressure and participate in a prison riot even though they believe that riots do not resolve problems.

Attitude Formation

Attitudes are formed mainly by the learning principles of classical conditioning, operant conditioning, modelling, and other forms of social learning (see Chapter 5). As children, people learn what they should think and feel about themselves and other aspects of life, and how they should act toward the various life domains.

Attitude Change

Social psychologists identify four key components to persuasion: the communicator, the message, the medium, and the target. Together, these components can persuade someone to change his or her attitude about something.

The *communicator* is the person who conveys the message. Six characteristics contribute to a communicator's ability to change people's attitudes:

- expertise and credibility,

- power or clout,

- attractiveness,

- likableness,

- similarity to the recipient of the message or ability of the recipient to relate to the communicator, and

- gender (in favour of males at present).

The *message* is what is conveyed to a target audience for it to be persuasive. Appeals to change attitudes may be rational or emotional. Rational appeals target people's reasoning and logical thinking. Emotional appeals target people's feelings. Negative emotional appeals arouse unpleasant feelings (such as fear) and stimulate attitude change. The less people know about an issue, the more likely they will respond to negative emotional appeals. Similarly, the more people are frightened, the more likely they will respond to negative emotional appeals. Positive emotional appeals arouse pleasant feelings (such as joy) and stimulate attitude change.

A message may also be one-sided or two-sided. A one-sided message presents only the views of the communicator and is more likely to be effective with an audience that is sympathetic to those views. A two-sided message presents the communicator's and the opposition's views and is more likely to be effective with a well-informed and intelligent audience.

The *medium* is the means by which a persuasive message is delivered. For example, television is a powerful medium.

The *target* is the intended audience for the message. To be effective, a message should consider the following audience characteristics:

- age,

- gender,

- self-esteem, and

- strength of the audience's attitude.

SOCIAL PERCEPTION

Social perception or cognition is the process of making sense of people. It has five critical aspects: how people form impressions of others, how people present themselves to others, how people attribute causes to the behaviours of others, why people are attracted to others, and why people dislike or even hate others.

social perception
process of making sense of people

Perception of People

FIRST IMPRESSIONS

People form impressions of others on the basis of their own mood and the availability of information on the others. People's impressions of others are more positive when their own mood is positive—that is, happy or relaxed. Similarly, people's impressions of others are more negative when their own mood is negative—for example, sad or angry.

Attributes that affect people's impressions of others are sex, age, diversity (for example, ethnicity or race), physical appearance, physical attractiveness, personal status (for example, marital status or occupation), and verbal and non-verbal behaviours.

People's overall impressions or judgments of others are heavily based on first impressions rather than on careful consideration of all the facts. The **primacy effect** refers to the process in which people's first impressions of other people are more dominant than later impressions. It seems likely that people pay more attention to initial information and create a framework or schema (see below) to interpret later information. New information that is consistent with a first impression or a schema is accepted. Similarly, new information that is inconsistent with initial information is rejected or distorted to fit the established schema. In either case, initial impressions are retained or strengthened.

primacy effect
process in which people's first impressions of other people are more dominant than later impressions

EXPECTATIONS

Expectations also affect people's perceptions of others. First, expectations colour people's attitudes and conduct toward others. People see what they expect to see—that is, what they pay attention to and what they ignore—and respond accordingly. Second, expectations serve a self-fulfilling prophecy function. They bring about the very behaviours that people expect from others. Expectations develop on the basis of a variety of human attributes, including age, sex, cultural or racial group, occupation, and social class. A law enforcement officer who expects that a long-haired male suspect is going to give her a hard time may act in a way that induces that suspect to give her a hard time.

SCHEMAS

A **schema** is an integrated set of cognitions or a knowledge base about objects, people, and events. Schemas are influenced by culture (Ridley, Chih, & Olivera, 2000) and may or may not be accurate. Nevertheless, they are important because they organize the way people recall, recognize, and categorize the social world. People fit others into schemas even when there is limited information about the others or gaps in knowledge of them. Five kinds of schemas relate to people and events:

schema
integrated set of cognitions or knowledge base about objects, people, and events

social stereotypes
beliefs people have about the characteristics of a group of people

- *Group schemas*, or **social stereotypes**, refer to beliefs people have about the characteristics of a group of people. These beliefs about how members of the group think and act are not proven even though they may be widely held.

- *Person schemas* refer to people's beliefs about particular individuals. "Musical" is a likely person schema of U2 singer Bono. "Flirt," "jerk," and "nice guy" are other examples of person schemas. People process and remember information that is consistent with their schemas. People's beliefs about individuals are based on social stereotypes, preconceptions, and expectations of the individuals. Mutambo, who is expected to be a warm person, is perceived as being warm. Abigail, who is expected to be a cold person, is perceived as being cold. Law enforcement officers who expect that black suspects will be friendly and respectful will probably perceive black suspects as friendly and respectful, and will react to them as if they are friendly and respectful.

- *Self-schemas* involve self-knowledge—that is, personality traits and behavioural patterns that are central to our own self-definitions. The self-schemas of Western cultures tend to be more individualistic than those of Asian, Latino, and African cultures. The self-schemas of many non-Western cultures are more collectivistic, meaning that interdependence in social relationships is more highly valued and expected.

- *Role schemas* refer to people's knowledge about norms and behaviours expected of them in particular social or occupational positions. Law enforcement work, for example, is connected with such behaviours as self-control and respect for authority.

- *Event schemas*, or *scripts*, involve organized sequences of well-known activities in well-known situations. For example, a police officer's encounter with the chief of police entails a script, as does dining in a restaurant. The restaurant script involves waiting to be seated, looking at the menu, ordering the meal, eating, paying the bill, and leaving the restaurant.

Self-Presentation

People present themselves in ways that are meant to influence the impressions they make on others.

Ingratiation is a self-presentation strategy in which people make deliberate efforts to impress others or to get other people to like them. Officer Dean seems to agree with everything his boss says or thinks. He goes out of his way to praise her and point out her accomplishments. Officer Dean also tries to impress his boss by doing as many favours for her as possible. Officer Dean ingratiates himself subtly and successfully without raising his boss's suspicion that his efforts are deliberate and calculated.

Self-promotion is a self-presentation strategy in which people present themselves as competent to gain the respect of others.

Intimidation is a self-presentation strategy in which people present themselves as dangerous to get what they want from others.

— *Exemplification* is a self-presentation strategy in which people advance themselves as people of integrity and moral purity.

— *Supplication* is a self-presentation strategy in which people project an image of weakness and dependency to elicit sympathy from others.

Attribution

Attribution is a social cognitive process in which an individual observes the actions of another and makes an inference about the reasons for those actions. Attributions are not always accurate. There are five types of attribution errors.

The **fundamental attribution error** refers to the process in which people attribute their own actions to situational or external environmental factors, but they attribute other people's actions to their personality traits. This error has been demonstrated so many times that it has been suggested half-jokingly that only extraterrestrials may be free from it (cited in Choi, Nisbett, & Norenzayan, 1999). According to the fundamental attribution error, the shooting of Amadou Diallo was more likely due to the personality traits of police (for example, a tendency to stereotype) rather than to the external factors confronting the officers at the time of the shooting. Of course, it is quite possible that the shooting was not due to a fundamental attribution error but that the police were in fact driven by racism.

The fundamental attribution error seems to operate more in individualistic cultures (for example, Canadian and American) than in collectivistic cultures (for example, Asian, Aboriginal, and Latino), which place greater emphasis on social responsibility and social obligation (Miller, 1984; Choi et al., 1999). Needless to say, differences in attribution, whether personal or cultural, are a potential source of conflict. For example, the higher crime rates among some groups may be attributed to blood or genes when in fact criminal behaviour may have to do more with life conditions, such as poverty.

 Defensive attribution is a second form of attribution error. It refers to the process in which an individual or a group is blamed or held responsible for a misfortune. Blaming Armenians for the Armenian Genocide and Jews for the Holocaust are examples of defensive attribution. Similarly, women who are raped are sometimes accused of "asking for it." Victims who are held responsible for their victimization are perceived as bad people who deserve their fate. Those who blame them consider themselves immune from misfortune. Defensive attribution is a form of disguised prejudice.

Self-serving bias is an attribution error in which people take credit for their successes. That is, they attribute their successes to internal or personality factors, and they blame their failures on external or situational causes. For example, Officer Shani attributes her promotion to her superior conflict resolution skills. When she is passed over for an interesting job, she blames it on "politics." The self-serving bias may be healthy in that it boosts a person's ego, but it may also be unhealthy because it distorts reality.

Halo effect is the process in which people attribute positive traits to others on the basis of their initial knowledge that the others have positive traits. For example, Officer Amira believes that Officer Sacha is compassionate based on her initial understanding that he is good-looking, kind, and smart. Similarly, Officer Paula

attribution
social cognitive process in which an individual observes the actions of another and makes an inference about the reasons for those actions

fundamental attribution error
process in which people attribute their own actions to situational or external environmental factors, but they attribute other people's actions to their personality traits

defensive attribution
process in which an individual or a group is blamed or held responsible for a misfortune

self-serving bias
attribution error in which people take credit for their successes

halo effect
process in which people attribute positive traits to others on the basis of their initial knowledge that the others have positive traits

infers that inmate Suzanne is lazy based on her prior knowledge that Suzanne is obnoxious and rude.

Assumed-similarity bias refers to the tendency of people to believe that others they know or meet for the first time are similar to themselves.

Interpersonal Attraction

interpersonal attraction
aspect of social perception that looks at people's positive feelings toward others

Interpersonal attraction, such as falling in love or being in love, is a major topic in social psychology (Berscheid & Hatfield, 1978; Orbuch & Sprecher, 2006). **Interpersonal attraction** is the aspect of social perception that looks at people's positive feelings toward others. People are attracted to others for two major reasons: they enjoy the company of others and they need intimacy. People become the object of the affection of other people (for example, friends or romantic partners) because of personal attributes and situational considerations. Specific factors that determine attraction to others include the following:

- Physical proximity: Boys and girls are more likely to be attracted to the next-door boys and girls than those outside their neighbourhood.

- Similarity: People are more likely to feel attracted to those who have similar views and tastes.

- Physical attractiveness: People are more likely to feel attracted to those who are physically attractive than to those who are not.

- Mere exposure: The more people see someone or the more that person becomes familiar, the more they like that person.

- Reciprocal liking: People are more likely to like someone who likes them.

Social Prejudice

social prejudice
widespread and inflexible negative attitude toward members of an "out-group" that is based on incorrect or incomplete information

Prejudice, stereotyping, and discrimination are related concepts (Nelson, 2009). Social prejudice is the aspect of social perception that examines people's negative feelings toward other people. **Social prejudice** is a widespread and inflexible negative attitude toward members of an "out-group" that is based on incorrect or incomplete information. There are four aspects to prejudice. First, it involves negative and hostile feelings toward all members of a target group. Second, while social psychologists traditionally identify "minority" groups as the usual target groups for prejudice, the definition here stresses out-groups (minority or majority) as potential targets. It can be argued, for example, that black people can be as prejudiced against white people as white people are against black people. The definition also allows the possibility of "minority" against "minority" prejudice. For example, black people can be as prejudiced against Korean people as they are against white people. Third, negative attitudes are likely unfounded and unwarranted. Fourth, prejudicial attitudes are like seasoned politicians—they are tough to crack.

COMPONENTS OF SOCIAL PREJUDICE

stereotyping
holding preconceived and unfavourable beliefs about a particular group or individuals in the group

Dislike and hate are the affective expressions of social prejudice. **Stereotyping** is the cognitive expression of social prejudice. It refers to holding preconceived and unfavourable beliefs about a particular group or the individuals in the group. Stereo-types can relate to sex, age, sexual orientation, mental health or capacity, and racial, religious, and ethnic groups. Over the years, Jews have been stereotyped as shrewd and Italians as overly emotional. Similarly, Americans believe that the typical American is very assertive, whereas Canadians believe that the typical Canadian is submissive, even though both groups show identical scores in objective assessments of assertiveness (Debusmann, 2009).

Discrimination is the behavioural expression of social prejudice. Discriminatory practices by the public and law enforcement on the basis of race, religion, or national or ethnic origin increased in both Canada and the United States in the wake of 9/11 (Kazarian, Crichlow, & Bradford, 2007). Discriminatory behaviours included people being called "terrorist" or "Osama bin Laden" while walking the streets, police wiretapping of telephone lines, and racial profiling through which airlines prevented passengers from boarding flights. In one case, a Sikh psychiatrist who was mistaken for an Arab was yelled at by a patient during an office visit: "You diaper-headed Arab. Go back to your country" (Lewis, 2009). Discrimination is harmful and illegal behaviour that deprives groups or group members of their civil rights.

discrimination
illegal and negative behaviour that deprives a group or its members of their civil rights

FORMS OF SOCIAL PREJUDICE

Racism refers to prejudice against members of a particular racial group. It may be overt (obvious) or disguised. Racism is unlikely to be eliminated under weak antiracism policies and social and economic conditions that keep people unequal. As a first step, Canadians must stop categorizing people into minority and majority cultures and referring to them as ethnic or racial minorities. A more acceptable form of address is hyphenation of the culture of origin (for example, Ukrainian-Canadian). Second, Canadians need to reject the recent ideology that multiculturalism is racism. Rather, misinterpreting and misapplying the principles of multiculturalism is racism. Third, Canadians must develop aggressive laws against racist acts and act swiftly against racist conduct. Fourth, Canadians need to work to decrease differences in socio-economic status so that people can encounter one another in equal-status roles. Finally, Canadians need to develop initiatives that foster interracial cooperation among school-age children in the school system. Racial prejudices can be overcome early in life under the right circumstances and the development of accurate schemas.

racism
prejudice against members of a particular racial group

Sexism is prejudice against members of one of the sexes, but usually refers to prejudice against women. When women are underrepresented in positions of power, relegated to low-status and low-paying jobs, and denied equal pay for work of equal value, all of society loses.

sexism
prejudice against members of one of the sexes

Finally, **diversism** is prejudice against people of diversity and includes racism, sexism, ageism, youthism, homophobia, and discrimination against mentally and physically disabled people (Kazarian, 2001; Kazarian et al., 2007). Diversism contributes to victimization, exploitation, and exclusion from full citizenry.

diversism
prejudice against people of diversity

EXPLANATIONS OF SOCIAL PREJUDICE

Social prejudice can be explained in terms of motivational, cognitive, and learning theories.

Motivational theories propose that prejudice against others enhances the self-esteem or sense of security of those who are prejudiced. These theories also suggest that prejudice is more likely among people with authoritarian personalities. An **authoritarian personality** is one that views the world as a threatening place or jungle. This negative view of the world is a result of some people's upbringing in a harsh and punitive home.

authoritarian personality
personality that views the world as a threatening place or jungle

Cognitive theories of prejudice propose that people develop schemas to make sense of their social world. Schemas may or may not provide accurate summaries of this world or other people. Cognitive theories also suggest that social categorization is a basic human process. **Social categorization** is the process of putting other people into groups or categories. People are grouped on the basis of sex, age, ethnicity, citizenry, race, occupation or political party. For example, "pigs" is a social categorization of police. Social categories serve five functions:

social categorization
process of putting other people into groups or categories

- They minimize the differences among in-group members.
- They emphasize the differences between in-group members and out-group members.
- They lump together members of the out-group more so than members of the in-group.
- They affect how information about individuals belonging to a particular group is received (information about an individual that is consistent with the social category is remembered easily, whether it is accurate or not).
- They may draw people's attention to distinctive characteristics of a group and lead people to believe that there is a correlation between these characteristics and the group. For example, a person may encounter a few law enforcement officers who act in a way that seems racist and conclude incorrectly that most or all officers are racist.

Learning theories of prejudice propose that prejudice is learned. Learning occurs when children are rewarded for expressing prejudicial attitudes and are exposed to prejudice in parents, friends, and media portrayals.

SOCIAL INFLUENCE

social influence
social pressure; the effect that social situations have on the way people think and act

Social influence, or social pressure, refers to the effect that social situations have on the way people think and act. Social pressure may be so powerful that it may result in people supporting views they do not really condone or committing acts they would normally consider unthinkable. It is highly likely that those who went along with the extermination of millions of Armenians and Jews in the First World War and the Second World War, respectively, were heavily influenced by prevailing social forces. The concept of social influence is not an apology or forgiveness for the horrific actions (or inaction) of people, but instead illustrates the vulnerability of people to social forces. Social influence is highly relevant to many aspects of law enforcement work. (See Box 12.1.)

conformity
behavioural pattern of going along with or giving in to the opinions and actions of others

Three behavioural patterns are influenced by social pressure: conformity, compliance, and obedience. **Conformity** is the behavioural pattern of going along with or giving in to the opinions and actions of others. The following are some factors that relate to conformity:

BOX 12.1   Police Interrogations

Law enforcement interrogators are highly trained in the psychological tactics of social influence for the purpose of obtaining confessions from suspects. Police officers in the United States for the past four decades, and more recently in Canada, have been receiving formal training in the Reid Technique, an interrogation approach developed and described by John E. Reid and colleagues in the authoritative text *Criminal Interrogation and Confessions* and considered a more liberal and humane alternative to the traditional "third-degree" interrogative approach.

The Reid Technique views interrogation as a "psychological undoing of deception," using a three-part process to obtain an admission of guilt from suspects.

The first stage is *factual analysis*, in which a highly structured interview is conducted to gain insight into the possible offender and to determine the direction of the investigation.

The second stage is the *behaviour analysis interview*, a non-accusatory question-and-answer session for the purposes of eliciting information in a controlled environment and to provide the investigator with verbal, paralinguistic, and non-verbal behaviour indicators that support either probable truthfulness or deception.

The third part of the technique, the *accusatory interrogation*, is employed for the purpose of eliciting the truth from someone whom the investigator believes lied during the non-accusatory interview. When properly employed, the persuasive efforts used in the accusatory interrogation stage are "effective enough to persuade a guilty suspect to tell the truth but not so powerful as to cause an innocent person to confess."

The accusatory interrogation stage is associated with nine steps based on principles related to deception and the criminal mind (avoidance of the consequences of telling the truth, justification of the crime, and victim mentality). The nine steps include direct positive confrontation to persuade the guilty suspect to tell the truth; theme development, in which moral or psychological excuses for the suspect's criminal behaviour are offered; presentation of an alternative question (for example, "Was this whole thing your idea or did you get talked into it?"); development of the oral confession; and conversion of the oral confession to a court-admissible document. Guilty suspects subjected successfully to the Reid *nine steps of interrogation* go through identifiable stages, including initial denial, a state of quiet and withdrawal, mental debate whether or not to confess, admission of guilt, and disclosure of the details of the crime.

In the wake of 9/11, police interrogation techniques, including the Reid Technique, have been under more intense scrutiny by the courts, scientists, and the public. While proponents point to the effectiveness of police interrogations in solving crimes and preventing terrorist attacks, police interrogation techniques have been criticized on the grounds that they are psychologically manipulative and coercive in the use of violence or physical intimidation, and that their effectiveness lends empirical support to the argument that the process is likely to evoke more false confessions than true admissions of guilt.

Needless to say, police interrogations that violate the constitutional and human rights of suspects are deterrents to justice and a major obstacle to the ideal of a global peace culture.

Sources: Inbau et al. (2001); Jayne and Buckley (2009).

- Gender: Men and women are equally conforming in situations that are familiar to the sexes. There is some evidence that women may conform more in public situations than in private ones.

- Group identification: The more people are attracted to a group, the more likely they will conform with the group's opinions and actions.

- Public announcement: People are more likely to conform in situations that require publicly announcing their actions—for example, voting by raising their hands as opposed to voting by secret ballot.

- Ambiguity of task: People are more likely to conform in ambiguous situations or when working with others on tasks that have no clearcut answers or solutions. That is, people go along with the group when they're not sure what to do in a situation.

- Personal competence: People are more likely to give in to social pressure when they feel less competent than other group members.

- Social supporter: People are less likely to conform when they have a social supporter within a group who backs them up in an unpopular minority opinion or action.

compliance
behavioural pattern of giving in or saying yes to an explicit request from someone who is not in authority

Compliance is the behavioural pattern of giving in or saying yes to an explicit request from someone who is not in authority. Two techniques that are used in sales to gain compliance from prospective customers are:

- The *foot-in-the door technique* involves asking for a small favour and then following it with a much bigger request. Advertisers make small requests of customers (for example, scratching a card or answering simple questions) to try to lure them into purchasing the advertised products.

- The *door-in-the face technique* involves asking for a big favour first and then following it with a more realistic request. Officer Julius receives an emergency call from his daughter, who informs him that she desperately needs $500 right away. When he tells her that all he can offer is $100, she readily accepts his "generous" offer to bail her out!

obedience
behavioural pattern of giving in to the commands of a person in authority

Obedience is the behavioural pattern of giving in to the commands of a person in authority. Instances of blind obedience or "only following orders" include Turkish officers carrying out the Armenian Genocide and Nazi officers carrying out the Jewish Holocaust. Factors that influence obedience are:

- Prestige: People are more likely to obey reputable or distinguished authority figures.

- Dissenters: People are less likely to obey authority figures in the presence of others who disobey orders.

- Personality: Authoritarian people or people who believe they have no control over what happens to them are more likely to obey people in authority.

GROUP INFLUENCE

A group is a collection of two or more people who identify with the collective, a common goal, and regular interaction. Groups can influence individual performance, decision making, and social roles.

Individual Performance in Groups

Social facilitation is the tendency of people's performance to improve when other people are around. Social facilitation usually occurs with well-learned or rehearsed tasks but not with new, complex, or difficult tasks (Zajonc, 1965). **Social loafing** is the tendency of group members to slack off or not pull their weight when working as part of the group. Social loafing lowers the performance of a group (Latané, 1981) and is seen in a variety of cultures. The negative effect of social loafing can be reduced by decreasing group size, increasing the sense of responsibility of each group member, and building in a process of group performance evaluation.

Deindividuation is the tendency of group members to lose their individual identity, to become less inhibited, and to care less about being evaluated by others. Deindividuated people are highly emotionally aroused, have intense feelings of cohesiveness with the "herd," are likely to do things they would not do otherwise, and are difficult to stop. Deindividuated behaviours range from the wild celebrations of English soccer fans (seen by some people as hooligans) to the violent actions of the Ku Klux Klan. Deindividuation is caused by the belief that people cannot be held personally accountable for their behaviour and by the focus on the external environment rather than on internal thoughts and standards (Prentice-Dunn & Rogers, 1989).

social loafing
tendency of group members to slack off or not pull their weight when working as a part of the group

deindividuation
tendency of group members to lose their individual identity, to become less inhibited, and to care less about being evaluated by others

Group Influence on Decision Making

Risky shift is the tendency of group members to make riskier decisions in a group than when alone. **Group polarization effect** refers to the tendency of people to strengthen and solidify their positions as a result of group discussion. **Groupthink** is the tendency of a cohesive or close-knit group to arrive at unanimous but poorly thought-out decisions to avoid disharmony. A famous case of groupthink is the fatal launch of the space shuttle *Challenger* in January 1986 despite knowledge of faults in its construction. The shuttle exploded shortly after take-off, killing all of the astronauts. Other examples are the escalation of the war in Vietnam during the 1960s and the Watergate coverup in the United States in the 1970s. These disastrous situations involved highly cohesive groups with a strong desire for group unity and consensual decision making. Groupthink can be avoided if groups acknowledge that they can exist and are open to critical thinking, allow group members to disagree or take on the role of "devil's advocate," assign independent groups to work on the same issue, and consider the advantages and disadvantages of all the available options (Janis, 1982).

Minority influence refers to the process in which a single group member or a minority of group members swings the majority. Minority influence is the opposite of majority influence, in which the larger group wins and even gives the boot to those who do not go along with the majority decision. A historical example of min-

risky shift
tendency of group members to make riskier decisions in a group than when alone

group polarization effect
tendency of people to strengthen and solidify their positions as a result of group discussion

groupthink
tendency of a cohesive or close-knit group to arrive at unanimous but poorly thought-out decisions to avoid disharmony

minority influence
process in which a single group member or a minority of group members swings the majority

ority influence is the black civil rights movement in the United States in the 1950s. While going against the majority can be a painful experience, minority influence contributes to new, creative, and often high-quality solutions to problems. An approach that contributes to minority influence is *informational pressure*, the process of presenting the minority view consistently and confidently to shape and direct the majority view.

Group Influence on Social Roles

Social roles are also influenced by groups. People take on different roles in life. A law enforcement officer may also be a sister, friend, lover, tourist, volunteer, and instructor. Groups define roles for their members, behaviours that are considered appropriate for the people occupying various positions within the group. Roles are powerful dictators of actions, as illustrated in a two-week experiment on prison life (Zimbardo et al., 1973). White, middle-class college students who were considered emotionally stable, physically healthy, and law-abiding were volunteer participants in the study. Recruited through ads placed in a city newspaper, they were randomly assigned by the flip of a coin to either the prison guard role or the prisoner role.

Neither "prisoners" nor "prison guards" received any training in their respective roles. The prisoners did not even know that the experiment was beginning when they were arrested by city police on a quiet Sunday morning. The nine college students who were picked up in a surprise mass arrest were each charged with a felony, read their constitutional rights, spread-eagled against the police car, searched, handcuffed, and hauled off to the police station for booking. After being fingerprinted and blindfolded, the students were transported to the "Stanford County Prison" (the basement of the Stanford University psychology building) where they were stripped naked, skin-searched, deloused, issued a uniform and a number, and each placed in a cell with two other prisoners.

The prison guards were fitted with military khaki uniforms, billy clubs, whistles, handcuffs, and cell keys, and were allowed to wear silver reflector sunglasses to make eye contact with them impossible. They were not given any special training in how to be prison guards, but were merely instructed to "maintain law and order" in the prison and not to take any nonsense from the prisoners.

Because of the behaviour of the prisoners and the guards, what was to be a two-week experiment was instead terminated after six days. The normal, sane, and emotionally stable students developed "perverted relationships" in a remarkably short time (Zimbardo & Ruch, 1976). An initial prisoner revolt was crushed by the guards. The mild-mannered guards quickly fell into their roles and became abusive, authoritarian, and sadistic. They dealt with prisoners using "commands, insults, degrading references, verbal and physical aggression, and threats" (Zimbardo & Ruch, 1976, p. 372). One of the guards made prisoners "call each other names and clean the toilets out with their hands." The initially autonomous and self-respecting prisoners fell into subservient and debased roles. They related to the guards in terms of "resistance, giving information when asked questions, questioning, and (initially) deprecating the guards" (Zimbardo & Ruch, 1976, p. 372). One of the prisoners had to be released in less than 36 hours after developing "uncontrolled crying, fits of rage, disorganized thinking and severe depression" (Zimbardo & Ruch, 1976, p. 372).

While the mock prison experiment is not typical of studies in social psychology, it demonstrates the powerful influence that roles can exert on social behaviour.

PROSOCIAL BEHAVIOUR

Prosocial behaviour refers to people's willingness to help other people. For example, Oscar Schindler helped Jews escape from Nazi death camps during the Second World War. Schindler most likely followed the four basic steps to helping behaviour later identified by Latané and Darley (1970):

1. noticing an event or a situation that may require help,

2. perceiving or interpreting the event as requiring help,

3. assuming responsibility for providing the help, and

4. deciding on a plan to help and implementing the plan.

Helping behaviour is likely influenced by both personality characteristics and situational factors. People who help other people are described as caring, helpful, empathic, self-assured, and altruistic. However, people who seemingly fail to help other people may not necessarily be unkind, uncaring, or unhelpful. Their failure to help may be due to other reasons, such as the situations they find themselves in. Situational factors that are likely to influence helping behaviour include the specific needs of the person who needs help, the emotional and financial costs associated with helping that person, the level of expectation of reciprocity ("You scratch my back and I'll scratch yours"), and the number of people involved in the situation.

A situational factor that plays a major role in helping behaviour is the **bystander effect**, which is the tendency of people who witness an emergency situation to help *less* when others are present than when they are alone.

The murder of Kitty Genovese in New York City is a famous example of the bystander effect. In 1964, *The New York Times* reported that Genovese was returning home late at night when she was stalked and stabbed by a man in three separate attacks. Thirty-eight respectable, law-abiding neighbours in a nearby apartment complex watched the more than half-hour ordeal and did nothing. The "sound of their voices and the sudden glow of their lights" (Latané & Darley, 1970) interrupted the assailant twice and frightened him off. Nevertheless, the attacker returned each time, sought Genovese out, and stabbed her again. Not one person called the police during the ordeal. One witness called the police after Genovese died.

Kitty Genovese's death and the apathy shown by the witnesses shocked the nation. Social psychologists concluded that people's failure to help others is not due to their having a defective personality. Rather, their failure to intervene may be due to **diffusion of responsibility** (Latané & Darley, 1970), the process in which feelings of responsibility to offer assistance are spread across all witnesses. A person may decide not to call the police for help thinking that other witnesses have already done so. Alternatively, the person may interpret the inaction of others as evidence that no action is needed.

The following is a list of situations in which bystanders are *less* likely to help a person in distress:

prosocial behaviour
people's willingness to help other people

bystander effect
tendency of people who witness an emergency situation to help less when others are present than when they are alone

diffusion of responsibility
process in which feelings of responsibility to offer assistance are spread across all witnesses to an emergency situation

- The situation is ambiguous (for example, the bystander can't tell whether a fight between two teenagers is real or just play fighting).

- The person in distress is not physically attractive in the eyes of the bystander.

- The bystander sees the person in distress as being different or from a different cultural or racial group.

- The bystander thinks the person in distress is drunk.

- The bystander witnesses family members fighting.

- The bystander is a woman rather than a man.

- There is a possibility that the perpetrator will retaliate against the bystander.

- There is a possibility that the bystander will get hurt.

- The bystander believes that victims are responsible for their problems and deserve their fate.

- The bystander has no history of being helped.

- The bystander has no experience with crime and intervention efforts.

- The bystander lacks helping skills (for example, training in first aid).

- The costs of helping outweigh the rewards of helping.

- The bystander is in a bad mood.

- The bystander is in a hurry.

- The weather is bad.

AGGRESSIVE BEHAVIOUR

Aggression and violence are multifaceted, manifesting themselves in domestic conflict and in acts of terrorism (Flannery, Vazsonyi, & Waldman, 2007). Aggression is a serious issue for law enforcement officers, who may be the victims of aggressive behaviour or the perpetrators of violence. As victims of violence, law enforcement officers may be taken hostage or killed in the line of duty. Aggression in the form of abuse of authority and power is also unfortunately well documented among law enforcement officers, and police abuse and brutality continue as a persistent and widespread issue (CBC News, 2008; Weisburd et al., 2000).

Aggression Defined

aggression
intentional infliction of physical or emotional harm on another person who does not consent to it

Aggression is the intentional infliction of physical or emotional harm on another person who does not consent to it. This definition excludes consensual sado-masochistic acts; sports that involve violence, such as hockey and boxing; and medical procedures that are painful but are carried out for the benefit and well-being of the patient.

Causes of Aggression

BIOLOGICAL THEORIES

In the past, morphologists tried to identify physical features that distinguished criminals and violent people. As early as the 16th century, violent men were identified as having thickened open lips, small ears and noses, bushy eyebrows, and long, thin fingers. Similarly, Italian criminals in the 19th century were differentiated on the basis of having high cheek bones, large jaws, and tattoos.

Today, biological theorists look for genetic clues to and physical causes of aggression. These include defective genes, inherited traits, defects in brain structure or function, and hormonal imbalances. Aggression is believed to be influenced by heredity even though the exact mechanism of the inheritance is not known. It is possible that people inherit the tendency to be aggressive or that they inherit the tendency to be impulsive, which in turn makes aggression more likely.

Several parts of the brain are thought to influence aggression: the amygdala (part of the limbic system), the hypothalamus, and the prefrontal cortex (see Chapter 2). Damage to these areas of the brain increase aggression.

The hormone testosterone seems to play an important role in aggressive behaviour during the formative years (early brain development) and in adulthood. Violent criminals seem to have higher levels of testosterone than non-violent criminals.

Other substances can also affect the brain and influence aggression. For example, alcohol intoxication is linked to murder, stabbing, domestic violence, and child abuse.

INSTINCT THEORIES

Instinct theories propose that people are naturally brutal and cruel. The events of the First World War convinced Sigmund Freud (see Chapter 8) of the existence of **thanatos** (the Greek word for death), the death instinct whose energy is directed toward self-destruction or the termination of life. Freud proposed that aggression is the death instinct redirected away from the self and toward other people.

thanatos
death instinct

Konrad Lorenz theorized that the innate fighting instinct is the primary source of aggressive behaviour (Lorenz, 1966). He explained that the aggressive energy that springs from the fighting instinct builds up over time and needs to be released to prevent a full reservoir of aggression. People who fail to express their fighting instinct periodically may commit a spontaneous violent act to empty their aggression reservoir. Lorenz was more optimistic about human nature than Freud, believing that the fighting instinct can be expressed in socially acceptable forms, such as sports and games. He also proposed that aggression can be inhibited by engaging in behaviours that are incompatible with the fighting instinct, such as giving love and helping others.

PERSONALITY THEORIES

Personality theorists view aggression as behaviour that endures over time and manifests itself across situations. Personality psychologists attempt to classify violent people into different personality types. Two that have received considerable atten-

undercontrolled personality type
violent person who shows minimal internal inhibitions against aggression

overcontrolled personality type
violent person who shows extreme inhibition against aggressive behaviour

tion are the **undercontrolled personality type** and the **overcontrolled personality type**. The undercontrolled type is the violent person who shows minimal internal inhibitions against aggression. Such an individual is impulsive and gets angry easily. The overcontrolled type is the violent person who shows extreme inhibition against aggressive behaviour. However, this individual may experience stress from ongoing frustration that is inescapable, become overwhelmed by it, and explode in a violent outburst or a hideously violent crime.

SOCIAL PSYCHOLOGICAL THEORIES

Social psychological theories focus on modelling (see Chapter 5) and on frustration. The *frustration–aggression theory* proposes that all aggressive behaviour is the result of frustration and that frustration always leads to aggression. Frustration is any interference with ongoing behaviour. The frustration–aggression theory doesn't hold up under the evidence. For example, people aggress against others without being frustrated or provoked (such as assassins), and they may aggress against others for reasons other than frustration. Bullies pick fights with weaker people in the absence of frustration, for example. People also act in ways other than aggressively in the face of frustration. Non-aggressive ways of dealing with frustration include withdrawing, feeling depressed, or letting off steam through physical exercise.

Leonard Berkowitz (1989) offered a revised frustration–aggression theory. He proposed that unpleasant or aversive events (not just frustration) or anger can lead to readiness to act aggressively. Unpleasant or aversive events include pain, heat, noise, or crowding. People who are ready to respond aggressively are likely to behave violently when aggressive cues are available. An aggressive cue is an object, situation, or target that is associated with aggression in the past and can trigger aggression in the present. Examples are knives, guns, or people in authority, such as law enforcement officers.

SOCIAL LEARNING THEORY

The *social learning theory* of aggression proposes that people learn aggressive behaviour by being exposed to aggressive models and the reinforcement or punishment of aggressive responses. Social learning theory identifies the family, the media, and aggressive models in groups or subcultures as cradles of violence. Cultures that emphasize individuality seem to show more aggressive behaviour than those that emphasize collectivity (Oatley, 1993).

Preventing Aggression

Biological, personal, environmental, social, and cultural factors that are known to set off aggression need to be identified and eliminated. People who are treated unjustly or deprived of a decent quality of life today are likely to be the aggressors of tomorrow. Those with aggression problems need to develop the capacity for empathy toward others and the skills to negotiate what they want using all means except violence. Peace culture as an ideal also needs to be embraced by all communities that collectively constitute the global village.

POINTS TO REMEMBER

Social psychologists attempt to explain attitudes, social perception, social influence, group influence, prosocial behaviour, and aggressive behaviour. Attitudes are predispositions to respond favourably or unfavourably toward objects, individuals, events, places, ideas, and situations. Social perception or cognition is the process of making sense of people. Social influence is the process of people influencing the ways other people think, feel, and act.

Groups can influence individual performance, decision making, and social roles. Prosocial behaviour is people's willingness to help other people. Aggression is intentionally inflicting physical or emotional harm on another person who does not consent to such harm. It is explained in terms of biological, instinct, personality, and social psychological theories. The prevention of aggression and violence is an imperative for safe communities and a global village committed to a peace culture.

KEY TERMS

aggression

attitude

attribution

authoritarian personality

bystander effect

cognitive dissonance

compliance

conformity

defensive attribution

deindividuation

diffusion of responsibility

discrimination

diversism

fundamental attribution error

group polarization effect

groupthink

halo effect

interpersonal attraction

minority influence

obedience

overcontrolled personality type

primacy effect

prosocial behaviour

racism

risky shift

schema

self-serving bias

sexism

social categorization

social influence

social loafing

social perception

social prejudice

social psychology

social stereotypes

stereotyping

thanatos

undercontrolled personality type

REFERENCES

Albarracin, D., B.T. Johnson, & M.P. Zanna (Eds.). (2005). *The handbook of attitudes*. Mahwah, NJ: Lawrence Erlbaum.

Associated Press. (2000a, February 22). Debate by Democrats turns angry. *The London Free Press*, p. A8.

Associated Press. (2000b, February 26). Four NY cops acquitted in slaying. *The London Free Press*, p. A7.

Berkowitz, L. (1989). Frustration–aggression hypothesis: Examination and reformulation. *Psychological Bulletin, 106,* 59–73.

Berscheid, E., & E. Hatfield. (1978). *Interpersonal attraction* (2nd ed.). Reading, MA: Addison-Wesley.

CBC News (2008, January 23). Two investigations ordered following alleged police abuse of Victoria teen. http://www.cbc.ca/canada/british-columbia/story/2008/01/23/bc-victoria-police-tether-inquiry.html.

Choi, I., R.E. Nisbett, & A. Norenzayan. (1999, January). Causal attribution across cultures: Variation and universality. *Psychological Bulletin, 125* (1), 47–63.

Chua-Eoan, H. (2000, March 6). Black and blue. *Time,* pp. 22–26.

CNN. (2000, February 25). *Larry King live.* Television program.

Debusmann, B. (2009, July 16). The Ugly American and other stereotypes. http://blogs.reuters.com/great-debate/2009/07/16/the-ugly-american-and-other-stereotypes/.

Festinger, L. (1957). *A theory of cognitive dissonance.* Evanston, IL: Row Peterson.

Flannery, D.J., A.T. Vazsonyi, & I.D. Waldman (Eds.). (2007). *The Cambridge handbook of violence behaviour and aggression.* Cambridge, UK: Cambridge University Press.

Inbau, F.E., J.E. Reid, J.P. Buckley, & B.C. Jayne (2001). *Criminal interrogation and confessions.* Baltimore: Aspen Publishers.

Janis, I.L. (1982). Counteracting the adverse effects of concurrence-seeking in policy-planning groups: Theory and research perspectives. In H. Brandstatter & J. Davis (Eds.), *Group decision making.* New York: Academic Press.

Jayne, B.C., & J.P. Buckley (2009, June 29). The Reid Technique of interrogation. http://www.reid.com/educational_info/r_tips.html.

Kazarian, S.S. (2001). *Diversity issues in law enforcement* (2nd ed.). Toronto: Emond Montgomery.

Kazarian, S.S., W. Crichlow, & S. Bradford. (2007). *Diversity issues in law enforcement* (3rd ed.). Toronto: Emond Montgomery.

Latané, B. (1981). The psychology of social impact. *American Psychologist, 36* (4), 343–56.

Latané, B., & J. Darley. (1970). *The unresponsive bystander: Why doesn't he help?* New York: Appleton.

Lewis, S.D. (2009, September 11). Post-9/11 discrimination plagues Detroit area Sikhs. *The Detroit News.* http://detnews.com/article/20090911/ METRO02/909110344.

Lorenz, K. (1966). *On aggression.* New York: Harcourt, Brace and World.

Miller, J.G. (1984). Culture and the development of everyday social explanation. *Journal of Personality and Social Psychology, 46,* 961–78.

Nelson, T.D. (Ed.). (2009). *Handbook of prejudice, stereotyping, and discrimination.* New York: Psychology Press.

Oatley, K. (1993). Those to whom evil is done. In R.S. Wyer & T.K. Srull (Eds.), *Toward a general theory of anger and emotional aggression: Advances in social cognition: Vol. 6.* Hillsdale, NJ: Lawrence Erlbaum Associates.

Orbuch, T.L., & S. Sprecher. (2006). Attraction and interpersonal relationships. In J. Delamater (Ed.), *Handbook of social psychology* (pp. 339–62). New York: Springer.

Prentice-Dunn, S., & R.W. Rogers. (1989). Deindividuation and self-regulation of behavior. In P.B. Paulus (Ed.), *Psychology of group influence.* Hillsdale, NJ: Lawrence Erlbaum Associates.

Ridley, C.T., D.W. Chih, & R.J. Olivera. (2000, January). Training in cultural schemas: An antidote to unintentional racism in clinical practice. *American Journal of Orthopsychiatry, 70* (1): 65–72.

Weisburd, D., R. Greenspan, E.E. Hamilton, H. Williams, & K.A. Bryant. (2000). Police attitudes toward abuse of authority: Findings from a national study. http://www.ncjrs.gov/pdffiles1/nij/ 181312.pdf.

Zajonc, R.B. (1965). Social facilitation. *Science, 149,* 269–74.

Zimbardo, P.G., C. Haney, W.C. Banks, & D. Jaffe. (1973, April 8). The mind is a formidable jailer: A Pirandellian prison. *The New York Times,* pp. 38–60.

Zimbardo, P.G., & F.L. Ruch. (1976). *Psychology and life.* Dallas: Scott Foresman.

EXERCISES AND REVIEW

Self-Test

Circle the correct answer.

1. Holding a woman responsible for being raped is an example of

    a. the fundamental attribution error

    b. defensive attribution

    c. telling it as it is

    d. none of the above

2. On the basis of the primacy effect, it is best to

    a. present your positive qualities first

    b. present your negative qualities first

    c. present your positive and negative qualities together

    d. keep quiet and say nothing

3. A police officer who persuades a suspect to sit in the cruiser for a few minutes and then seeks the suspect's cooperation to go to the police station is using

    a. the foot-in-the-door strategy

    b. the door-in-the-face strategy

    c. a one-sided argument to elicit the suspect's cooperation

    d. an emotional appeal to persuade the suspect

4. A law enforcement officer who wants to learn a complex task (for example, golf, or billiards) is best to

    a. learn the task while her children are playing around her

    b. work things out on her own before trying them in a group

    c. learn the difficult task when other officers are watching

    d. visualize the task in bed before going to sleep

5. Asian-Canadians attribute their children's success in school to their effort and hard work. Euro-Canadians attribute their children's success in school to their innate abilities. Which of the following is true about the discrepancy in attributional style between the two groups?

    a. Asian-Canadians are committing the fundamental attribution error

    b. Asian-Canadian children may outperform Euro-Canadian children because Asian-Canadian parents are more likely to push their children to achieve than their Euro-Canadian counterparts

   c. discrepancy in attribution is not real because all cultures commit the fundamental attribution error

   d. Asian-Canadian children are unlikely to outperform Euro-Canadian children even though Asian-Canadian parents are more likely than their Euro-Canadian counterparts to push their children to achieve

6. During a political protest, normally mild-mannered people start throwing rocks and fire bombs at police. Which of the following is a likely group influence explanation for the behaviour of these people?

   a. social loafing

   b. social facilitation

   c. deindividuation

   d. mass hysteria

7. Which of the following is likely to make a person better liked?

   a. the person's looks

   b. the person's geographic closeness

   c. seeing the person frequently

   d. all of the above

8. A "devil's advocate," or someone who opposes majority opinion, is most needed in which of the following situations?

   a. groupthink

   b. learning of an easy task

   c. risky shift

   d. group polarization

9. Which of the following represents social influence?

   a. obedience

   b. compliance

   c. conformity

   d. all of the above

10. Law enforcement officers who are unhappy with their pay

   a. are likely a frustrated bunch

   b. will invariably take out their frustrations on suspects

   c. will invariably take out their frustrations on their bosses

   d. all of the above

Thinking About Psychology and Law Enforcement

1. Inmates frequently complain about the prison system—the unhygienic living and segregated conditions, the use of excessive force, and the poor training of prison guards. What approaches should be considered to address these issues other than the approach that states that those who commit crimes shouldn't complain when they're imprisoned?

2. How might you explain in psychological terms the following incidents? How could similar events be prevented from happening again?

    a. In June 2000, police clash with more than 1,000 protesters demonstrating against homelessness outside the Ontario legislature. The baton-wielding riot police dodge bricks, paint bombs, and Molotov cocktails, while peaceful protesters are injured by police nightsticks.

    b. Allen Ho, 21, collapses after ingesting the designer drug ecstasy at a Toronto rave. A coroner's inquest jury does not recommend banning the all-night dance parties. Rather, it recommends that public health officials educate young people about the risks associated with ecstasy, marijuana, and other drugs associated with raves; that raves be restricted to people at least 16 years old; that any suggestion of drug use be eliminated in advertising raves; and that permits be required to hold raves.

    c. At school, a six-year-old boy pulls out a concealed semi-automatic handgun and informs his classmate Kayla that he does not like her. When she turns back and says "So?" he fires a single bullet that enters her right arm and travels through her vital organs. The boy runs to the bathroom to toss the pistol into the trash and hide. Kayla dies later at the hospital.

    d. A married mother of four who is a teacher has a sexual affair with a 12-year-old male student, allowing him to father two of her children.

Glossary

abnormal behaviour behaviour that is distressing, dysfunctional, and deviant

abnormal psychology scientific study of behaviours that are seemingly unhealthy, strange, or unusual

absolute threshold minimum sensory stimulation required for detection

acculturation process of adaptation or change that results from people of diverse cultures being in continuous contact with one another

acculturative stress negative consequence of acculturation

action potential the firing of a neuron

acute stressors stressors that are temporary or last a short time

aggression intentional infliction of physical or emotional harm on another person who does not consent to it

amygdala part of limbic system involved in unpleasant sensations and learning of fear

anterograde amnesia the inability to store new long-term memories

antidepressants drugs that are used in treating depression and select anxiety disorders

antipsychotic drugs drugs that are used to control severe mental disturbances such as delusions and hallucinations

anxiety disorders psychological disorders in which anxiety is the major disturbance

applied research research that aims to advance new knowledge that has immediate real-world uses

arousal state of physical and mental stimulation

attitude predisposition to respond favourably or unfavourably toward objects, individuals, events, places, ideas, and situations

attribution social cognitive process in which an individual observes the actions of another and makes an inference about the reasons for those actions

authoritarian personality personality that views the world as a threatening place or jungle

autonomic nervous system division of the peripheral nervous system that controls the involuntary muscles and glands

basic anxiety pervasive feeling of isolation, loneliness, and helplessness in a hostile world

behaviour observable actions; what people actually do

behaviour therapies a psychotherapeutic approach that focuses on "unlearning" maladaptive behaviours and learning new, more adaptive behaviours

biological approach approach to psychological disorders that assumes they are the result of underlying diseases that require biological treatments

blackout inability to remember events that occurred during a drinking bout

brain fingerprinting the use of brain activity as a physical marker indicating deception

Broca's area part of frontal lobe involved in muscle movements that produce speech or verbal sounds

bystander effect tendency of people who witness an emergency situation to help less when others are present than when they are alone

cancer disease in which cells become abnormal and keep dividing and forming more cells without order or control

case study research approach that involves exploring a single individual in depth to obtain a detailed portrayal of a particular behaviour or phenomenon, or to identify the co-occurrences of two or more events or variables

central nervous system major division of the nervous system that interprets sensory information and sends orders to the body to respond

cerebellum part of hindbrain involved in maintaining balance, coordinating movement, and regulating muscle tone

cerebral cortex part of forebrain involved in language, memory, and thinking

chronic stressors stressors that are continuous or last a long time

chunking grouping individual pieces of information into larger, meaningful units to aid memory

circadian rhythm daily behavioural or bodily cycle that occurs repeatedly about every 24 hours

classical conditioning learning in which a stimulus begins to elicit a reflexive response when that stimulus becomes associated with another stimulus that naturally evokes the reflexive response

code of ethics set of rules by which a group of people, often members of a profession, agree to abide

cognitive disorders psychological disorders characterized by significant disturbances and deterioration in cognition and memory

cognitive dissonance mental discomfort or pain a person experiences that is associated with being aware of attitude inconsistency

cognitive psychotherapy psychological treatment to change maladaptive behaviours and feelings by changing irrational thoughts, beliefs, and ideas

collective efficacy a group's shared beliefs about their competency

collective unconscious evolutionary reservoir for the universal experiences of humanity

compliance behavioural pattern of giving in or saying "yes" to an explicit request from someone who is not in authority

conditional positive regard people's belief that they are worthy of love, acceptance, and respect only when they think, feel, and act as others want them to

conditioned compensatory response physiological changes that counteract a drug effect and that result from the association of a drug effect with environmental cues

conformity behavioural pattern of going along with or giving in to the opinions and actions of others

consciousness people's state of awareness of their external and internal worlds

consequence event or stimulus that follows an operant and determines its future probability

continuous reinforcement reinforcement of all responses

coping process of dealing with stressors to minimize, reduce, or learn to tolerate physical and psychological wear and tear

correlational method research approach that involves gathering multiple case studies to identify co-occurrences of events that are generalizable to more than one individual

couple therapy psychological treatment in which the two partners in a relationship are involved in therapy

critical thinking ability and willingness to ask questions, to wonder, to assess claims, to evaluate assumptions, biases, and evidence to make objective judgments on the basis of well-supported reasons, to look for flaws in arguments and resist claims that have no supporting evidence, and to tolerate uncertainty

cutaneous senses skin senses

declarative memory a person's store of long-term factual knowledge

deductive reasoning application of general principles or findings to reach a specific conclusion

defence mechanism coping strategy that wards off anxiety

defensive attribution process in which an individual or a group is blamed or held responsible for a misfortune

deindividuation tendency of group members to lose their individual identity, to become less inhibited, and to care less about being evaluated by others

delusion fixed belief that is real only to the person holding it

dependent variable measurable indicator that is presumed to change (increase or decrease) at the conclusion of an experiment; the change in this variable is attributed to the independent variable

depressant drug that decreases central nervous system arousal, slows down bodily functions, and impairs sensitivity to external sensory stimuli

depression mood disturbance characterized by persistent feelings of sadness and loss of interest

difference threshold smallest detectable difference between two sensory stimuli

diffusion of responsibility process in which feelings of responsibility to offer assistance are spread across all witnesses to an emergency situation

discrimination illegal and negative behaviour that deprives a group or its members of their civil rights

display rules principles followed by different cultures for expressing emotion—what, how, when, and where emotions should be expressed

dissociative disorders psychological disorders in which people's identity, memory, and consciousness are changed or disrupted

dissociative identity disorder disorder in which two or more separate personalities exist in the same individual

diversism prejudice against people of diversity

divided attention perceptual ability to focus on more than one stimulus at a time

drive internal state of tension that motivates a behaviour that satisfies a need

economically compulsive violence criminal activity committed for the purpose of supporting a drug habit

electroconvulsive therapy biological treatment in which an electrical current is passed through the brain to induce seizure and abort depression

emotion experience of pleasant or unpleasant feelings

emotion-focused coping approach to dealing with stress that involves consciously regulating the feelings evoked by stressful events

encoding-specificity principle the rule that memories are more easily recalled in environmental conditions that match those experienced during encoding

encoding transformation of information into a form that can be stored in memory

endocrine system chemical communication network of the body that stimulates and regulates human behaviour through hormones produced by the glands

epidemiological method research approach that uses data on incidence or prevalence of behaviours or events to determine their extent, possible causes, and trends over time

episodic memory long-term knowledge of one's personal experiences

errors of commission the recall of inaccurate or unwanted information

errors of omission information that cannot be retrieved by short-term memory

experimental method research approach that randomly assigns experimental participants to two or more groups or conditions to compare them on one or more measures

extinction weakening and eventual disappearance of the conditioned response

extrasensory perception perception that relies on means other than the known sensory systems

extraversion personality of sociability, exuberance, impulsivity, and craving for excitement

extrinsic motivation doing things to gain tangible rewards or to avoid undesirable consequences

factitious disorders psychological conditions in which physical or mental symptoms are induced or simulated for no apparent reason

family therapy psychological treatment in which the entire family is involved in therapy

five-factor theory trait model that suggests that personality can be explained using five broad dimensions: neuroticism, extraversion, openness to experience, consciousness, and agreeableness

fixation process of "getting stuck" at a particular stage of development

frontal lobe part of cerebral cortex involved in voluntary body movement, thinking, motivation, and planning

fundamental attribution error process in which people attribute their own actions to situational or external environmental factors, but they attribute other people's actions to their personality traits

gate-control theory theory that explains the role of psychological factors in pain

General Adaptation Syndrome sequence of reactions to stressors

general intelligence the view of intelligence as a single, generalized ability that applies in all situations

gland organ that secretes hormones into the bloodstream

group polarization effect tendency of people to strengthen and solidify their positions as a result of group discussion

group therapy psychological treatment in which several clients meet regularly to resolve personal issues

groupthink tendency of a cohesive or close-knit group to arrive at unanimous but poorly thought-out decisions to avoid disharmony

gustation sense of taste

hallucination sensory experience that is disturbed or disturbing and is real only to the person experiencing it

hallucinogen drug that is mind-expanding, mind-altering, and perception-distorting

halo effect process in which people attribute positive traits to others on the basis of their initial knowledge that the others have positive traits

hardiness personal characteristics of commitment, willingness to face challenge, and sense of control that help to make a person more resistant to stress

health the absence of disease; a positive state of physical, mental, and social well-being; a resource that can be used to influence the quality of life

health psychology scientific and practice field that contributes to understanding health behaviour and the treatment, rehabilitation, and prevention approaches that evolve from such an understanding

hierarchy of needs Maslow's model of motivation that presents human needs in hierarchical order from lower-order needs to higher-order needs

hippocampus part of limbic system involved in memory

homeostasis tendency of the body to maintain an internal balanced state

hormone chemical substance produced and released into the bloodstream for the purpose of affecting the growth and functioning of other parts of the body

humanistic psychology personality theory that emphasizes the goodness of human nature and people's potential for growth and actualization

hypnosis altered state of consciousness in which a person is highly receptive to suggestion

hypothalamus part of forebrain that regulates a wide range of bodily functions and emotional behaviours, including hunger, thirst, and sexual behaviour

hypothesis statement of prediction that can be tested empirically

identity people's understanding of themselves as discrete entities

incentive external stimulus or event that is positive or negative and that motivates behaviour

incongruence state of discrepancy between the self-concept and aspects of an individual's experience

independent variable condition that is manipulated to examine its effect on the dependent variable

inductive reasoning analysis of specific facts to arrive at a conclusion

inferiority complex inability to solve life's problems

insight-oriented psychotherapy psychological treatment to increase psychological well-being through self-understanding

instinct inborn rather than learned pattern of behaviour

intermittent reinforcement reinforcement of some but not all responses

interpersonal attraction aspect of social perception that looks at people's positive feelings toward others

intrinsic motivation doing things because they are enjoyable to do

introversion personality of shyness, quietness, self-control, introspection, and inhibition

kinesthetic senses senses that provide information about movement, orientation, and posture

laboratory observation research approach that involves observing and recording behaviour as it occurs in a laboratory rather than a natural setting, with minimal researcher influence or control

lateralization functional differences between the two brain hemispheres

learning change in behaviour that is relatively permanent and is due to experience

left hemisphere side of brain involved in verbal ability

limbic system part of forebrain that plays a vital role in emotional behaviour during periods of stress

lineup a recognition test in which a suspect appears among others known to be innocent

long-term memory the store of long-lasting, relatively permanent memories

mania mood disturbance characterized by persistent feelings of emotional high, agitation, pressured speech, and impulsivity

medulla part of hindbrain that coordinates the basic life-support systems of the body

memory the processes involved in the acquisition, storage, and retrieval of information

mental processes internal activities (physiological activities, thoughts, and feelings) that cannot be observed directly but can be measured with recording instruments or inferred from self-report measures and performance

minority influence process in which a single group member or a minority of group members swings the majority

misinformation effect distortion of a witness's memory after receiving misleading information

model person who demonstrates a behaviour to be learned by an observer

mood disorders psychological disorders in which the primary symptom is mood disturbance

motivation force behind human behaviour that explains why people do what they do

multiple intelligence the view of intelligence as a variety of independent abilities of greater or lesser effectiveness

naturalistic observation research approach that involves observing and recording behaviour as it occurs in a natural setting, with minimal researcher influence or control

need biological requirement that demands satisfaction

negative reinforcement process in which a response that terminates an unpleasant stimulus increases the probability of the behaviour being repeated

neopsychoanalytic perspective personality theory that stresses social and cultural rather than sexual influences in personality development

nervous system communication network of the body that controls thoughts, feelings, and actions

neuron specialized cell that transmits electrical signals throughout the nervous system through an electrochemical process

neuroticism personality dimension that differentiates between normal people and those who are neurotic

neurotransmitter chemical that transmits messages between neurons

non-declarative memory a person's store of knowledge not easily expressed or verbalized, such as skills and actions

obedience behavioural pattern of giving in to the commands of a person in authority

observational learning learning by observing

observer person who learns by observing and imitating a model

obsessive–compulsive disorder disorder characterized by obsessions and compulsions

occipital lobe part of cerebral cortex involved in vision

Oedipus complex boy's unconscious incestuous desires for his mother and murderous wishes to get rid of his father

olfaction sense of smell

operant behaviour emitted voluntarily

operant conditioning changing the probability of an existing voluntary behaviour and learning an entirely new behaviour

opiate drug that kills pain and alters mood, sometimes producing euphoria

overcontrolled personality type violent person who shows extreme inhibition against aggressive behaviour

panic disorder recurrent and unexpected panic attacks

paraphilias group of sexual and gender identity disorders in which people have recurrent and intense sexual urges, fantasies, and behaviours

parasympathetic system division of the autonomic nervous system that restores the body to a normal state after a threat has passed

parietal lobe part of cerebral cortex involved in touch, pressure, temperature, pain, body awareness, and spatial orientation

perception process in which a sensory stimulus is sorted out and interpreted by the brain

peripheral nervous system major division of the nervous system that relays information from sensory receptors to central nervous system

personality disorders psychological disorders in which people show enduring, pervasive, and inflexible patterns of inner experiences and behaviours that deviate from cultural expectations and cause distress or impairment

personality unique and stable patterns of thoughts, feelings, and behaviours characteristic of an individual

pharmacological violence violence committed under the influence of a particular drug

phobia persistent and unrealistic fear of an object or situation

photo bias source confusion produced by familiarity with an often-viewed image

physical dependence continued abuse of a drug to avoid unpleasant withdrawal symptoms

pleasure principle immediate gratification of needs

pons part of hindbrain involved in maintaining a state of alertness

positive regard pervasive need for acceptance, love, and approval from significant people in one's life

positive reinforcement process in which a positive consequence follows a behaviour and increases the probability of the behaviour being repeated

post-traumatic stress disorder severe anxiety disorder that occurs after exposure to a traumatic event

prefrontal cortex part of frontal lobe involved in intellectual abilities and personality traits

primacy effect process in which people's first impressions of other people are more dominant than later impressions

problem-focused coping approach to dealing with stress that involves facing the stressor for the purpose of solution and resolution

prosocial behaviour people's willingness to help other people

psychoactive drug drug that affects behaviour, feelings, perceptions, and thoughts

psychoanalysis the first comprehensive personality theory that emphasized unconscious motives in human behaviour

psychological approach approach to psychological disorders that relies on psychotherapy or talk therapy to improve biological, psychological, social, cultural, and spiritual functioning

psychological dependence craving for the pleasurable effects of a drug

psychological treatment a psychotherapeutic approach to help people change maladaptive thoughts, feelings, and behaviours and to improve their psychological, biological, social, cultural, and spiritual functioning

psychology science and profession that strives to understand human behaviour by studying all aspects of the human experience; the scientific study of behaviour and mental processes

psychopharmacology study of the use of drugs for psychological disorders

psychosurgery biological treatment in which brain surgery is performed to treat severe, unremitting, and debilitating psychological disorders such as obsessive–compulsive disorder

psychotherapy process in which a client and a trained professional interact for the purpose of improving the client's quality of life

psychoticism personality dimension that differentiates between normal people and those who are psychotic

punishment application of an aversive stimulus or withdrawal of a pleasant stimulus to decrease the probability of a response

pure research basic research that aims to develop new knowledge without immediate concern for the practical uses of this knowledge

racism prejudice against members of a particular racial group

reality principle balances the needs of the id and the superego against the needs of society

reciprocal determinism belief in interaction of behavioural, cognitive, and environmental influences

reflex involuntary response to a particular stimulus

rehearsal repetition of information to keep it active in short-term memory

reliability consistency in test results when administered to the same individuals on different occasions

retrieval cue a stimulus that triggers a forgotten long-term memory

retrograde amnesia the inability to remember anything before the event that resulted in loss of memory

right hemisphere side of brain involved in visual–spatial abilities

risky shift tendency of group members to make riskier decisions in a group than when alone

schema integrated set of cognitions or knowledge base about objects, people, and events

schizophrenia psychological disorder characterized by psychotic thoughts, perceptions, feelings, and actions

scientific method method of doing research that involves (1) forming a research question, (2) framing the research question as a hypothesis, (3) developing the methodology for testing the hypothesis, and (4) drawing conclusions about the hypothesis

selective attention perceptual ability to focus on particular stimuli while ignoring all other stimuli

self-concept view that people develop about themselves

self-control people's ability to regulate their own behaviour

self-efficacy people's beliefs about their ability to exercise control over events that affect their lives

self-serving bias attribution error in which people take credit for their successes

semantic memory long-term knowledge that is general and impersonal in nature

sensation process in which a sensory stimulus is detected and transmitted to the brain for interpretation

sensory adaptation process in which people become less responsive to a sensory stimulus to which they are exposed for a prolonged time

sensory memory information from the bodily senses, stored for a brief time

sequential lineup a lineup in which members are presented to the witness one at a time

sexism prejudice against members of one of the sexes

shaping process in which a complex behaviour is learned when only those responses that successively approximate the desired behaviour are reinforced

short-term (working) memory recently acquired information stored in limited capacity

signal detection theory theory that considers detection of sensory stimuli in the context of background noise

simultaneous lineup a lineup in which the suspect and distractors appear before a witness at the same time

social categorization process of putting other people into groups or categories

social–cognitive approach personality theory that emphasizes the importance of social-environmental and cognitive factors in understanding personality and human behaviour

social influence social pressure; the effect that social situations have on the way people think and act

social loafing tendency of group members to slack off or not pull their weight when working as a part of the group

social perception process of making sense of people

social prejudice widespread and inflexible negative attitude toward members of an "out-group" that is based on incorrect or incomplete information

social psychology study of social situations that affect the thoughts, feelings, and actions of individuals

social stereotypes beliefs people have about the characteristics of a group of people

somatic nervous system division of the peripheral nervous system that controls the voluntary muscles

somatoform disorders psychological disorders in which people experience physical symptoms that have no apparent physical cause

source confusion flawed recall due to previous exposure to similar stimuli

spontaneous recovery re-emergence of an extinguished response

standardization the establishment of norms to guide administration of tests and interpretation of their scores

stereotyping holding preconceived and unfavourable beliefs about a particular group or individuals in the group

stigma a label that causes the labelled person to be perceived as different, and in negative light

stimulant drug that speeds up the central nervous system, makes a person feel rushed or energetic, and increases anxiety

stimulus source of physical energy that elicits a response in the sensory system

stimulus discrimination responding only to the original stimulus

stimulus generalization responding to a stimulus that is similar to the original unconditioned stimulus

stress buffers factors that reduce the negative outcomes of high stress

stress physical or psychological reaction to threat

stressors events that cause stress reactions or responses

sublimation child's efforts to channel sexual energy into non-sexual activities

subliminal perception perception of sensory messages without conscious awareness

substantia nigra part of the midbrain involved in controlling body movements

suicide the action of willfully taking one's own life

suicide by cop suicide committed by a person by provoking police into shooting him or her

suprachiasmatic nucleus part of the hypothalamus that controls circadian (daily) rhythmic cycles, such as the sleep–wake cycle

survey method research approach that uses questionnaires, interviews, and opinion polls to learn about people's attitudes, beliefs, values, opinions, feelings, actions, and experiences

sympathetic system division of the autonomic nervous system that makes a person alert and ready to use energy when there is an internal or external threat

systemic violence violence that originates from a network of drug trafficking and distribution

T-helper cell type of white blood cell that is important in regulating the immune system and stimulating other cells to attack invading germs

temporal lobe part of cerebral cortex involved in audition

thanatos death instinct

theory statement of a general principle or set of principles for the purpose of explaining how a number of separate facts are interrelated

tolerance diminishing effect of a drug over repeated use, necessitating higher doses of the drug

toxicity physical or psychological harm the quantity of a drug presents to the user

trait relatively stable and consistent personal feature

trait perspective personality theory that defines personality in terms of traits or internal dispositions

traumatic event disastrous or extremely painful stressor with severe psychological and physiological consequences

Type A personality personality that is generally aggressive, competitive, hostile, in a rush all the time, doing several things at once, and constantly striving for achievement

Type B personality personality that is generally easygoing, patient, and relaxed

Type C personality personality that is generally inhibited about talking with others about problems, uptight, emotionally unexpressive, and constrained

unconditional positive regard process in which individuals are accepted, loved, and respected for what they are, independent of their behaviour

undercontrolled personality type violent person who shows minimal internal inhibitions against aggression

uplift positive minor life event

validity the degree to which a test measures what it purports to measure

variable any factor or condition that can be manipulated, controlled, or measured

vestibular senses senses that provide information about balance and movement

vicarious positive reinforcement occurs when an observer's behaviour increases as a result of observing the positive reinforcement of the model's behaviour

vicarious punishment occurs when an observer's behaviour is reduced as a result of observing the punishment of the model's behaviour

weapon focus impairment of a witness's recall due to distraction caused by the perpetrator's use of a weapon

Index